Joseph Addison. Drawing by George Vertue.
(The William Andrews Clark Memorial Library, University of California, Los Angeles.)

EDWARD A. BLOOM AND
LILLIAN D. BLOOM

Joseph Addison's Sociable Animal

IN THE MARKET PLACE
ON THE HUSTINGS
IN THE PULPIT

BROWN UNIVERSITY PRESS
PROVIDENCE

International Standard Book Number: 0-87057-120-6
Library of Congress Catalog Card Number: 73-111455
Brown University Press, Providence, Rhode Island 02912

Published 1971
Printed in the United States of America
By Connecticut Printers, Incorporated
On Warren's Olde Style
Bound by Stanhope Bindery
Designed by Richard Hendel

To Herbert Davis, 1893–1967

Man is said to be a Sociable Animal.
Addison

CONTENTS

PREFACE

THIS troubled age needs Joseph Addison, but not, as the late Mr. C. S. Lewis would have it, because he is "an admirable cure for the fidgets." With due respect to Mr. Lewis, the "Addisonian world" is not simply a refuge, "a good one to fall back into when the day's work is over and a man's feet on the fire and his pipe in his mouth." For many, like Lewis, Addison undoubtedly still lives upon "some tranquil middle ground of quiet sentiments and pleasing melancholies and gentle humour to come in between our restless idealisms and our equally restless dissipations" ("Addison," in *Essays on the Eighteenth Century Presented to David Nichol Smith in Honour of His Seventieth Birthday* [Oxford, 1945], pp. 1–14). That is to see him outside the range of historic perspective; that is to make him a *Spectator* character, charmingly idiosyncratic but not to be taken seriously.

The anxieties of Addison's era were less complex and urgent than ours, but they were complex and urgent enough to provoke their own tensions. Addison flourished in his age, standing, it must be agreed, "on the common ground of daily life and deal[ing] only with middle things" (Lewis, p. 14). But the middle things are always crucial; they are at the center of dynamic events and change. For all his professions of disinterest, he did not merely observe the drama of his world; he participated in it. What brings him at times close to the twentieth-century reader is his struggle for a stable world that lay just beyond his reach. Ironically, although he contributed to the restoration of national order, he was already dead when it became a reality under Walpole.

Everyone knows that Addison chided bad manners, popularized Milton, discoursed on the imagination, and became a prose stylist whom Johnson admired. Even if nobody were to read Addison today, these achievements have assured him a place in literary history. But he is more than a relic or a tranquilizer, and he should be read as Dryden, Swift, and Pope are read, as part and parcel of the Augustan period. By analyzing his pamphlets and journals, his background, and the many influences that helped mature him, we have attempted to present a whole view of Addison, the age whose values he reflected and refined, and the social and moral seriousness with which he anchored himself to his times.

There is an odd contradiction in the fact that several astute critics of the eighteenth century read Addison's essays admiringly yet treat the man himself with attitudes that range from patronizing amusement to contempt. They find his writings a superb record of his times but reproach him for failures of personality and conviction. The vagaries of reputation are such that some of the literary and social qualities for which he was esteemed in the eighteenth and nineteenth centuries have now been turned against him as liabilities: witness the present, rather widespread suspicion of his reasonableness, politeness, and good nature as covers for a disposition toward compromise and expedience. This is not to suggest that he was flawless, but when flaws are magnified, as his have been, then the significance of his accomplishments cannot be clearly realized.

Little of what is known of his life would excite a Boswell, and further, what is essential to his life is subsumed under or effaced in his writings. Biography as such, therefore, has not been a concern here. Still, as generally sympathetic critics of the Addisonian legacy, we have used whatever biographical materials help to explicate his writings. Our involvement with the literature has made us neither Addison's apologists nor encomiasts, and certainly not his detractors.

He must, first of all, be seen as a part of the fabric of his times. But we, his interpreters, can hardly dissociate ourselves from our own position in the twentieth century. Hence, without attempting to stand between the reader and Addison, we occasionally speak out in our voice, using, for instance, terms that originated in the nineteenth century, like *middle class* and *mercantilism*. Both terms are frequently misunderstood, but it would be foolhardy to avoid words about which so much history and even controversy have grown. At other times in the following pages factual judgments are made that are warranted by the hindsight of history but that could not have been made had we documented Addison's political essays in a starkly descriptive way. An example of this is the analysis of his stand on a controversial measure like the Septennial Act of 1716. And moral judgments are made about matters in which values are unlikely to be affected by the passage of time. Addison's equivocating views on slavery and habeas corpus, as cases in point, make us extremely uncomfortable, and we have not been satisfied simply to state his position. We have consciously avoided any attempt, however, to let our judgments limit the evidence or shape the record; not everyone, we know, will agree with our ethical judgment. Therefore, we have tried to write in such a way that the reader, knowing how we think, will not feel bound to what are after all ancillary opinions.

The foundations of this study were set several years ago with some exploratory essays into Addison's political and religious convictions: "Addison's 'Enquiry after Truth': The Moral Assumptions of His Proof for Divine Existence," *PMLA* 65 (Mar. 1950):198–220; "Joseph Addison and Eighteenth-Century 'Liberalism,'" *JHI* 12 (Oct. 1951): 560–83; "Addison on 'Moral Habits of the Mind,'" *JHI* 21 (July–Sept. 1960):409–27. The essence of our discoveries and conclusions is incorporated in this book, but the earlier research was our point of departure, a stimulus that widened the boundaries of investigation rather than a neatly circumscribed terminus. What began as scrutiny of seemingly independent problems has turned out to have a common focus. The history that Addison compiled of his age and class indicates the scope of his unified interests; this we have tried to trace.

Addison was a man closely attuned to the spirit of his times. He drew much that was vital in his far-ranging social thought from the eighteenth-century repositories of public and private debate: that is, he read copiously—the classics, works of Renaissance scholarship, current political pamphlets, tradesmen's journals, newspapers, and sermons, which were often more polemical than religious. Although ephemeral, many of these publications were the popular measures of an age, the widely disseminated records of grand as well as commonplace rhetoric. To read them today can still be a vivid experience, for they are a means of identifying oneself with the past: they provide a window into the Augustan world that Addison knew. In sometimes extensive notes, therefore, at least a representative fraction of that vast outpouring is documented.

Except for Donald F. Bond's splendid presentation of the *Spectator,* which is our authority, a definitive edition of Addison's works has yet to be produced. For consistency throughout this book, therefore, whether quoting Addison or any other seventeenth- or eighteenth-century author, we have uniformly followed modern usage with respect to capital letters, italics, and spelling. Without taking any other textual liberties, we have avoided the reproduction of the frequently arbitrary and eccentric practices of many printers, especially those who turned out myriads of pamphlets.

Most of the chronological details relevant to Addison we have drawn from Peter Smithers's comprehensive *Life of Joseph Addison* (2d ed. [Oxford, 1968]). These biographical details are used so frequently that a general acknowledgment of our indebtedness is appropriate here. Other modern studies that have helped to formulate our judgments and critical values are listed as secondary sources in the Bibliography rather than in the Notes, where they might disappear among the many primary sources.

We are grateful for the wise counsel of several scholars: Professor Richmond P. Bond of the University of North Carolina, Professor Donald F. Bond of the University of Chicago, and Dr. John M. Steadman of the Henry E. Huntington Library. Here, also, we wish to express appreciation to Dr. Ian Roy of King's College, University of London, for helping us understand the politics of Queen Anne's reign, and to Professor Horton Davies of Princeton University and Professor William A. Clebsch of Stanford University, who taught us much about religion in that period. Most of all we are indebted to the late Professor Herbert Davis of Oxford University and Professor Maynard Mack of Yale University, who set aside more important work to read the entire typescript. We have profited from their unparalleled knowledge of the eighteenth century. The ultimate responsibility is ours, but the friendly interest of these scholars has enhanced whatever value this book may have.

In addition we acknowledge the aid of Lois D. Atwood of the Brown University Press, who participated in the thankless checking of details. We also thank the staffs of the libraries in which we did our research: those of Yale, Brown, and Harvard universities; the British Museum; the Bodleian Library; and the Huntington Library.

And finally, we thank the Corporation of Brown University for several research grants, the American Council of Learned Societies for a grant-in-aid; and the Trustees of the Huntington Library for a research fellowship in 1963–64 and 1967–68.

INTRODUCTION

THE MIDDLE PATH

LIKE Samuel Johnson a half century later, Joseph Addison tried to fortify his generation against "the whispers of fancy, . . . the phantoms of hope." And he too resisted the illusion "that the deficiencies of the present day will be supplied by the morrow."[1] He could not take shelter behind such blinkered optimism because he had too clear an insight into man's limitations and nature's hardships. "Man is subject to innumerable pains and sorrows by the very condition of humanity," he said in *Spectator* 169, "and yet, as if nature had not sown evils enough in life, we are continually adding grief to grief, and aggravating the common calamity by our cruel treatment of one another. . . . At the same time that the storm beats upon the whole species, we are falling foul upon one another." Helpless before the brutality of nature, Addison concentrated on his fellow beings who, vicious in society, also flagellated themselves. All about him he saw fickle, self-destructive creatures who allowed the mind to lie fallow and so to sprout "up in follies, that are only to be killed by a constant and assiduous culture" (*S* 10). Since this discipline was rare, there could be no unalloyed well-being for most individuals, a fact that by his admission dejected and terrified him.[2] But like his own Cato he steeled himself against sentimental whimpering; he dismissed as inane all "enquiries after happiness, and rules for attaining it" (*S* 163). The truth for him was simply that human behavior was unpredictable, happiness at best a sometime thing beyond general expectation. Misery, if one surrendered to it, was the true reality.

But Addison's portrait of man, though gray, was by no means hopeless. Short of happiness, man could still quest for contentment, and this was the mark of complaisance and of honorable regard for secular and divine authority. Contentment, at once a virtue and the reward of virtue, demanded submission to rank and duty. In this dual role it satisfied the pragmatic and ideal end of human striving. To "aim at anything higher," Addison argued, could bring man "nothing but grief and disappointments," and his social world nothing but unsettling change (*S* 163).

Despite bleak moments he admitted that he did not know "what it [was] to be melancholy" (*S* 26). This is of a piece with his conviction that man, if not precisely *animal ridens,* was still "the merriest species of the creation" and had "a very good counterpoise to the spleen" in laughter. Risibility, to be sure, was never Addison's strong suit; he even distrusted it, preferring the modified alternative of studied cheerfulness. Laughter, however, when restrained, seemed to him a way to push aside "the gloom which is apt to depress the mind" (*S* 249). Yet with man's penchant for frustrating his own best interests, the argument for good cheer was far simpler than its attainment. Self-pity and restlessness were always barriers; erroneous judgment and sinfulness remained obstacles to the life of contentment. But he refused to deface his portrait of regenerate man, ultimately at peace with himself, his world, and his God.

His hope sprang from faith in God's power to translate evil into good and in man's faculties of self-restoration. As the indispensable link between the spiritual and animal creations of the universe, man was never "so sunk in vice and ignorance, but there [were] still some hidden seeds of goodness and knowledge in him" (*S* 262). These seeds Addison wanted to cultivate as a "moral habit of the mind" (*S* 387). The whole process of regeneration, as he saw it, was one of self-analysis made rigorously and humbly before God. In that process he would act as the husbandman to speed a wholesome moral growth.

The whole man, he insisted, carries a burden of obligation on two related planes: the first, described in the preceding paragraph, is private; the other is public, the totemic bonds of society. The individual can no more justify his separation from the rules of society than he can escape from the watchful eye of God. Even as the private obligation begins with a sense of reverence, the public one begins with a sense of affiliation. Instincts contrary to man's gregarious nature—melancholy or pride or selfishness—must be stifled. But the reward more than compensates for the effort: obedience to communal law brings substance, gains both material and spiritual. The individual may push past the constraints of loneliness through friendship, family life, and even the empathic observation of human activity on the Exchange or at a busy street corner. He may share in a peaceful world by participating in international commerce; he may adore God by recognizing the heavenly kingdom in his own body politic.

In short, Addison respected what Aristotle called "the best of animals"—the "political."[3] At the same time he apparently feared that *political,* which in his own day often meant the same as *factional,* would be misconstrued. Therefore, without altering the philosopher's humane intention, he adopted the less ambiguous but slightly more polite metaphor "sociable animal" (*S* 9) to connote one who properly discriminates between good and evil, just and unjust, indigent and idle. The sociable animal, further, is in harmony with his neighbor; the harmony, as Pope stated it, of "creature link'd to creature, man to man."[4] Yet he is a sociable animal, Addison concluded, only because as a mere man he is incapable of self-sufficiency. He has moments of creativity and accomplishment, but these do not soften the fact that he is too fragile to survive by himself. He knows neither his limitations nor his ultimate fate. For all his achievement and activity, he is a subject for pathos. Addison lamented particularly that man, bored with the present and unable to realize its richness, likes to hide himself in a mythical golden age or to escape from reality into chimeric hopes for the future.

Without the trait of sociability man would be destroyed. In gratitude for it he must recognize that his social role begins with knowledge: each man, as Addison points out, has to know himself as best he can, and he has to know his universe as a divine contrivance descending from the angelic hosts to microscopic animate matter. Such order demands of all creatures—and especially of rational man—acceptance of an assigned station and its corresponding duties. All fit into the whole design and are in that sense equal; all are bound one to another, whether they are inferior or superior to the forms above and below. All are secure as long as the whole remains unchanged. For the practical world of the sociable animal, order becomes the goal. Like the universe of which it is a part, this world too is meaningful and planned, designed for good rather than evil.

Only an innocent, however, would assume that a social ideal need merely be formulated to become operative. Addison was aware of the human reluctance to submit; and he knew that when men abandon reason for anarchy, they endanger the common good. To clinch even a philosophical point he was not above resorting to jingoism; that is why he called upon rebels against stability and moderation to take a lesson from English heroes. If a hero happened to be a Whig leader, so much the better. He pointed thus to Lord Somers, whose "character was uniform and consistent with itself, and his whole conduct of a piece. His principles were founded in reason, and supported by virtue; and therefore did not lie at the mercy of ambition, avarice, or resentment" (*F* 39). Moving outward from the individual to the nation, Addison described comparable principles of equipoise in the structure of British government: her constitution based on a limited monarchy and the three estates, her rational church balanced between coldness and zeal, her class organization dominated by a tolerant middle class.

Human shortcomings were a nagging concern, which he judged firmly but always with the forbearance of a gentleman. Himself an example of one "whose very best actions must be seen with grains of allowance," he concluded that his criticism of others could not be "too mild, moderate and forgiving" (*S* 169). Sensible and realistic, Addison was not weighing the traits of either rascals or saints. He knew that even good men have faults that sometimes run counter to the social good, and of these aberrations he was critical. What was more important to him was the overbalance of virtues that might prompt each individual to communal performance. Hence he sympathized with the acquisitive spirit of the English freeholders but would never approve of an amour-propre that choked off altruism. He praised man's dream of responsible liberty but deplored license that would end in either anarchy or tyranny. Similarly he respected piety but detested false zeal and bigotry. He saw the good man as one who walks a middle path of self-reliance, inner harmony, and public duty.

It was a path he himself followed despite the political rowdyism and religious bickering that blurred its boundaries. Forced to walk in such confusion, he nonetheless remained the well-bred censor who was almost always urbane and dignified. With quiet civility he exposed abuses of fellowship and obligation that endangered the social whole—that undermined church and state and that slowed England's trading advantage and her aggressive military machine. And then he tried a cure with benevolent cautery, the age-old therapy of bland satire. His eye was fixed on the world of the sociable animal, but only as the prelude to a glorious immortality, which has been promised to men redeemed from baseness:

> The cast of mind which is natural to a discreet man makes him look forward into futurity, and consider what will be his condition millions of ages hence, as well as what it is at present. He knows that the misery or hap-

piness which are reserved for him in another world, lose nothing of their reality by being placed at so great a distance from him. The objects do not appear little to him because they are remote. . . . For this reason he is careful to secure to himself that which is the proper happiness of his nature, and the ultimate design of his being. He carries his thoughts to the end of every action, and considers the most distant as well as the most immediate effects of it. He supersedes every little prospect of gain and advantage which offers itself here, if he does not find it consistent with his views of an hereafter. In a word, his hopes are full of immortality, his schemes are large and glorious, and his conduct suitable to one who knows his true interest, and how to pursue it by proper methods. [*S* 225]

For all its compromises, his social criticism became a religious act, directed to a reconciliation of man and God. He never obscured his vision of a deity, a being necessary and sophisticated who provides order and eternal design to all worldly achievement. As optimistic in this respect as Pope, he spread even more widely the truth that despite appearances not everything was

> together crush'd and bruis'd,
> But, as the world, harmoniously confus'd:
> Where order in variety we see,
> And where, tho' all things differ, all agree.[5]

Addison would not—indeed, could not—compartmentalize his views of the world in which he lived. His standards of behavior are grounded in convictions that adjust a Calvinistlike morality to Augustan common sense, reason, and pragmatic need. His ethic is directed to the literate whole: to the coffeehouse politicians and those who decide England's destiny, to the fox hunters and the urban idlers who inhabit fashionable salons, to the shopkeepers and the merchants moving restlessly from countinghouses to wharves, and to the atheists and deists and those who sink to their knees in the house of God. Animating his ethic is a spirit of calculated, necessity-driven benevolence. And it is this spirit as much as anything else that unifies his concern with the diversities of politesse, economic law, Whiggism, and rational piety.

His ethic, woven of many strands, lends itself to convenient stretching. A disciple of Sir Andrew and his mercantile code, Addison is also respectful of Sir Roger and the "landed" principle. He is a traditionalist who stands on the side of change when the new contributes to national order and prosperity and to learning and civility. He is a Whig who moves with ease among moderate Tories. He praises the beauty of faith, but his is a belief derived more often than not from earth-bound demonstrations. Arguing for tolerance as a token of good nature, he is a staunch Anglican who extends the hand of Christian fellowship to orthodox dissenters and turns his back on Catholics. He himself is rarely tormented by doubts; still, he admires and encourages the probing spirit of others as long as it disrupts neither personal nor communal stability. He is a paradox, yet predictable.

He concentrated his ethic on man, and first on economic man who devoted himself to being enterprising, diligent, and thrifty. But Addison's vision, although intense, was not narrow; it moved constantly outward from the single, acquisitive man to the social organization, then to the conglomerate of political men who reconciled their private wants with the public good. Ultimately, he turned his vision toward even larger perspectives. That is to say, he was absorbed by the endeavors of a secular though spiritually minded people who performed acts of charity and good will, observed the faith and natural piety of trinitarian Protestantism, and revered the Deity as the loving source of all mankind. The sociable animal was a fixed center from which Addison initiated his concept of interrelated activities and obligations as though he were making concentric circles with a stone cast into water. His gesture was sweeping, from the one to the many, from the temporal to the eternal, and from the lowest to the highest of human passions. It was this outward-flowing movement of Addison's mind, energy, and hope that dictated the arrangement of the chapters in this book, which is focused on Addison's effort to work out a comprehensive ethic for himself and his society.

PART I

IN THE MARKET PLACE

CHAPTER ONE

THE SQUIRE AND THE MERCHANT

NO English Augustan was more delicately attuned than Addison to the values and destiny of his own social group, which we would call the middle class. Faithful to the terminology of his time, he called it the "middle condition." Others spoke of it as the "middle station" or the "middle state." Whatever phrase is used to designate the structure, it refers to the "moneyed interest," the "new" men whose substance was largely self-made in domestic trade or international commerce (*S* 126, *G* 137). Addison himself was assimilated into this median society, thrived in it, and became its supreme historian. In this role he examined his subject with objectivity and amiable criticism. He devoted his skill as an essayist to analyzing the values of his class, which he admired, and its conduct, which he often deplored. But whether he praised or condemned, he wrote with a familiar politeness that skirted condescension and dogmatism. Many twentieth-century critics, however, have been so intent on creating the myth of Addison as middle-class propagandist, indeed, as apologist, that they have been blind to his role as its moral judge. The myth must be discredited on at least two counts: it falsely estimates his position as a social commentator; and it wholly ignores the modulated idealism with which he viewed his class and the ambitions of its members.

A solid class structure, he knew, is based on wholesome traditions as well as political and economic strength, but in the middle class the latter dominated. He himself would not have crossed the line from one social stratum to another, for all his ease in moving from the management of his country estate to that of his City investments. Yet he would never repress his attachment, at once reasonable and sentimental, to the "upper stations" where tradition still had meaning. They had for him what the middle class either lacked or scorned: they had—like Sir Roger de Coverley—a sense of their own worth rooted in the past and flowering in the present, a respect for their heritage of land, family, and stewardship. Indeed, Addison stood in one world and looked to another, but never with envy. What he sought was their reconciliation or at least a reduction of the friction that alienated "the landed" from "the moneyed interest" (*S* 126). In his periodicals he worked as a peacemaker but never challenged his station or doubted that its future was the future of England.

He often quoted from Holy Writ to confirm his social predilection. The appeal to scriptural authority was a well-known technique, common in the writing of such conspicuous apologists as Defoe and the clergyman Richard Steele.[1] For Addison, these quotations had a purpose beyond that of mere class vindication. He thought of them as a device for emphasizing the moral force of the "middle condition," for reminding its members of their heritage, and so for molding class behavior in piety and virtue. On 22 August 1712, for example, he said that "the middle condition seems to be the most advantageously situated for the gaining of wisdom" and for the procurement of virtue and contented well-being. He fortified this assured yet tentative statement with a passage from Proverbs 30:7–9, which defers to the will and omnipotence of the Deity: "Two things have I required of thee, deny me them not before I die. Remove far from me vanity and lies; give me neither poverty, nor riches; feed me with food convenient for me. Lest I be full and deny thee, and say, Who is the Lord? or lest I be poor and steal, and take the name of my God in vain" (*S* 464). Out of moderation, the very heart of the middle-class ideal, he educed man's freedom from bias and the enticements of sensuality, greed, and worldliness. Addison preached the relentless message that for every good there must be indebtedness; in return for its comfort, the middle class owed its Creator loving gratitude and obedience, its social superiors respect, and its underlings a steward's care.[2]

Whether in defense or criticism of the middle class, Addison's prose was brilliantly lucid. A master of painless exhortation, he insinuated where others were stridulous and dogmatic. Unlike Defoe, he persuaded without rhetorical hammer blows. And unlike his friend Steele, he argued without sentimentality. But then his task was also more complex: while Defoe and Steele hewed without question to the middle-class line, Addison meant to give the impression of being the uncommitted observer and impartial voice of reason. Hence Mr. Spectator assures his readers "that there is no rank or degree . . . who have not their representative in this club, and that there is always somebody present who will take care of their respective interests, that nothing may be written or published to the prejudice or infringement of their just rights and privileges" (*S* 34). Despite these brave words, Addison did not play host freely to divergent points of view and concerns. As his characterizations show, the Spectator Club is a genial fiction devised for the sake of inducement. The attentive reader of the *Spectator* soon discovers that Addison, contrary to his claims for a social cross section, has restricted the class lines. These are represented primarily by two members of the club: the squire Sir Roger de Coverley and the business man Sir Andrew Freeport. By the simple act of bringing these two opposed types into the club, Addison was in effect arguing for an *entente cordiale* between the classes that produced them. The gentry, he insisted, must relax its stiff-necked snobbery and often-calcified sense of tradition and find its place in a modern England. The middle class must in turn give up its greed and social indifference and admit the gentry's superior breeding.

Addison naturally preferred Sir Andrew to the squire, although he had his reasons for treating the merchant lightly: a serious depiction would have been an admission of partiality, and the literary context dictated a fictional touch. Addison made the semicomic tones of Sir Andrew's portrait consistent with those of the other club members. All of them, from Sir Roger to the deliberately featureless Mr. Spectator, evoke amusement as well as thought. Hence there is a playfully ironic cast to the name "Freeport" that belies Sir Andrew's advocacy of high protective tariffs and stringently regulated commerce. He is neither a manufacturer nor a tradesman, but one of those "merchants of foreign traffic" who have for their "great benefit to the public, and their great endowments and generous living been of best repute in England." He is the most useful and responsible of sociable animals, laboring to fulfill his dreams of financial glory for himself and of a favorable balance of trade for England. On the golden scales of heaven—a metaphor that Addison might have used in this context—Sir Andrew would not "have been found wanting" (*S* 321); his merit would have outweighed his eccentricity.[3]

The personalities of Sir Andrew and Sir Roger are not fixed. The one may lean toward the "landed interest," the other toward the "moneyed," but beyond these proclivities neither is confined by a ruling passion. Had Addison restricted them to singular drives, they would have lost their complexity and their association with the fluid ideas they represent. They would furthermore have been precariously deterministic and thus incapable of free moral choice. Instead Addison made both knights credibly multiplex; they go their literary ways as thinking individuals who choose between ethical alternatives and bear the responsibility for their choices.

The portrait of Sir Roger is complicated also by Addison's ambivalence toward his subject. Yet critics, ignoring this, have dehumanized the squire as an archetype of the egregious Tory fox hunter who later appears in the *Freeholder;* indeed, they have simplified Sir Roger as a deliberate blind "for throwing ridicule" upon the gentry, an interpretation, substantially unchanged since its first statement in 1800, that reduces him to an abstraction.[4] It violates Addison's intention of presenting the knight as a distinct personality, a mixture of rectitude and folly. In the words of Mr. Spectator, "His virtues, as well as imperfections, are as it were tinged by a certain extravagance, which makes them particularly *his*" (*S* 106). Sir Roger is a human being, laughable and noble, dignified and petty, rational and perverse. Only after we recognize his humanity can we see him as the symbolic representative of his class.

Addison constructed the figure of the squire upon a series of paradoxes and thereby defined him as a man. Sir Roger, for example, wavers between tolerance and prejudice. Although gregarious himself, he respects another's desire for solitude. Mr. Spectator especially was grateful for the old man's capacity to live and let live. "Sir Roger," said the ubiquitous observer, "who is very well acquainted with my humour, lets me rise and go to bed when I please, dine at his own table or in my chamber as I think fit, sit still and say nothing without bidding me be merry" (*S* 106). The squire's hospitality is divorced from whim; it is in the biblical spirit and indeed a virtue. This generosity, however, is counterbalanced by his political idiosyncracy and bigotry. When, according to Mr. Spectator, he and Sir Roger journeyed from London to the country,

> we did not so much as bait at a Whig inn; or if by chance the coachman stopped at a wrong place, one of Sir Roger's servants would ride up to his master full speed, and whisper to him that the master of the house was against such an one in the last election. This often betrayed us into hard beds and bad cheer; for we were not so inquisitive about the inn as the

inn-keeper; and provided our landlord's principles were sound, did not take any notice of the staleness of his provisions. [*S* 126]

But before dismissing the knight as a symbol of adamant Toryism and little else, we should remember that he shuns "the mischief" set in motion by parties in the country and is alert to "how they spoil good neighbourhood, and make honest gentlemen hate one another" (*S* 125). He finds it expedient to be a much more vehement Tory in the country than in London. His sense of friendship always transcends his political allegiance. He loves Sir Andrew despite a groundless suspicion that the merchant broadcasts "republican doctrines" and even has "a hand in the Pope's Procession," which the Tory ministry in 1711 condemned as an example of "Presbyterian" subversion (*S* 269, Steele).

The squire for all his liberality exacts deference from those he regards as inferiors. So "the good old knight," walking among his servants, betrays "a mixture of the father and the master of the family" (*S* 106). His benevolence—directed with little discrimination toward his parson, Moll White, his old servants, the gypsy fortune teller—is whimsical, operating on instinct rather than reason. Sometimes his charity is only condescension, boastful and wrong-headed. Addison forces his readers to ask questions: By what fiat can Sir Roger assume that in the house of God he "is landlord to the whole congregation," and by what presumption will he "suffer nobody to sleep in it besides himself?" (*S* 112). He is at once selfless and vain. For example, "he caught his death the last county sessions, where he would go to see justice done to a poor widow woman, and her fatherless children that had been wronged by a neighbouring gentleman." He was "always the poor man's friend" (*S* 517). Nonetheless he was often a posturer, orating at the assizes "with a look of much business and great intrepidity" when, with nothing to say, he wanted only to "keep up his credit in the country" (*S* 122). In another instance he scorns the gypsies as an "idle profligate people" but liberally pays one of their "Cassandra[s]" to flatter his amorous propensities (*S* 130).

Sir Roger de Coverley lives up to the merry connotations of his family name; he radiates countrybred heartiness and cheer. He is one of those rare persons, says Mr. Spectator, "who is not only at peace within himself, but beloved and esteemed by all about him. He receives a suitable tribute for his universal benevolence to mankind, in the returns of affection and good will, which are paid him by every one that lives within his neighbourhood" (*S* 122). Yet Mr. Spectator had forewarned his audience that the residents of the knight's country parish are as simple as the old man; they are really "not polite enough to see anything ridiculous in his behaviour" (*S* 112). He is a harmless eccentric. His conduct in church—his loud hymn-singing and thrice-repeated amens—emphasizes his singularity. His clothes, treated symbolically by Addison, are the anachronistic mark of a man who continues to wear a coat and doublet fashionable during the Restoration. He is silly enough to believe he can induce piety among his people with hassocks and pulpit cloths and itinerant singing masters. His lighthearted abandonment of reason to superstition dances through his juridical advice to poor Moll White "to avoid all communication with the Devil, and never to hurt any of her neighbours' cattle" (*S* 117).

No wonder that in bustling London he is because of the "mirthful cast in his behaviour . . . rather beloved than esteemed" (*S* 2, Steele). To be sure, his friends want to be agreeable to him, even as one delights in children or tries to please the senile. Addison himself would have liked Sir Roger to enjoy what was left of a privileged way of life that would soon be no more, but the knight had to be killed off. Despite his virtue he is functionless in a society that gauges everyone by his performance. And despite his enterprise, represented by the antlers that ornament the hall and the patchwork of fox noses on the stable doors, he is unable to compete in a mercantile world. The complex portrait of Sir Roger is built contrapuntally upon "singularities as foils that rather set off than blemish his good qualities" (*S* 112). In his portrait of a human being who is also a symbol of the landed tradition, Addison is both conciliatory and patronizing. His loyalty to middle-class values, on the other hand, is assured, although he himself is never so uncritical of middle-class activity as to believe with Defoe "that the tradesmen were the only gentry in England."[5]

Addison, who always respected a vital tradition, objected to radical realignments in the English social structure. He did not advocate ancestor worship, but he did believe that the wellborn inherited prestige and substance. Hence to writers like Horace, Juvenal, Boileau, and others who deprecated the "vanity of a man's valuing himself upon his ancestors," he retorted, "a man bids fairer for greatness of soul, who is the descendant of worthy ancestors, and has good blood in his veins, than one who is come of an ignoble and obscure parentage." As a Christian he believed that there was a scheme for equal opportunity in eternity, but experience taught him that Providence had not equalized man's temporal condition. Consequently "a man of merit, who is derived from an illustrious line, is very justly to be regarded more than a man of equal merit who has no claim to hereditary honours" (*G* 137). Addison accepts the privilege of birth—if it is supported by good works—and is as reasonably deferential to it as befits a free Englishman.

For him, unlike Defoe and even Steele, all "the great and noble monuments of charity and public spirit which have been erected by merchants since the Reformation" could not give "hereditary honours" to a Sir Andrew. This was a deficiency that the merchant and tradesman, however successful, would have to live with for generations to come; but this was the least of their shortcomings. Far more serious was a moral laxity that Addison exposed and analyzed, not vindictively but as a spur to reformation. He was disaffected by the fussy preoccupation of businessmen with ledgers. He yawned before their tedious repetition of maxims and superpragmatic belief that frugality was surely next to godliness. He was ashamed of their lust for profit, especially when it came from "fraud or cosenage" (*S* 174, Steele). Practical and direct, he urged them to tread between greed and profligacy, self-interest and indiscriminate altruism. He accepted Barbon's frank rationale that "the chief end of business or trade," though never indifferent to the public good, "is to make a profitable bargain." He nevertheless rejected out of hand Defoe's belief that gain is "the essence of [the tradesman's] being . . . the pole-star and guide, the aim and design of all his motions; . . . the center and point to which all his actions tend."[6]

Even as a pamphleteer, who in 1707 still talked and walked gingerly, he was offended by such greed. He saw it as a form of vulturism nullifying those old values that had helped to strengthen and refine the middle condition. He therefore recalled the mercantile ideal of trade motivated by communal as well as personal need. But that ideal, he admitted, seemed to lie in the past; in his own time, "minds that are altogether set on trade and profit, often contract a certain narrowness of temper, and at length become uncapable of great and generous resolutions" (*War,* p. 256). His conclusion, though hedged with euphemism, implies a sensitive concern for the individual and anxiety about the state. It silently admits that self-interest fetters man in the bonds of his depravity and restrains the nobility that should be part of his nature. It also echoes the economic truism that some forms of trade may benefit the individual but harm the country, swelling private bank accounts but depleting the national treasury and weakening public credit. Addison was appalled by the specter of an England picked bare by men "uncapable of great and generous resolutions."[7]

The members of the English merchant class were not the only fiscal scavengers to worry him. He found the mercantile Dutch with their cheap and grasping ways equally disturbing. He thought them unimaginative penny pinchers whose love of money had turned them into narrow, dull, coarse men. Relying upon personification, he described an artist who "was dressed in the habit of a Dutchman, and known by the name of Industry. His figures were wonderfully laboured: if he drew the portraiture of a man, he did not omit a single hair in his face; if the figure of a ship, there was not a rope among the tackle that escaped him" (*S* 83).[8] Thus he indicted the middle station's dreary literalism, whether manifested in Englishmen or Hollanders. No matter what useful ends diligence may serve, it is a poor faculty when unaccompanied by vision that rises above the commonplace. Such vision, he felt, is no less necessary to the merchant than to the artist.

If drudging application sometimes haltered the merchant on whom depended the "safety, strength, and prosperity of our nation" (*F* 42), so too did prudence. This was not an opinion calculated to soothe preachers of caution like Defoe, for example, who commended the "plodding fair-driving" man of commerce in his "safe and sure" enterprise. Addison for his part was sceptical of middle-class prudence as the cure-all for personal and national affairs. Occasionally he held prudence, in the Aristotelian sense, to be a virtue deserving of material reward, but he was equally convinced that wariness could be carried too far. "It very often happens," he wrote, "that prudence, which has always in it a great mixture of caution, hinders a man from being so fortunate, as he might possibly have been without it. A person who only aims at what is likely to succeed, and follows closely the dictates of human prudence, never meets with those great and unforeseen successes, which are often the effect of a sanguine temper, or a more happy rashness" (*S* 293).[9]

Perhaps Addison became caught up in the subject, because his demurrer is in itself so prudential that the meaning of his remarks does not emerge easily. He knew that the word *prudence* was often a slippery tag subject to more than one interpretation. Ethically it was a way of alluding to discreet conduct or practical wisdom. Given an economic context, however, it had a submerged meaning that suggested the acquisitiveness to which merchants abandoned their country's welfare or the sordid buccaneering by which they ravished foreign lands. It allowed greed without audacity and cruelty without courage; it ignored foresight and moral concentration upon things necessary for the work of the world. Addison, though not unaware of the ethical, was especially concerned with the economic implications of *prudence*. Selfish indifference to the needs of others, at home or abroad, repelled him as a failure in religious duty and also alarmed him because it menaced existing world order with the specter of chaos.

He was too earnest a Christian to praise indiscriminate prudence and too good an economist, for he sensed that merchants "tenacious of old laws and customs" were headed toward bankruptcy. He restated the idea positively in asserting that members of "a trading nation must be still for new changes and expedients, as different junctures and emergencies arise" (*Remarks,* p. 53). However roundabout his criticism of economic prudence, his working position is unambiguous. Longer in memory than many mercantile princes of his day, he still associated wealth and power with a bold spirit. And valiance, even of concept, is hostile to caution. For this reason he urged a return to daring individualism—which, as he tried to remind his countrymen, had advanced England's international prestige after her trade revolution. But he had no reason to be confident that his appeal for economic vigor and imagination would be successful, especially as he foresaw in the merchant class the onset of a flawed traditionalism that might in time inhibit England's commercial power and trading empire.

Economic timidity, it seemed to him, was like a parasitic vine; specifically, he feared that commerce had begun to feed itself destructively at the expense of its spiritual origin and purpose. He was inevitably disenchanted by a middle-class tendency to make security a greater good than piety and to sacrifice devotion to personal prosperity and comfort. This disenchantment proliferated, driving him to further censure. He felt even more put upon by a middle-class desire to hide spiritual lack under pious claims and mannerisms. This was hypocrisy, he observed, that "assumes a face of sanctity, and covers a multitude of vices under a seeming religious deportment." The tone may be frosty, but the mood is as much one of disappointment as of disapproval; he sought to understand the sources of this cant. He found a partial answer in the militant self-righteousness that clung to the middle class from its Puritan past. He recognized, further, that worldly pressures and sincere reverence are often antithetical. Such understanding allowed him to be forbearing, to feel "care and compassion" for those "who are walking in the paths of death, while they fancy themselves engaged in a course of virtue" (*S* 399).[10]

Theirs was nevertheless a pharisaical self-deception to be exposed, even if he had to bruise feelings and preach sermons. A Sir Andrew might complain about attacks on the middle class, but Addison would not be sidetracked. No "order of persons," he insisted throughout the *Spectator,* was "too considerable to be advised" (*S* 34). Like a secularist turned parson, he therefore urged all to invite the pain of honest self-scrutiny and impartially included himself among those who would profit from it. Sprinkling his statement with all-encompassing pronouns, he wrote: "There is nothing of greater importance to us, than thus diligently to sift our thoughts, and examine all these dark recesses of the mind, if we would establish our souls in such a solid and substantial virtue, as will turn to account in that great day, when it must stand the test of infinite wisdom and justice" (*S* 399). This is a worldly man speaking, who defines metaphysical truths in the idiom of finance and commerce: *establish, solid, substantial, account.* The point is that he brought his worldliness and piety into conjunction. No daily preoccupation, he implied, was ever so demanding that it should turn one's thoughts away from eternal judgment. Hence he argued that to peer into the covert ways of the soul was man's greatest obligation, for that act of self-distrust and of trust in God was the proof of conscience. Addison believed that self-analysis was the means by which a man rose above his limitations into the circle of divine love and never-ending life.

Whatever failings he attributed to himself, he was confident of his religious stability since it was anchored in Anglican authority. That is why he felt qualified to measure the greater shortcomings of others with either pity or contempt. Today we can respect his forthright intention, but our esteem is lessened by what appears thereafter to be a retreat from disinterested judgment: Addison juggled with forms of hypocrisy until he arrived at an acceptable choice. He preferred the hypocrisy of hyperreligiosity to that of blatant impiety, which he described as the exhibitionism of those who frequented "the fashionable end of town" and hid their belief behind a façade of irreligion. He laid bare such behavior as a conscious lie, a threat not only to the individual soul but to civil morality as well. When he condemned this "modish" fraudulence as worse than that practiced by the middle class, he resorted to dubious if not fallacious judgment (*S* 399).[11] He may have rationalized that in setting up ranks of hypocrisy, he would meliorate his own criticism of the middle station, or he may have convinced himself that middle-class pretense was less damaging to social order than that of the gentry. Whatever the case, ambiguous though it is, Addison had a scale for measuring differences in religious hypocrisy.

Although caste identity was important to him, he would not enter the noisy, long-running paper war over the merits of the middle and the landed classes. His obvious commitment bound him to conciliatory rather than divisive action. The two classes, he felt, must be brought to understanding or at least indulgence. His effort was formidable; but his cool nature was an advantage in counteracting bombast, as was his ability to use judicious rather than vehement language and implication rather than diatribe. He urged social harmony, as Defoe petulantly said, with "soft touches, the fineness of a clean turn," a keen satire "dressed up in, and couched under gentle and genteel expressions." His methods and goal differed from those of his critic, who wanted total victory at any price for his class. But Addison was just as perceptive as the older man in tracing the opposition between the two groups to their suspicion of each other's origin and destiny. Moreover, he shared with Defoe the knowledge that under cover of this distrust the two classes met in reluctant association and that there were even such acceptable oddities as Whig country gentlemen and Tory moneyed men. "As so many of our noble and wealthy families are raised by, and derive from trade," said Defoe, and Addison concurred, "so it is true, and indeed it cannot well be otherwise, that many of the younger branches of our gentry, and even of the nobility itself, have descended again into the spring from whence they flowed, and have become tradesmen."[12]

This was a point of connection but a feeble one, which Addison feared would be ignored in times of verbal rage and manufactured issues. He knew how mischievously words could create public disorder and strengthen demagogues. It was not so long since the Sacheverell incident, when the inflammatory rhetoric of political adventurers had almost achieved what many of the Whigs believed to be the triumph of anarchy. With the memory of that assault on reason and law still fresh, he again had cause to worry. He was depressed to see the gentry and middle class being goaded into an open "spirit of dissension." This was a calamitous spectacle, "not only as it destroys virtue and common sense, and renders us in a manner barbarians toward one another, but as it perpetuates our animosities, widens our breaches, and transmits our present passions and prejudices to our posterity" (*S* 126).[13] Anticipating the abortive Jacobite rebellion as early as 1711, he was oppressed by the gathering clouds of civil war. He saw the fury of that "unnatural conspiracy"—the epithet is his—aroused in part by the gentry's loyalty to the Stuart cause. But he knew that it had also been fanned by malicious wordmongers, rabid Whig journalists who accused the squirearchy of subverting mercantile ambition and, especially, Tory propagandists who hoped to frighten a hardpressed gentry into thinking itself imperiled by a militant tribe of "new" men.

In an environment made uneasy by class skirmishing the middle station was thought of by many as a bully taking unfair advantage of his strength. But Addison's image of the middle station was of a brawny youth who is bewildered by the contempt of his sophisticated elders. Addison wanted the middle class to harness its awkward power and settle into its constructive social role. But he realized that its members had to fix their identity; they had to stand firm against landowners fearful of displacement; they had to wear down the prejudice of the Tory fox hunter, his well-fed innkeeper, and all other grumblers against "the inconveniences of trade, that carried from us the commodities of our country, and made a parcel of upstarts as rich as men of the most ancient families of England" (*F* 22). The fox hunter and his publican are caricatures without the variable human qualities of Sir Roger. Like him, nevertheless, they epitomize class bias hardened by time and distrust. For many years there existed the suspicion enunciated, for example, by Berkeley that "a man whose passion for money runs high bids fair for being no patriot."[14] Disputing such a maxim, Addison tried to relax the trepidation of the gentry and to arouse the middle class to a sense of its own worth.

Implicitly he realized that his class was no longer as complacent as it had been in Elizabethan and Puritan days, that on the contrary it had begun during the Restoration to suffer an uneasy self-consciousness, which time had not alleviated. For several generations the middle class had been doing the right things for social acceptance—practicing Anglicanism and philanthropy and making a virtue of education. Still it was not permitted to live down its origins in dissent or its reputation for greed and boorishness. Addison ignored these reflections on the middle class; to debate them would have complicated his scheme of social peace. As it was, his literary goal of a practical union between the merchant and squire was simple, though the tones by which it was to be achieved were varied. At times he was mildly satiric, pinking his figures of either class delicately but nonetheless drawing blood. He laughed at those who were ashamed of their middle condition, whether they called themselves "Sir John Anvil," ironmonger, or "John Enville, Knt." (*S* 299). Occasionally he twitted the pseudo gentlemen who forced themselves to forget their commercial roots and suppress what was painful to remember. He could smile at such behavior only because he judged it a form of pretense that did no lasting harm to either the individual or the state.[15]

He conceded that illustrious ancestry lends distinction to "a man of merit" who conducts himself virtuously and wisely, but he mocked those who claimed honor for no better reason than the accident of good birth. He leavened his wit with pity and ridiculed the "empty man of a great family" who in worthlessness betrayed his descent "from a long line of patriots and heroes." From behind the mask of Nestor Ironside, he gently mocked the indomitable yet futile pride of Mrs. Martha, "who would never marry beneath herself" and so, having achieved a lonely death as a spinster of quality, "now lies buried among the family of the Ironsides, with a stone over her, acquainting the reader, that she died at the age of eighty years . . . and that she was descended of the ancient family of the Ironsides." In his satire of class rigidity, Addison never depended for his effectiveness on either viciousness or visible anger. He obviously delighted in using his quiet rhetoric not to flay (in the ripping manner of Swift) but to peel away the hypocritical layers of those who justified their lineage by reacting with "pious indignation . . . at the sight of a man who lived plentifully on an estate of his own getting" (*G* 137).

If Addison's critical tone was generally good-natured, it was on some occasions sober and reproachful. He showed little patience with the arrogant gentry who forced their sons willy-nilly into one of the learned professions. He wondered in fact at the freakish "humour of parents, who will not rather choose to place their sons in a way of life where an honest industry cannot but thrive, than in stations where the greatest probity, learning and good sense may miscarry. How many men are country-curates, that might have made themselves aldermen of London, by a right improvement of a smaller sum of money than what is usually laid out upon a learned education?" (*S* 21). Like other Addisonian observations, this one is subtly prudential. It makes a moral issue of false pride, demonstrating its evil in the arithmetic of red-inked debits. Yet its creator recognized that no expository statement, however persuasive, would carry the full force of his accusation. Several months later he repeated the idea, pushed to its logical fatuity in the personification of Will Wimble.[16]

This country gallant becomes a case study, a composite of "many a younger brother of a great family, [whose parents] had rather see their children starve like gentlemen, than thrive in a trade or profession that is beneath their quality." He is significantly named after an instrument designed to dig in soft ground or to extract rubbish from a borehole. Yet neither the name nor the comic dramatization of the figure bars sympathy with this middle-aged boy who is adept at "finding out a hare" and exercises "all the little handicrafts of an idle man": net weaving, knitting, and other "gentlemanlike manufactures." His life, stifled by excessive good breeding, is wasted on trivia; it is valueless to himself and his country. Will Wimble, who at first was intended to function only as an *exemplum,* assumed enough vitality to arouse compassion from both Addison and his readers. Were the essayist a man of less discipline and more passion, he would have wept for Wimble as a futile sacrifice in commercial England, where "the younger sons, though uncapable of any liberal art or profession, may be placed in such a way of life, as may perhaps enable them to vie with the best of their family: Accordingly we find several citizens that were launched into the world with narrow fortunes, rising by an honest industry to greater estates than those of their elder brothers" (*S* 108). One wonders, of course, whether a Will Wimble ever had the resilience to survive the competition of the market place. Perhaps Addison wondered also, but it was the moral principle, not the realistic possibility, that gave social dimension to the portrait.

Throughout the *Spectator* he repudiates both the false pride of the gentry and the false humility of the middle condition. He states without qualification that England is a mercantile power, a "trading nation" of ships and businessmen (*S* 21). There is no wavering in the conclusion that for him was empirically grounded and morally right: the good old days to which Sir Roger and Will Wimble clung so precariously were finished, and nothing could resurrect them. The task before Addison and other Englishmen was to salvage the wholesome traditions of the past and blend them with a modernity purified of rawness and greed. The task began for him specifically in an appeal, not for the erasing of class lines or the subservience of the gentry to the middle station, but for a rapprochement between the two ranks. The accord as he defined it, however, is no accord at all. Its conditions are economic and thus create an overbalance in favor of the middle class. Blandly, without any suggestion that his convictions might be biased or even questionable, he asked England's landed families to consider trade as meritorious as the genteel professions. In return he invited the Will Wimbles and their sponsors to partake of the manna dispensed by a commerce smiled on by Heaven.

This one-sided rapprochement was nonetheless socially and politically beneficial to both gentry and merchants. Addison dramatized these benefits in many numbers of the *Spectator* and the *Freeholder*. He stressed the ability of the two classes to live together in peace by making both Andrew Freeport and Roger de Coverley titled commoners and members of the Spectator Club. Whatever difference might exist between them is so "moderate . . . that it proceeds no farther than to an agreeable raillery, which very often diverts the rest of the club" (*S* 126). More to the point, this difference, although indelible, can support friendship. Sir Andrew, when he opened the book willed to him by the squire, "found it to be a collection of acts of Parliament. There was in particular the Act of Uniformity, with some passages in it marked by Sir Roger's own hand. Sir Andrew found that they related to two or three points, which he had disputed with Sir Roger the last time he appeared at the club. Sir Andrew, who would have been merry at such an incident on another occasion, at the sight of the old man's handwriting burst into tears, and put the book into his pocket" (*S* 517). In this vignette—its poignancy rare in the *Spectator*—there is no longer any separation in principles between the two men who, like all humanity, partake of mortality. No wonder then that Sir Andrew can move at will from the City to his country estate. He is at ease in either environment, just as he and Sir Roger were once at ease with each other.

Even the Tory fox hunter had been able to rise to the challenge of rational argument; his prejudices abandoned, he had undergone a conversion. His private apocalypse had come appropriately and symbolically atop the Monument erected to celebrate London's triumphant rise from near extinction during the Great Fire. High above its base, where two offensive inscriptions indicted the Catholics as traitorous arsonists, he had looked out over the murky, sinuous thread of England's river, which reaches the uttermost ends of the earth. From this perspective he could see that "trade and merchandise . . . had filled the Thames with such crowds of ships, and covered the shore with such swarms of people" (*F* 47).

Mercantilism and all its appurtenances attracted Addison as the magnet of English life. Merchants who honorably exercised their calling were his heroes, the protagonists of an unfolding success story. As an individual he never denied his affinity with the world of trade. As the influential Mr. Spectator, however, he played down his personal commitment to fulfill a critic's apparent disinterest. Nowhere is this spectatorial objectivity better achieved than in the periodical's early view of Sir Andrew as a merchant of credible strength and idiosyncracy. Possessing "indefatigable industry, strong reason, and great experience," this man of commerce whose "notions of trade are noble and generous" is made indistinguishable from others with kindred notions. Like those in his profession, he mouths the axiom that "true [national] power is to be got by arts and industry" (*S* 2, Steele). And he reveals thereby that peace is an investment more profitable than war. Certainly Addison encouraged his readers to equate beneficial trade with English heroism. He wanted them to accept trade as an activity that enhances the social good. But he also wanted them to see through Sir Andrew's deceptions and weaknesses, to respect the merchant's mastery of trade even when wearied by his tedious fulminations against idleness and his celebrations of frugality.

The portrait of Sir Andrew clarifies Addison's literary technique of balanced appraisal. With the merchant as with Sir Roger, nuances of personality—faults dovetailing merits—contribute to the gradual development of character. Out of Addison's deft treatment, Sir Andrew emerges as an individual as well as a representative of his class. As would be true of any individual, isolated situations fail to do justice to his total personality. His chauvinism and self-righteousness are only details in a whole portrait. Unsuspected complexities develop, which indicate, when taken all together, that Addison had not intended to create a mere stock figure but a vulnerable human being, more good than bad and more right than wrong, who is also an expert in his calling.

Sir Andrew's redemptive qualities, unfortunately, are often obscured by venality. An undue appetite for property and wealth promotes almost every one of his questionable actions and attitudes. Even scriptural authority becomes his personal text, providing a benedicite for his material comfort. His self-assurance is augmented by the unvoiced hope that God and mercantile rule favor him and that nature will magnify his already impressive prosperity. This is the unenviable side of Sir Andrew although there is the other, humane and decent, which should not be overlooked. For example, if he esteems possessions for their contribution to his private well-being, he also values them for their social benefit. If he is a tough-minded competitor, he also knows and observes the rules of fair play.

Addison accepted Sir Andrew's overall soundness, the probity of his mind and his good sense. Throughout the periodicals—from the *Spectator* to the *Old Whig*—the essayist shared many mercantile values, criticizing only their distortion. By the time he wrote the *Freeholder* his advocacy of mercantile goals makes the journal as representative of the middle class as of the Whig party. Still, in that same periodical his alignment is more to principles than to particulars of the class or its behavior. Like the merchant, then, he consistently praises the doctrine of labor as a religious and social virtue; he argues for the amassing of money and its power; he venerates habits of frugality and prudent charity; he pleads for toleration and contentment as adjuncts of economics; and he identifies the family, church, and constitution as the triad of English strength.

Addison's values may offend modern readers or make them uneasy. They may wonder how much of his praise of toil and thrift is prompted by an inordinate respect for property; they may bristle at euphemisms that seem to conceal a calculating justification of good works; and they may object to the materialism that Addison shares with contemporaries of his class. Modern readers may also find him priggish and too prone to see personal tranquility as the reward for communal obedience, especially among the poor.

It cannot be denied that Addison often lacks the magnanimity of greatness; indeed, his vision is sometimes as myopic and his thinking as biased as Sir Andrew's. Still, Addison's moral capacity, if flawed, is ever-present and active; and his often-critical grasp of reality must be acknowledged. Like Sir Andrew, he accepts his world, accepts the process of living as a challenge to be resolved by self-examination, reason, and discipline. Like Sir Andrew, he may regret that the answers to all of the daily problems that harass man are elusive, but persistence and integrity nonetheless compel him to search.[17]

CHAPTER TWO

THE SOCIAL VIRTUES

WHEN Addison described the two faces of morality—good and evil—he addressed his large audience with the assurance of a professional essayist. As anonymous as he was genteel, he drew a curtain between himself and the fictional censor, Bickerstaff or Mr. Spectator or Nestor Ironside. His was the seemingly divided self of the journalist who conceals the private individual behind the persona. Nonetheless, he was always a felt presence; he was the author who, inseparable from his subject, defines the moral life with utter familiarity. We know remarkably little of Addison the man but a great deal of Addison the essayist, who wrote of virtue as if he had mastered each of its manifestations. In this capacity he is a public performer who rarely becomes overbearing. Yet he is dauntless in his suave celebration of the good as an instrument of personal and civic well-being.

This was no philosophy of asceticism: his system of values is fully fleshed, born in this world and meant to stay here. Like many of his City friends, he believed that the final accounting, which awaits all men, must take place in eternity. Meanwhile, they thought it possible to reconcile temporal reality with metaphysical futurity and to adjust Christian behavior to the profit motive. Even while working diligently in the countinghouse for personal advantage, therefore, they radiated good will by employing the poor and contributing to charity schools and workhouses. For all their talk of compassion, theirs was a bleak and formal humanity, of a kind to which Coleridge later objected as "cold beneficence." It was practiced by busy, successful men whose gospel was obligation and performance rather than sympathy and contemplation. For Addison these were worthy men, their rectitude measured by power and comfort, not by humility and self-doubt. He saw them as men who were destined to win, no matter what cards they threw down; every one of their virtuous actions carried its own packet of rewards. His moral code is a program of studied cheerfulness.

Spontaneity was barred from an ethic in which motivation and act were tested for rational purpose. With reason as both means and end, Addison sometimes squeezed goodness into a strait jacket of necessity. His view of charity, for example, is constricted by requiring that the need of the individual be secondary to that of the community. On rare occasions he depersonalized virtue, as in his appeal for subordination. But if his ethic is sometimes narrowed by a slanted interpretation of particular virtues, it frequently has the breadth of "habitual good intention" and deed; it aims all its "thoughts, words and actions at some laudable end"—the glory of God, the welfare of mankind, or the benefit of his own soul (*S* 213). The Addison of the *Tatler* and the *Spectator* is a man of integrity who more often than not allows social altruism to supersede self-interest, as the Addison of the *Guardian* and the *Freeholder* is a man of political probity who usually permits liberal idealism to override party demands and the lure of high office.

In the eighteenth century the moneyed interest accepted the Protestant doctrine that everyone must willingly pursue a trade or profession. Diligence, efficiency, and perseverance in one's station—these were the sine qua non of obligation. They alone warded off poverty and ignorance, evils that sapped the energy of man and the order of his society. Many merchants and tradesmen, without denying the practicality of the doctrine, saw their labor as an exacted oblation, for "the Lord commands every one of us, in all the actions of life, to regard his vocation . . . [his] calling." Humble before God but aggressive in the market place, the individual who heeded the rule of labor would be rewarded with grace and profit.[1] Addison also acknowledged that conscientious toil, of the head or of the hands, was a responsibility owed to God and society. Conversely, he suspected solitude as a rejection of communal obligation and discipline. He either would not or could not concern himself with poets and artists, those lonely thinkers and gift bearers only able to work apart from the social group. A retreat from secular performance, no matter how austere or productive, in his judgment denoted civic failure and profanation.

He harmonized his lively regard for the doctrine of work with the aims of the popular essay. Although many of his ideas were drawn from the abstractions of philosophy and religion, he approached the doctrine as a pragmatic reality to be used for the reform of laggards in society, for the correction of delinquents who contributed nothing to the good of the whole. His purpose, then, was that of a schoolmaster. Sometimes he flicked the rod lightly, sometimes menacingly; sometimes he threw it aside altogether. His text was often Locke's *Thoughts concerning Education,* its lessons translated into an idiom that was familiar to many of Addison's readers. The philosopher was the concealed tutor, unmentioned yet pervasive, and Addison was an improvisor who elaborated Locke's proposals and remedies with a variety of literary methods, among them comedy, satire, *exemplum,* parable, and realistic anecdote.

His critical tone, which alternates between easy sophistication and earnest simplicity, is seldom so obvious as when he tags the ne'er-do-wells embryos, idols, or blanks of society. These metaphors gave him the double satisfaction of expressing his own disapproval and of catering to popular biases; similar pejorative names for the idle were current in a world that was far more Calvinistic than he would have admitted. For example, they were stigmatized as "the ciphers in their generation," "moth[s] in the commonwealths," "drones" deserving expulsion from a "well-governed state."[2] These epithets are directed to no single social group. Addison's criticism similarly disregards class. He speaks without discrimination to the beaux and coquettes, the Will Wimbles, the affluent of the middle station, and even the upholsterer who neglects his trade. He urges them all to mend their slothful ways and find their total identity in a vocation before time runs out. Addressing himself to the "youth of Great Britain," he asks them to remove themselves from their "deplorable state of nonexistence and . . . to come into the world" through industry and good will (*T* 97).

But he was not so naïve as to think his embryos could be trusted to undertake their redemption without external help nor so modest as to underrate his own services as a guide. The proper tool for reconstruction, he decided, was a course of discipline to expose and correct childish frivolity and posturing. He was convinced that in spite of puerility they were capable of mature adjustment and dignity. It is this element of confidence that makes his censoriousness palatable to a general audience. Like Locke, he proposed to restrain his embryos from acts of mere self-gratification and to attract them to tasks that, although difficult or even repellent, are part of the "condition of humanity." Then with firmness eased by understanding he would teach his students—as Locke had urged—that "all virtue and excellency lie in the power of denying ourselves the satisfaction of our own desires, where reason does not authorize them." Indeed, Addison seems almost fervent in imaging embryos and idols brought to moral action; he revels—paradoxically—in a vision of self-restraint triumphant over temptation. His specific aim, less exuberant and always pragmatic, was to excite them into a desire for a calling. To accomplish this, he worked out a system of rewards and punishments relevant to what Locke called a child's "love of credit" and "apprehension of shame and disgrace." Then, like Locke, he praised or chided his pupils, entertained or frightened them, according to their achievement.[3]

His literary technique varies with his pedagogical method. Sometimes he identifies himself with those he means to teach and mocks himself along with them as "the fraternity of spectators who live in the world without having any thing to do in it; and either by the affluence of their fortunes, or laziness of their dispositions, have no other business with the rest of mankind but to look upon them" (*S* 10). As time passes, however, the laughter becomes less jovial, the mood more disillusioned. He becomes fretful rather than amused by lives frittered away over pipes and chocolate, by the vacuum of days that are a succession of dittoes. Satire is more to the point than bland wit for one who presides over the dissection of a beau's head or a coquette's heart. But he also knew how far he could carry his satire before losing its object in either irritability or overrefinement. Hence he often turns to the *exemplum* as a means of teaching the joys of a productive life. A comparison between the domesticized Aurelia and the mercurial Fulvia, for instance, simplifies the reader's choice in wifeliness. As Mr. Spectator he also clarifies the didactic purpose of his satires and character sketches through direct exposition, berating those guilty of asocial behavior as ciphers who are as superfluous to the rich and learned as they are to the poor. Productive of nothing, "they are neither missed in the commonwealth, nor lamented by private persons. Their actions are of no significancy to mankind, and might have been performed by creatures of much less dignity, than those who are distinguished by the faculty of reason" (*S* 317).[4]

Despite intervals of unadorned reproach, Addison was by and large a benign censor who counted on man's desire to respond to moral stimuli. He therefore used his superb talent as a translator to reproduce literally Xenophon's account of the compensations that would follow a job well done: the sound of "the most delicious music, which is the praise of one's self; . . . [the sight of] the most beautiful object, which is the work of one's hands." Unlike some of his contemporaries, he did not guarantee salvation to his regenerate pupils; but he did tantalize them with the sure expectation of inner peace as a reward for secular virtue. Those who contribute to the world's business are "favoured by the gods, beloved by their acquaintance, esteemed by their country and (after the close of their labours) honoured by posterity" (*T* 97).[5] Again and again he stressed for his embryos the triumph of self-realization, which emerges from participation in a calling. While he came close to sentimentalizing the rewards of honest toil, he forgot—as a teacher or propagandist must—the fatigue, frustration, and failure that can accompany such effort. On the other hand, his role demanded one-sided concentration on positive results. And the role pleased him, for with an insight rare in his age he understood that labor offered the wholesome reality of routine and so displaced morbidity. He understood also that work often allowed man to restrain his depravity and made possible not only the assurance of identity but the hope of redemption.[6]

Certain that human labor fulfills divine intention, he spurned the possibility of debate and asserted that "every station of life has duties which are proper to it." Whether one's duties are assumed through choice or necessity matters little; all men "are under an equal obligation of fixing on employments which may be either useful to themselves or beneficial to others." To support what he saw as religious law, Addison sometimes abandoned his intellectual defense of the rule of labor. Instead he referred to Scripture and built his lesson upon man's fall from grace. That is, he involved his embryos directly in the disobedience of Adam and forced them to share their sinfulness with the father and representative of the race; they were not to think themselves exempt from "labour and industry," part of divine retribution (*S* 583).[7] When he uses this lesson and its biblical authority he strains against his own cheerfulness and implies for the moment that human nature is defective at its center. But he would not have dwelt on this imperfection; almost immediately he would have remembered that human dignity arises in part from man's recognition of his own weakness.

Addison's ethic is grounded in a sense of obligation. As a result, he calls insistently for a vocation that will impart the multiple benefits of vigor to the body, clarity to the mind, and joy to the soul. Fruitful labor, in short, is a requisite condition of healthy human existence. Although he makes allowance, as in *Spectator* 115, for pleasurable respites from productivity, such respites are only temporary. Accordingly they should not be permitted to distract from the pervasive spiritual and material reality that "the earth must be laboured before it gives its increase." To represent the ultimate folly of which man is capable when he ignores his duty, Addison interjects a description of Sir Roger's passion for hunting. Obliquely, through *exemplum* by antithesis, he ridicules the knight for having corrupted the doctrine of work. As one of "those who are not obliged to labour, by the condition in which they are born," Sir Roger is an indefatigable spendthrift of time and energy. His hunting trophies are "the most valuable furniture of his house," gratifying proof in his simple mind "that he has not been idle." Addison does not overtly condemn such behavior, but his mild irony speaks for his distaste of activity as useless and undirected as Sir Roger's. The implication is a serious one indeed, for in violating the doctrine of labor Sir Roger also violates the orthodox image of man as a "compound of soul and body ... obliged to a double scheme of duties," both spiritual and worldly, private and social.[8]

These comments on Sir Roger are introduced so unobtrusively as to give the impression of being an amiable aside in the midst of more serious business. In part, at least, Addison probably intended the knight's portion of the essay to be an amusing little entr'acte. Light moments like these were welcomed by the *Spectator*'s audience, and Sir Roger's oddities never failed to please. Yet for all his good nature, Addison is passing severe judgment on those members of the gentry who fail to respect a covenant with their fellow men. He does not impose a blanket indictment on the entire class and all of its pleasures; he is too discriminating and too just for that. He does, however, castigate selectively, finding Sir Roger symptomatic of a disproportionate concern with cause over effect and with means over ends. In his full-scale preoccupation with trivia, he has filled his house with stuffed animals to create a perpetual memento mori, of which he is himself unaware. The criticism in *Spectator* 115 strikes at any attempt to validate leisure divorced from toil. Work is the good, leisure the salutary interruption, the respite in which we renew ourselves for the continuation of labor.[9]

Anyone guilty of contravening the command to work was subject to Addison's attack. When the fault warranted it, he turned the edge of his scorn against the tradesman as well as the gentleman. One of his memorable malingerers was an upholsterer so eager for news of England's continental war that he neglected his family and, more important, his shop, which in time became bankrupt. Addison's narrative places a heavy burden of guilt on the derelict shopkeeper. Although he is aware of the commandment to labor and was at one time obedient to it, he now ignores his obligation while he indulges himself to no purpose in rooting out military rumor and gossip. As Hurd with unexpected discernment notes of *Tatler* 155: "The ridicule of this paper is incomparably fine and well placed." And so it is. Addison, however, needed something stronger than derision to point a moral and composed an ending as explicit as the message in a tradesman's manual of conduct. "This paper," he said, "I design for the particular benefit of those worthy citizens who live more in a coffeehouse than in their shops, and whose thoughts are so taken up with the affairs of the allies, that they forget their customers."

Among those who would have supported the censure of the upholsterer and his kind were Richard Steele (the clergyman) and Daniel Defoe. The latter filched the sketch and stressed its theme, asserting that no pleasures or interests are innocent "when they turn away either the body or the mind of a tradesman from the one needful thing which his calling makes necessary, and that necessity makes his duty; I mean, the application both of his hands and head to his business." This was the moral Addison proposed, less bluntly than Defoe, in a mixture of satire and exposition. Several years later his upholsterer is recalled in two *Freeholder* axioms: "the making of the politician is the breaking of the tradesman" and the "citizen turn[ed] a Machiavel . . . grows too cunning to mind his own business" (*F* 53).[10]

In both abstraction and anecdote, deliberate ambiguity shades Addison's definition of the doctrine of labor. The pleasures that he ascribed to a calling were balanced against the penitential burden of labor. In effect, he concluded that toil, like religion, has regenerative power; it is an act of contrition that brings its performer the joy of God's blessing; it is an individual's performance motivated by and directed to brotherly love. The gifts entrusted to every Christian, Calvin wrote, are shared by all other Christians. To uphold this doctrine, freed of its dissenting taint, Addison examined the ways of the ant and preceded his reworking of the parable with a statement of its thesis: An idle man is "a kind of monster in the creation. All nature is busy about him; every animal he sees reproaches him." He altered the intent of his biblical source by concentrating on the community spirit of the insects: "Everything is common among them; . . . they have nothing of their own: a grain of corn which an ant carries home, is deposited in a common stock: it is not designed for her own use, but for the whole community: there is no distinction between a private and a common interest. An ant never works for herself, but for the society" (*G* 157). The enthusiasm of Addison's statement (evident in its repetition of ideas) is at odds with the essayist's usual calm. To account for it we must move from the scriptural to the rhetorical tradition. Exposed to the latter at both grammar school and university, he learned from Quintilian how to use the *exemplum* of the ant or other "tiny insects [who] still toil for the common weal" as a valuable aid in oratorical appeal, one that would effectively establish a tone of convincing exhortation. But for Addison, even more than for Quintilian, polemic gusto had to be checked by prudence. He therefore imitated the rhetorician's use of the ant image and used it to persuade his audience "to enter the service of the state." With greater caution than Quintilian exercised he warned them not to copy the selfless industry of the ant but to adapt it to the human requirement—not to merge "a private and a common interest" but to make a "complacent" adjustment between them. His treatment of the rule of labor is complex, embracing thematic subtlety and tonal refinement. Yet it asserts as a simple truth that man's voluntary engagement in a calling is a touchstone of the moral life.[11]

Addison in his journals portrays generic man as sometimes capable of greatness though a composite of frailty and strength; he is unmistakably human, as variable as the sun in the dappled leaves of a tree. Occasionally the essayist saw him as a weakling who clung desperately to the ideal of order, occasionally as a victim of *hamartia* torn between gross worldliness and the "unsocial state" or between "his two capital enemies," the extremes of self-indulgence and miserliness. At the same time Addison saw as heroic beings "tradesmen" and "men of estates" who avoided either extreme to become models of frugality (*S* 191). Others might laugh at so niggling a creed, summed up in terms of pennies saved and pennies got, but in Addison's eyes such men were radiant with the virtues of industry and moderate self-denial. He applauded the rewards—a full purse and God's preferment—that followed upon such goodness.[12]

His argument for thrift is drawn from a tradition hallowed by time and gain, for he recommended financial temperance with the stern fiat of Roman Stoicism modified by the ethos of Protestantism and mercantile economics. Like the Stoics, he was critical of such luxuries as food, clothing, and decoration that gratify without being essential to comfort or health. Like the Stoics, too, he was occasionally willing to judge such extravagance as mindless indulgence rather than sin. He thus dismissed foppish ornaments, the "superfluities of garniture and equipage" as only "indications of vice, not criminal in themselves." He emphasized their transience by comparing them to short-lived and gaudy blossoms. Just as such blossoms "fall of themselves, when the root that nourishes them is destroyed," so flamboyant display and ostentation, the offshoots of intellectual error, will not endure once the mind is pruned of its folly (*S* 16).[13]

This is the relaxed mood in which he at times allowed himself to express his confidence in English good sense, moderation, and conscience. At such times at least, he was tolerant of worldly temptations and their spell. His tolerance, however, preceded a call to action, for when he wrote in this vein, he did not intend to condone the fault, only to plead that it be redressed through rational analysis and self-scrutiny. But such forbearance was not typical. More often he echoed Protestant hostility to luxuriant frivolity, which he feared as a despoiler that ravaged human energy and social fortitude. To forestall its effects—if he could—he laughed, ridiculed, and chided in an unobtrusive literary war against extravagance, which will, as Calvin asserted, "either seduce or disturb . . . thoughts of the heavenly life" and attention to the improvement of man's soul.[14]

Such austerity lies just below the surface of Addison's view that undisciplined appetency flouts divine benevolence. Property, regardless of who holds title at the moment, belongs to God and may not be abused by man. "It is a great presumption," he said, "to ascribe our successes to our own management, and not to esteem our selves upon any blessing, rather as it is the bounty of heaven, than the acquisition of our own prudence" (*S* 293). Because he believed vast wealth in the hands of an individual or a single family was necessary to both cosmic and social harmony, he deplored any kind of profligacy as an affront to God. Pragmatic cause, in other words, terminated in spiritual effect: proper use of wealth he equated with rectitude, improper use with the sins of unfaithfulness, disobedience, and ingratitude.[15]

Extravagance he found sinful not only in a private context but in a public as well. The affluent man who diverted an excessive share of his wealth to pleasure was indifferent to the needs of others and thus was socially deficient. In journals as diverse as the *Spectator* and the *Freeholder,* Addison repeatedly argued that abundance must find its way into public as well as private channels. While he held that benefit must accrue to all, his conviction was firmer than his solution. How, he asked, are Englishmen to be assured of the moral disposition of coin and bullion and trading investments; what indeed are the guarantees that such treasure will function for communal well-being? Sumptuary legislation, which might have been an answer, was distasteful to him. To favor it would have been embarrassing, like making an inventory of another man's wallet. Through scattered innuendo rather than direct or consistent statement, he denied the effectiveness of sumptuary legislation, which he saw as a curb on moral choice, as contrary to human impulse, and a depressant on English affluence.[16]

On the other hand, he felt that something positive must be done to halt the wastefulness that had already infected the world of the well-bred and was beginning to send its virus into the middle station. Hence he undertook "to look into the manners of the people, and to check any growing luxury, whether in diet, dress, or building" (*T* 162). Only a confident writer would have adopted this tone, which, though assured, is informed by neither personal superiority nor Grundyism. He was no Puritan provoked by pique and sour disposition. He was in fact motivated by a kind of patriotism typical of his world, committed to a simple code, which Berkeley later synthesized: "Frugality of manners is the nourishment and strength of bodies politic."[17]

Addison identified frugality with the human power to steer clear of penury and wastefulness. According to his thesis, it is sensitive to religious and political obligation but without conscious strain adjusts to the mercantile argument that wise spending brings prosperity to the individual and abundance to the state. He laughed, for instance, at the petticoat as a billowing emblem of female conceit. Still, like Goodman Fact's suit of English broadcloth, it would bring about "a prodigious improvement of the woollen trade! and what could not fail to sink the power of France in a few years" (*T* 116).

This same seriocomic tone animates his description of a fashionable lady's toilette. Her clothes may be prodigal of effort and time; but they are an economic triumph, "the product of an hundred climates. The muff and the fan come together from the different ends of the earth. The scarf is sent from the torrid zone, and the tippet from beneath the pole. The brocade petticoat rises out of the mines of Peru, and the diamond necklace out of the bowels of Indostan"; men are sacrificed, ships are lost, and the earth is ravished to satisfy the high fashion of a single "woman of quality" (*S* 69).[18] Ecclesiastes notwithstanding, all is not vanity, and ego may yet serve the social good. Addison brings off a half-serious proof that even a primping woman contributes to England's well-regulated trade and its favorable balance in the markets of the world. By deferring to mercantile good, he navigated the mainstream of his age and eased what might have become spectatorial austerity.

Addison was aware that he often presented the merchant as dull, one who, circumspect and successful, toils with indefatigable steadiness. As a human being, however, he is limited. Knowing that he must choose between good and ill, the merchant often oversimplifies the complexities of such a choice, and he glorifies discretion for its competitive strength. He embodies every trait of the so-called civilized man whom Rousseau was later to deride: "Always moving, sweating, toiling, and racking his brains to find still more laborious occupations: he goes on in drudgery to his last moment, and even seeks death to put himself in a position to live."[19] But Rousseau's subjective language would have been alien to Addison's sense of restraint and respect for quiet security. The essayist, as familiar with the merchant's virtues as his deficiencies, gave the former the resilience of his own politeness, sometimes bending them to social and political need but never stripping them of their rational benevolence. Behind his printed words, Addison was not so virtuous as to be selfless, yet he was sufficiently an altruist to feel that he must do everything possible to reduce human suffering and promote order within the family and state. He was a fallible but decent man who stood with both feet on the middle ground of reality, and despite contradictory critical judgments that run from Macaulay to Dobrée, he was neither saint nor villain.

He argued, for example, that the businessman must above all else be honest. "There is," he wrote in *Spectator* 469, "no man so improper to be employed in business, as he who is in any degree capable of corruption." He was thin-skinned on this subject because he knew that many merchant princes and tradesmen esteemed a reputation for honesty only as the basis for expanded credit. Defensively he both anticipated and responded to attacks by the gentry on sharp trading. Agreeing that these reproofs were often justified, he underscored his contempt for façade morality. Defoe might in the main allow the shopkeeper a certain latitude, but not Addison. As Isaac Bickerstaff and Mr. Spectator, who never had to worry about remaining on the black side of a tradesman's ledger, he insisted that wealth acquired through deception, even if within the law, is evil. Although he never denigrated the profit motive, he set businessmen a goal of service; he asked them to behave toward the public with "justice and equity, [to find] a thousand occasions for all the good-natured offices of generosity and compassion" (*S* 469).[20] Integrity for him was a good beyond dilution, as real and lasting as the divine source from which it flowed. In expounding rectitude, he felt comfortably beyond the reach of controversy. He was in fact risking nothing. He knew that in theory all his readers felt about dishonesty as they did about sin—they were against it.

While Addison saw getting and giving as complementary, he was reluctant to see them as equal conditions. If, as he had no doubt, it was blessed to give and receive, the blessings seemed to him slightly in favor of the latter. Despite the high-flown sentiments of the cliché that "charity is a virtue of the heart, and not of the hands," he did not believe that the "general benevolence to mankind" should be boundless—or "universal," as Calvin did. Addison looked on charity as a "moral virtue" and not an "amiable instinct." Rational and objective, he rejected the idea of careless largesse; on the contrary, he wanted the charitable act tailored to a scale of need. Thus he judged benevolence misguided if "it makes no distinction between its objects, if it exerts itself promiscuously towards the deserving and the undeserving, if it relieves alike the idle and the indigent, if it gives itself up to the first petitioner, and lights upon any one rather by accident than choice" (*S* 177).[21]

This is a joyless manifesto that glosses over the physical and psychological hardships of poverty. It is insensitive to the moral apathy that persistent want imposes on those reduced to bare survival. Poverty for Addison is an inevitable condition that must be relieved by philanthropy since it cannot be cured by economic reform. Even when he gives his definition of charity a religious context, he is constrained by a debit-and-credit arithmetic. Charity he makes "an offering to Him who has a right to the whole, for the use of those, whom . . . He has described as his own representatives upon earth." Recalling the scriptural glorification of charity in the Book of Job, Proverbs, and Matthew, he endorsed acts of giving that harmonized business adroitness and devotion. "We should," he counseled, "manage our charity with such prudence and caution, that we may not hurt our own friends or relations, whilst we are doing good to those who are strangers to us" (*S* 177).[22]

A favorite outlet for middle-class bounty, the charity-school movement had an articulate champion in Addison. He saw the schools as a source of food, clothes, and even life for children who might otherwise perish as beggars and thieves on the streets and roads of England. His interest in this movement, however, was as much social as it was humane. The children of the poor, he felt, should be trained to serve society; and the charity schools could best promote this end not by imparting knowledge but by promoting obedience. The children were to be drilled in incontrovertible truths: neither to steal from their masters nor to waste time at work, to be dutiful servants, and to look forward to heavenly reward. In Addison's optimistic prediction, the charity school "seems to promise us an honest and virtuous posterity," a contented poor willing to accept the stewardship of their economic and political leaders (*G* 105). This harsh optimism, which denies the children of the poor the advantages of learning, was attacked many years later by Dr. Johnson, who demanded the "privileges of education" for all and denounced the "salutary restraints" implicit in the charity school as but "suggestions of pride."[23]

But Johnson's was to be a minority voice. Addison's, however, was representative of his century, particularly in his defense of the charity school as an instrument of political and social order. His appeal for the establishment of foundling hospitals, on the other hand, was radical, anticipating by several decades what was to become a new outlet for organized English charity. When he spoke out for such hospitals in 1714, only the Royal Hospital in Lisbon and writers as temperamentally disparate as Petty, Chamberlayne, and Berkeley gave him precedents for his program on behalf of England's illegitimate children.[24] The prevalence of bastardy did not anger him or even rouse him to moral anxiety; but he could not speak of one of its brutal consequences "without horror": the assizes provided him with a grisly record of parents—"monsters of inhumanity"—for whom infanticide was the answer to unwanted progeny (*G* 105).

Along with others of his civilized, Christian world, Addison detested such barbarity, although his public reaction is formal, almost impersonal. He recommends shelters for abandoned children, but seems emotionally untouched by the external evils that cause illegitimacy: poverty, ignorance, inadequate moral guidance, and the harsh drabness of a life of want. Never did he fail to label these conditions as evil or refuse to acknowledge them as an unfortunate source of human unhappiness. Nonetheless, like the other defenders of the status quo—and their number was legion—Addison convinced himself that such inadequacy and injustice were necessary to England's class structure, which for all its flaws was the best devised by the mind of man. Illegitimacy was not a problem about which he thought in terms of reconstruction. Rather, he could only promote foundling hospitals as institutionalized sanctuaries for the innocent. If, coincidentally, the hospitals proved to be in the interest of commerce and increased manufacture, so much the better. In his commitment to foundling hospitals Addison is at once the moralist and the mercantilist. These institutions as he conceived them would overlook the stigma of illegitimacy and bring the children to adulthood; they would arrest the despair and fear that rob "the commonwealth of its full number of citizens" or, more accurately, of its full number of productive ciphers (*G* 105).

Addison's attitude toward the poor is chillingly benevolent. He favors the group over the individual and the establishment over both, but this is consonant with the Latitudinarian spirit of his world. However, he never questioned the need for good works. Indeed, for merchants and tradesmen who fell too easily into the slough of denial, he recalled in *Spectator* 177 the story of a prosperous Job who "delivered the poor that cried, and the fatherless, and him that had none to help." If this ideal lay beyond Addison's consistent reach, he recognized it as an ideal and was drawn to it, magnetically and without volition, as the essence of good nature.

While there may have been an unbridgeable distance between him and the suffering of the needy, he was able to join with all men—rich and poor, learned and ordinary, squire and merchant—in their search for contentment. This is a good, he conceded, which does not provide wealth but drives away the hunger for it; contentment does not dispel anxiety but makes it endurable. The result is an equilibrium that "has indeed a kindly influence on the soul of man, in respect of every being to whom he stands related." His description of contentment is Stoic in origin but is eased by the less intellectual temper of Protestant Christianity. While the peace of the Stoics was passive almost to negation, offering only "silence" rather than satisfaction, that of orthodoxy was positive and dynamic. While the Stoics rarely used the word *happiness,* the Christians underscored it and its synonyms. Addison, when speaking of the rewards of contentment, used the term *gratification* to proclaim that "a contented mind is the greatest blessing a man can enjoy in this world" (*S* 574).[25]

At the same time he strips the idea of sentimental illusion and treats it with a realistic focus on human will. Contentment for him becomes the calm that follows man's submission to estimable ends: it is a reward that comes only after the individual has conquered unreasonable desires and has accepted his station in the community. Geared ultimately to public order, it is inseparable from Addison's principle of social hierarchy. Because he viewed England's social system as inviolable, he condemned any random shifting of vocation, any movement contrary to the "order and distinction" of his society. And yet he knew, when he faced the "truth of it," that "honours are in this world under no regulation; true quality is neglected, virtue is oppressed, and vice triumphant." He remained unangered by such injustice because he judged it "necessary in the present constitution of things." Instead, he turned attention from temporal inequities to the justice of eternity; there disorder is rectified and all imbalances of caste are "set right" according to the excellence of one's performance here on earth (*S* 219).

Several times he prompted the *Spectator*'s audience to remember that men are only strangers and sojourners upon earth, that life is merely a pilgrimage. But ascetic metaphor and abstraction nettled people who, dwelling in earthly comfort, were reluctant to die until they could exact their own conditions. To make the idea and image more palatable, Addison humanized both in the figure of Epictetus, the crippled philosopher, who, though he "lived and died a slave," performed his assigned role "in perfection" without complaint. Epictetus moves through the pages of the *Spectator* as an enviable human being, a hero conveniently distant, proving to Augustan Englishmen that superiority is founded in virtue and obedience to station (*S* 219).[26]

Hierarchy was as relevant in the home as in society, for Addison thought of families as "little domestic governments," which provided a stockpile of citizens for the prosperous state (*G* 165). The political analogy, though it reduces the family to a functional unit, appealed to many as the affirmation of a long-standing tradition. Since the large household was by general agreement a national asset, he did not sentimentalize the home as a center of love and forbearance. It was rather a training ground for social discipline. He silently rejected Locke's recommendation of natural law as the foundation of family life. Instead he denied his own liberalism, took sides with Filmer, and described the family as an authoritarian government in miniature, a "patriarchal sovereignty" (*S* 500).[27] It is not likely, however, that he himself would have seen this contradiction or worried about it if he had; in this instance he mirrored without distortion a culture that exalted domestic discipline as an absolute good. "The disobedience of children to parents," said Defoe in the *Review* for 2 October 1711, "like that of subjects to a prince, remain to be judicially resented; neither does the command of forgiveness take place here, at least the obligation to it cannot be the same."

Under Addison's direction a painter might have composed a typical family with its members displayed at three distinct levels of authority and submission, as though they were on a three-tiered dais. Grandly dominating the group from the master's seat on the uppermost platform would be the husband-father. At a slightly lower elevation would be the modest wife-mother. Seated beneath both, probably on the floor of the bottom tier, would be an assortment of docile children. As the family's chief source of material comfort, the Addisonian father is "king and priest" (*S* 500). Even Defoe's father-metaphor, "guide and governor," is inadequate for one who is not only an exemplar of financial astuteness and virtue but a ruler with unquestioned power. The matriarch has a secondary role, which involves educating the children, overseeing the household, and devoting herself to her husband in affection and duty. Addison's portrait of the ideal woman makes her as respectful of wealth as her husband and as concerned with its prudent use. She is a paragon of efficiency whose thrift is as natural and obligatory as her motherhood. Finally, the children. Their function in the familial scale is simply to defer to the will of their parents in "subjection and obedience"; to do otherwise would literally be sinful.[28]

As long as this ramrod morality remained abstract, Addison could accommodate himself to it, but in a real situation it made him uneasy. At the back of his mind, perhaps, was Locke's opinion that parents must allow a child freedom of action and election upon maturity. But at what point in the child's development, Addison wondered, does the transition to maturity take place? When, in short, must the parental grip be relaxed? To dramatize a dilemma that obviously touched upon many lives, he depicted a daughter who married without her parents' consent and thereafter "languished under the displeasure of an inexorable father" (*S* 181). Caught between theory and reality, he bent, as usual, toward the latter. The girl might have been a child within the family, but biology and instinct were on her side. In refusing to concede his daughter's maturity, the father was guilty of unnatural conduct and unchristian behavior. This was Addison's reluctant judgment on Thursday, 27 September 1711. Within a week, however, he was shaken by Defoe's accusation of moral laxity and prepared to beat a judicious retreat to his theoretical position. On 6 October he called up once more the metaphor of the family as a "patriarchal sovereignty" and in effect vindicated the "inexorable father." He bowed again to custom and insisted that "the obedience of children to their parents is the basis of all government, . . . set forth as the measure of that obedience which we owe to those whom Providence hath placed over us" (*S* 189).[29]

There was little softness or warmth in the Addisonian family. When he described it figuratively, he found images that stressed symmetry, efficiency, and discipline. Sometimes his language reflected a concern with trade, sometimes with society and war. On one occasion he compared his ideal family with an English trading ship, which being "duly trimmed, wants neither sail nor ballast" (*S* 128).

Its course was precise, predictable, steady, and gainful; the father—the most arrogant figure to appear in the *Spectator*—is of course the captain. On other occasions he is a militarist whose troops are always at attention. The metaphors are less important than Addison's ethical intention: he refused to separate parental leadership from rigid discipline and social duty. The father may indeed speak to his children in the peremptory voice of the centurion but only to fashion them into "a multitude of . . . reasonable creatures, citizens, and Christians" offered to the body politic (*S* 500).

The solid virtues admired by Addison—regulated attention to pew, ledger, and family—bring daily satisfactions. They also bring comfortable retirement as the climax of a busy, useful life. For Sir Andrew, "grown old in the heaping up of riches," this is one of the "mercies, favours of Providence, and blessings upon an honest industry" (*S* 549). In withdrawing from the City to a landed estate he tacitly acknowledges that it is time for him to convert energy into reflection; and by retirement he celebrates and caps his career. He does not change his values or his class; he merely readies himself for the last phase of his career.[30] With these final brush strokes Addison's portrait of the merchant can be seen whole.

When Sir Andrew makes his last appearance in *Spectator* 549, he is a contented man, at peace with himself and the world. He is also closer to the reader than ever before because Addison has allowed him the intimacy of a letter to Mr. Spectator. By shifting the point of view from witness to participant, Addison strikes a subjective note; the testament of a man in his twilight bespeaks sincerity. Sir Andrew's closing words are no exception. Not only is the letter revelatory, it is the basis of an unstrained empathy that results from the merchant's tranquility as he justifies a career of endeavor. He has had moments of ambition spotted with greed and arrogant self-satisfaction, but good intentions and charity have cleansed him. He has in the past shown a stony resistance to profitless change, but Addison now suggests flexibility by taking him away from the City. His retirement is symbolized as the act of a malleable individual who has come to terms with his destiny.

As the mark of success, retirement in Addison's eyes had a special, middle-class relevance. It was a tradition—still evolving, to be sure—formalized by an unstated protocol of honorable retreat. One did not enter into it simply by resting his oars after the long pull of competition. Rather, like Sir Andrew, one had to pass three trials of recognition and obligation, which validated the custom. First, having devoted one's life to substantial gain, one had to admit that accumulation has definable limits beyond which it becomes greed. In this spirit Addison has the old man see the error of his earlier aphorism "A merchant has never enough till he had got a little more." With new clarity he has come to think "he has enough, and is determined to pass the remainder of his life in the enjoyment of what he has."

Addison knew that wealth alone did not justify retirement. His merchant therefore had to pass a second trial; he had to admit that the demands of competition were now beyond him. Unwilling to impede progress, to stand like an old tree whose shadow stunts younger growth, Sir Andrew tacitly concurred with Defoe's tradesman that "an increasing love of wealth in the decline of life is a sight shocking to human nature."[31] And finally he had to pass the third trial, that of conceding his own mortality. Sir Andrew, because he must turn his eyes from the till to eternity, reckons that he "may find business enough on himself, by setting his mind in order, preparing it for another world, and reconciling it to the thoughts of death." In a burst of moral realism, his creator has him leave the earthly struggle to others and resign himself to the truth that eternity begins with the grave. Meanwhile the merchant has the satisfaction of a life well-spent and of a retirement well-earned.

Even though Addison has removed Sir Andrew from the sphere of action, he does not permit him to undergo a change of personality. The pace of his existence is now less brisk, but only death will immobilize him. He is contemplative and mellow, as is the right of an old man, but he is no dreamer. Sir Andrew continues to accommodate his experience to every situation. In *Spectator* 549 as at the beginning of the periodical, we are still expected to judge him realistically in the terms of his own useful wisdom. That is why Addison, noting the merchant's persistent habit of frugality, exacts a practical rather than idealized response from his readers.[32] The imminence of death purifies much of Sir Andrew's thinking, but he never forgets the efficacy of wealth. He finds fresh and safe sources of profit in the land. Canny investment "in substantial acres and tenements," furthermore, enables him to erase his mortal debts with good works. What was good for him was also good for the community, and Addison himself could hardly disapprove of such calculating altruism. "My gardens, my fishponds, my arable and pasture grounds," Sir Andrew grandly remarked, "shall be my several hospitals, or rather workhouses, in which I propose to maintain a great many indigent persons, who are now starving in my neighbourhood." For better or worse, Sir Andrew's charity remains businesslike, grounded in his time and class.

In *Spectator* 549 Addison depicts Sir Andrew's retirement as a profitable partnership with nature. "As in my mercantile employment," said the merchant, "I so disposed of my affairs, that from whatever corner of the compass the wind blew, it was bringing home one or other of my ships; I hope, as a husbandman, to contrive it so, that not a shower of rain, or a glimpse of sunshine, shall fall upon my estate without bettering some part of it, and contributing to the products of the season." Obviously, in retirement the merchant has changed only his physical locale, not his disposition. The English freeholder emerging from the industrious and thrifty merchant was an evolution deemed proper by Addison, by society, and undoubtedly by God. "*Finis coronat opus,*" Sir Andrew declared and with casual inaccuracy attributed the Ovidian quotation to either Vergil or Horace. He cared little who had first stated the thought; his business was only "to apply it." If Addison was amused by this ostentatious, shaky learning, he was reconciled to it. In his last appearance, as throughout the *Spectator,* the knight's achievement is presented as one of practical morality and sound finance. It is a triumph of good will, which in Addison's eyes makes minimal the merchant's cultural deficit.

CHAPTER THREE

THE MERCANTILIST PRINCIPLE

ADDISON'S quest for social order took him at times to heights of academic conjecture but not to linger; in his practical concern for English stability, he usually adjusted concept to action and ideal to reality. Certain abstract topics—the interdependence of ethics, political thought, and economic theory, for example—were pleasant for speculation in the library or coffeehouse, but hypothesis was only a prelude to action. The important thing, he had learned from Locke, was "to try such speculations . . . to see how they will prove when they are reduced into practice." That is to say, he was drawn toward the kind of demonstrable proof to be found in the market place, where, in his own period and for at least a century before, the coexistence of war and trade made for English affluence. This was reality; he could not stare it down nor extirpate the association of profit-making with slaughter.[1]

He had scruples about the amassing of private wealth, but far fewer about the nation's acquisitiveness. As a matter of conscience he was troubled by England's monetary expedience. Yet, in common with many of his era, he deduced that she had to capitalize on militant commerce if she were to assure her riches and hence her invincibility. Along with Sir Andrew, that paragon of lucrative logic, he believed that wealth rather than arms was England's best defense against attack and usurpation. His premise extends a pruned olive branch. While it does not deny peace as a moral good, it pleads—in a polite aside—for a solvent military machine equally prepared during periods of armistice and of conflict. Otherwise, perseverance, Marlborough's strategy, and even Shovell's death would have been mere romantic sacrifices in a real war fought for British destiny. Addison, who strongly believed that the courage of England's patriots contributed to her might, was convinced nevertheless that funds and public credit had played a more important role in defeating the enemy at Blenheim and Ramillies.[2]

He and his readers knew that England's strength lay in her ability to pay for naval vessels, sailors, munitions, horses, and trained military personnel; that money equals martial striking power, for gold and silver are the sinews of war. This knowledge they shared with most mercantilists of their day. Defoe, for example, prudently observed, " 'Tis the longest purse, and not the longest sword that conquers nations." And, as he put it still more bluntly, "they that have the *Gelt*" have ready access to the most professional armies in Europe.[3] Addison would never have uttered such crass statements, even in the national interest. But he understood that a powerful state cannot often allow itself the luxury of unassailable ethics; it must reconcile ideals with practicality.

In the *Spectator* he justified his country's pursuit of wealth as a defensive necessity, but in that nonpartisan periodical he was also on guard against his own chauvinism. Released from the yea-saying of hyperpatriotism, he freely excoriated Englishmen who lusted after wealth without respect for means or ends, equating their behavior with perversion of social morality. He wrote angrily against the cruel exploitation of Negro slaves and Indians in the American colonies: "What colour of excuse," he demanded, "can there be for the contempt with which we treat this part of our species; that we should not put them upon the common foot of humanity, that we should only set an insignificant fine upon the man who murders them; nay, that we should, as much as in us lies, cut them off from the prospects of happiness in another world as well as in this, and deny them that which we look upon as the proper means for attaining it?" (*S* 215). Behind this attack was his recognition that all people, whether primitive or sophisticated, enslaved or free, possess reason and are innately equal. To deny either the Negro or the Indian his humanity was to deny God's creation of man. He therefore accused Christian exploiters of profanation and criminal pride and placed them in a hell made of "several molten seas of gold, in which were plunged the souls of barbarous Europeans" who destroyed other human beings "for the sake of that precious metal" (*S* 56).[4]

His sense of the brotherhood of man was genuine. When—as a private subject—he could afford the freedom of moral judgment or even indignation, he never dissembled. His sympathies were never specious, but they were often divided, altering with his roles. As a propagandist and statesman he had values that were sometimes at odds with his personal convictions, because his own values were preempted by the demands of the national purse or his country's posture in war and peace. Thus his own qualms about slavery and conquest, stated in the *Spectator,* were real. In his role of public official and pamphleteer, however, he always remembered the truism that "in the present constitution of the world, wealth and power are but different names for the same thing" (*War,* p. 246).

Less than two years after his *Spectator* essays against capitalizing on primitive peoples, he again wrote of slavery, this time in *The Trial of Count Tariff,* a brief but significant pamphlet that has been ignored by biographers and critics. Here he is official Whig allegorist splashing vitriol on the Tory-negotiated Assiento, the agreement between England and Spain signed in March 1713. Into a courtroom drama he brings Don Assiento, "a tall, black, blustering person, dressed in a Spanish habit, with a plume of feathers on his head, a Golillio about his neck, and a long Toledo sticking out by his side: his garments were so covered with tinsel and spangles, that at a distance he seemed to be made up of silver and gold" (*Trial,* p. 271). The personification, obvious and polemic, was anchored in two equivalents in Britain's political life. One was the Assiento, which granted an English company under the patronage of Anne a thirty-year slave-trading monopoly; it empowered English merchants to transport forty-eight hundred African slaves annually and to sell them in the Spanish West Indies. The other equivalent was Arthur Moore, author of the Assiento, who was ridiculed by the Whig press as "Don Arturio . . . Marquis d'Assiento."[5]

Addison used the pamphlet to spread his party's hatred for Moore, an Irishman who, having begun his career as a footman, was therefore a fraud as a diplomat—"nothing but show and beggary" (*Trial,* p. 271). But Addison's Whiggish distaste for Moore as a person was mild in comparison with his contempt for Moore's handiwork. If the man was only a strutting, worthless agent, the document he had written was politically monstrous: it was as affected as the golillio about Don Assiento's neck, as vicious as the Toledo at his side, and as pro-Spanish as his habit. Or in a metaphor popular among the Whigs, the Assiento, "like the dog in the manger, . . . neither trades itself nor will suffer those that would."[6] Obviously the Whig attitude toward the Assiento—which was also Addison's—had nothing to do with scruples. He denounced the agreement as a restriction on the unlimited transportation of slaves in British ships from Africa to Spanish America. No matter how satisfactory the agreement might appear to opportunistic seaports like Bristol, Liverpool, Plymouth, and London, he declared that to settle for a mere forty-eight hundred multiplied by thirty was "worse than nothing" (*Trial*, p. 271). It is apparent that in this instance he subordinated people to pounds, conveniently separating his Christianity from England's activity in the market place.

His interest in human beings as salable commodities coincided with his awareness of England as an emerging commercial empire with territorial aspirations. Certainly he had no quarrel with his country in this posture; whatever augmented her strength, security, and prestige pleased him. At the same time, he would have had her administrators refrain from acting like piratical conquerors. Their roundup of slaves in Africa and their mistreatment of American Indians was, he complained, evidence of "rapaciousness and corruption" (*S* 55). Even though he was convinced that the conquest of primitive peoples was in the best interests of England, he would have preferred to avoid the accompanying brutality and license. Thus he asked that the conquest be carried out humanely, with some regard for those who differed from Englishmen only in the shape of their noses or the color of their skins. He asked not for the redress of a moral wrong but for a palliative of civilization's confusion of economic necessity, might, and right.

Nor did his humanity ever restrain his eagerness to take up "pen in the defence of property" or wealth (*F* 1). For him all personal order and all civilization depended on property and the state's acknowledgment of it as a natural right. Indeed, whatever philosophical warrant there may be for his veneration of property, his joyous pride in ownership is immoderate. He was probably thinking of his estate at Bilton, near Rugby, when he proclaimed, in the first number of the *Freeholder*, the "unspeakable pleasure" in "calling anything one's own. A freehold, though it be but in ice and snow, will make the owner pleased in the possession, and stout in the defence of it." That self-assured journal was begun as the triumphant Whigs settled in to distribute the spoils. Whereas in the *Spectator* he had asked his readers to remember that they were short-lived pilgrims on their way to eternity, within only a few years he was willing to postpone knocking at the gates of heaven until he had enjoyed the earthly pleasures granted by a title deed. But in an age of pensions, annuities, and retirement plans like our own we can scarcely appreciate eighteenth-century respect for property. It had indeed been the threat to property, as much as the threat to liberty, that provoked the Revolution. To preserve property, therefore, was to preserve the Revolution principle and the right of individual freedom as it was asserted in 1688–89.

Addison's political ethic was fixed in his concern for tangible goods and place. He argued that the state must assure to its people life and liberty, but he insisted that these rights were inseparable from that of property, whose preservation was also a fundamental responsibility of government. Using a stereotyped figure of speech to suggest vitality and growth, he described property as the source of freeholders' strength and the root of their humanity; it was "the substantial stock, that conveys to them their life, taste, and beauty; and, without which, they are no more than blossoms, that would fall away with every shake of wind" (*F* 1). And even this luxuriant metaphor does not convey the full intensity of a conviction that would withhold legal recognition from a state failing to build into its very structure reverence for private ownership. The right of property became for him an article of political belief; it was a tenet of material faith attuned to his respect for British law, which in the name of justice would hang a child for stealing a loaf of bread.

Addison was a good enough Aristotelian to correlate the form of the state with the character and distribution of property among its inhabitants. He asked himself Aristotle's question: "What is the best constitution for most states and the best life for most men, neither assuming a standard of virtue which is above ordinary persons, nor an education which is exceptionally favoured . . . nor yet an ideal state which is an aspiration only." Like Aristotle, he realized that the best answer lies in the mean, with a reduction of extremes and a broadening of the middle condition. He therefore distrusted absolute monarchy and republicanism, exalting instead government led by a limited monarch and based on a middle-class charter of rights—a constitutional system of law and equity. Only a state so constructed could uphold individual property rights or indeed be safe from political violence that threatened it. He assumed, as had Aristotle, "that the best political community is formed by citizens of the middle class," men of comfortable estate who had learned to live in easy condescension or deference to other ranks. Addison therefore looked to the moderation and self-discipline of all just and upright freeholders to give his world the stability it so much needed.[7]

His commitment to constitutional monarchy never seriously wavered. But as early as 1705, probably under the influence of Sidney's *Discourses,* he said that "there are no people in the world who live with more ease and prosperity than the subjects of little commonwealths" (*Remarks,* p. 195). Overtly he expressed his confidence in republicanism's potential for social good, yet he detracted from that confidence when he deliberately used the word *commonwealth,* which still bore the pejorative connotation of the Cromwellian Protectorate. Such ambivalence cannot be brushed aside as passing uncertainty, since three years later he repeated: "In a commonwealth there are not so many overgrown estates as in monarchies, the wealth of the country is so equally distributed, that most of the community are at their ease, though few are placed in extraordinary points of splendor and magnificence" (*War,* p. 262).[8] His admiration is restrained by misgivings and his praise moderated by loyalty to monarchical rule. No republican himself, he was reporting and interpreting for his countrymen what he had seen and understood on foreign soil.

His criticism of the republican state is often simplistic. When favorable, it is usually encapsulated in a word like *ease,* which is either equatable with prosperity or vaguely suggestive of commercial well-being. When unfavorable, it is tied to rivalry between England and those other European communities, Holland in particular, that vied with her for the spoils of trade. Even when it aims at objectivity, it lacks a speculative breadth that would free it from empirical conclusions. Unacceptable is his assurance, probably derived from James Harrington and Algernon Sidney, that republican principles were bred of necessity in land-hungry nations whose survival depended on planned frugality.[9] Nor is it possible any longer to take seriously the extension of his premise that a large and rich country could not tolerate a commonwealth. He was impelled by national prejudice and his sense of English superiority to deprecate republicanism as a source of grossness. He therefore attacked the Dutch, whose commercial power he distrusted, as a people who lived coarsely in order to peddle luxuries abroad, their lives a sacrifice to profit.[10]

He genuinely feared that the liberty evident in a commonwealth carried within itself the seeds of mob license and could in time reduce the exercise of individual enterprise and confound the right of property. He feared the tyranny of the many, which he associated with the latent self-destructiveness of republicanism. Drawing an illustration from Harrington's *Oceana,* he pointed to the Swiss, who divided "their estates equally among all their children, by which means every one lives at his ease without growing dangerous to the republic" (*Remarks,* p. 224).[11] This statement in part approves man's capacity to adapt himself to circumstances: the enclosed government of the Swiss cantons, dependent on the equality of their citizens, required the periodical redistribution of wealth to preserve uniformity. Still, the approval is grudging, held back by Addison's anxiety lest republicanism erase distinctions among men and classes. Such leveling, he was certain, could only violate individual freedom and a divinely ordered disproportion of abundance.

English constitutionality was the yardstick by which he measured alien governments. What he therefore admired about republicanism were those characteristics that it had in common with limited monarchy. In both he sought and found the moral equation of natural rights and civil liberties, an equation that led to commercial boldness and wealth. But when allegorically he contrasted the republican state with British monarchy, he found the former adequate but imperfect, a contradictory amalgam of bravura and drabness. In some of its characteristics he thought it was "exceeding bold and daring"; but in others "mean and vulgar" (*T* 161). From his English vantage point republicanism appeared bright with a promise never to be fulfilled.

Except for republics, however, he appears to have had no tolerance for any state that was not in the British mold. He hated absolutism as much for stifling economic freedom as for paralyzing religious and political liberty. Like Petty, he believed that an absolute monarch is one "who taketh from the people, where, when, and in what proportion he pleased."[12] But more sternly than Petty and as liberally as John Locke, he denied the compatibility of despotism and a prosperous civil society. He was prepared to stamp out the absolute monarch as a tyrant who held himself above the law and twisted it to his advantage. With his frankly jaundiced eye on France, he concluded that under a tyranny individual property rights are nullified: private fortunes, land, and even life are jeopardized.[13] To his City friends the threat to life was perhaps no more frightening than the prospect of emptied coffers or downward-flowing Exchange prices.

Constitutional monarchy equals economic solidity, and absolutism equals financial chaos: this was Addison's political arithmetic, to judge from his allegory in *Spectator* 3 on public credit. One of the rare pieces of propaganda in the periodical, it is his testimonial to the Bank of England as a commercial fortress created by Britain's political system. Charles Montagu, Whig chancellor of the exchequer and Addison's patron, and a group of London merchants had formed the bank in 1694 when large sums of money were needed quickly for the prosecution of King William's War. Subsequently the new bank, which had outlasted the military emergency, became the most influential economic institution in the country. The original nominal capital of £1.2 million had by 1710 been augmented to £5 million. During the War of the Spanish Succession, it came to be the exchequer's principal ally and, what Swift bitterly condemned, the stronghold of "moneyed" men and "Whiggery." This feeling was so strong among the Tories that they sought to weaken the Whigs' financial grip on the kingdom by destroying the bank. After rancorous journalism and a rival land bank failed to do this, they tried in the election of April 1711 to dislodge the Whiggish "pursemen" who directed the Bank of England and to seat their own directors.[14]

Addison strengthened the Whig cause, a month before the election, with his dream allegory on public credit. It insisted that the national economy could not survive either Tory manipulation or the absolutist restoration that the Tories would effect once they were in control of the kingdom's wealth. The heroine of the essay, Public Credit, is so prosperous that she sits upon a heap of moneybags in the Bank of England.[15] Like the heroine of a romance, she is a beautiful virgin, rather delicate in health and given to swooning. Her frailty merely points up her endowments, making her altogether alluring and mysterious. But she shuns frivolity and proclaims her sober patriotism by adorning her walls with the Magna Charta and the Act of Settlement, her moderation by displaying the Acts of Toleration and Uniformity. Addison's feminine ideal, a paragon of prosperous virtue and forbearance, is a tribute to British steadfastness.

Suddenly Public Credit is confronted by phantoms, among them Tyranny, the Genius of the Commonwealth, and, most frightening of all, a twenty-two-year-old person we guess to be the Pretender. Armed with sword and sponge, the young man has come to destroy the Act of Settlement and erase those other documents on her walls that symbolize political and religious freedom. In the face of such danger, Public Credit does what any respectable young virgin would do: she faints. Her possessions, attuned to her premonition of national bankruptcy—almost the ultimate in catastrophe—shrink before the apparition, and at the climactic moment the moneybags collapse. Just as all seems lost, a group of "amiable phantoms" arrive at the desolate scene in time to avert disaster, and hope rises once again for Whiggish Public Credit—and so for England. The agents of succor are "Liberty, with Monarchy at her right hand"; then comes Moderation accompanying Religion; and finally, to establish lasting and prosperous freedom, the Hanoverian heir approaches, escorted by the Genius of Great Britain. With the appearance of the future George I, optimism has succeeded despair in the counting room: "The bags swelled to their former bulk, the piles of faggots and heaps of paper changed into pyramids of guineas." Public Credit revitalized is once more the stewardess of England's wealth.

Within a few days of the *Spectator*'s inception, then, Addison participated in political debate, proving the urgency with which he and the Whig leaders awaited the bank elections. Only unusual pressure, from within himself as well as from his party, would have forced him to grapple with such an issue in a new periodical whose professed aims were nonpartisan. No one, least of all the touchy, hard-pressed Tories, would be fooled by the transparent allegory. Nevertheless, it allowed Addison to evade open statement and to modify his grave intention with a show of literary play—the melodrama of fainting beauty in peril, rampant villainy, and chivalric heroism. It also enabled him to soften his role as a propagandist, for with allegory he could at least go through the motions of accepted literary practice, letting the moral insinuate itself and surprising his reader into knowledge and wisdom.[16] The allegorical gesture was above all a pragmatic one, designed to strengthen and popularize a factional cause among his readers.

In *Spectator* 3 he dramatized several convictions that he shared with most men of the City and his party. First, only a limited monarchy could liberate the potential skills and productivity of its people and thus guarantee the nation's economic future. Second, the need for political stability, which nourished Britain's complex trade and mercantile structure, precluded Tory control of the Bank of England as the nation's pivotal financial institution. With deliberate emphasis on Tory enthusiasm for the French-bred Pretender, Addison implied that the coronation of James III would be an economic debacle. The image of the young Stuart arriving with his sponge, already familiar in official Whig journalism, symbolized Tory repudiation of loans made to the government by City men since the Revolution.[17] Third, there could be no separation between the financial and political health of England. As Burnet had written two years earlier, every successful bond issue of the Bank of England "showed both the wealth of the nation, and the confidence that all people had in the government." Or as Addison argued more abstractly, prosperity and good government are the demonstration of national progress. The equation he created had a mathematical simplicity. "Riches and plenty are the natural fruits of liberty," with *liberty* equivalent to the Revolution Settlement and the Hanoverian succession (*S* 287).[18] Finally, he used his allegory on public credit as a promissory note, an implied pledge of good fortune abounding under his party's influence. By stressing conventional nouns and adjectives which connote either towering height or huge area—*great, prodigious, infinitely, high, vast, pyramids, heaps, hill, bulk*—he suggested England's limitless resources made possible by Whig foresight with the Bank of England as its instrument.

Although the bank in 1694 answered a special need, some economists had advocated a similar financial institution even earlier. Nicholas Barbon, for instance, had appealed in 1690 for a national bank of credit, modeled after those at Amsterdam and Venice, to reduce the complexity of payments between England and the nations with which she traded. Such a bank, he surmised, could make even more aggressive the foreign commerce to which the British had dedicated themselves for some six generations past.[19] That dedication had long been patent to anyone economically aware. According to Defoe, for instance, England under Elizabeth "gave herself a loose in trade, and got the start of all her neighbours, and like a strong horse in a race, who having shot ahead of the rest at their first setting out, by the skill of the rider, holds it all the way, by mere strength, as well as speed."[20] Addison humanized the energy and initiative implicit in Defoe's equestrian simile. At the "great council" of the Royal Exchange, tears of English pride dampened the cheeks of the usually composed Mr. Spectator. In this vignette the English merchants, realistically characterized, merged surface sentimentality with clear-eyed cunning. They gloried in the patriotic fact that they and trade had made "this metropolis a kind of emporium for the whole earth" (*S* 69). At the same time, as they moved in friendly if competitive assembly with foreigners, they demanded that England hold her trading lead against all challengers and at any cost.

In the early eighteenth century it was axiomatic that England's power depended on her wealth and her wealth on her trade. At once more seductive and lavish than her kin Public Credit, Trade was banally personified as "the universal mistress of mankind, courted and caressed by all civilized nations." Rivals fought bloodily over the lady, knowing that she would reward her victors with "riches, honour, power, and all other earthly [rewards]."[21] Consequently, the business-minded lovers wooed their "universal mistress" with fierce devotion and computed their blessings. Yet Addison minimized the acquisitive militancy of the merchant class; when in *Spectator* 69 he considered the public ends to which its members applied their capital, he could persuade himself that they were among the nation's most "useful" subjects. They may be prosaic and without glamour, like Sir Andrew; but they "knit mankind together in a mutual intercourse of good offices, distribute the gifts of nature, find work for the poor, add wealth to the rich, and magnificence to the great." By the time he wrote the *Freeholder,* in 1715 and 1716, sensibility and literary elegance had yielded to propagandistic hyperbole. In the Whig journal his aim was to perfect the mercantile image, so he presented the man of commerce as devoid of peccadillo or greed. Ponderous documentation, drawn from history, statistics, and legal precedent, was mustered to show the merchant as the patriot's patriot and England's selfless benefactor.[22]

Addison's readiness to flatter the merchant class is of a piece with his faith in the economic system that, through an elaborate structure of restrictive commodity duties, was intended to insure England's advantageous balance of trade. But even while he justified mercantile strategy and ends, he felt blowing across the country a new economic wind, generated by the arguments of such Tories as Child, Barbon, North, and D'Avenant. Anticipating Adam Smith, they declared that trade was divinely sponsored and simply "a commutation of superfluities." They maintained further that countries were adapted by geography to different commercial pursuits. D'Avenant, who summed up the hypotheses of this radicalism in international commerce, remarked that "trade is in its own nature free, finds its own channel, and best directeth its own course."[23] By implication he charged that the rigidity of mercantile practice subverted England's need for a liberated flow of foreign traffic.

Addison shared with free-trade advocates a hope of England's millennium as "universal merchant." He borrowed still other ideas from them. Like Sir Dudley North, he regarded trade, at least in definition, as "a commutation of superfluities," a medium for insuring a national reserve that would be neither sparse in goods nor swollen. And like D'Avenant and others, he predicted divine approval for foreign trade that supplied a profitable exchange of necessities and luxuries among nations. He anthropomorphized a trade-conscious Nature, attributing to her the wise geographical distribution of the trading community and the scheme whereby "the natives of the several parts of the globe might have a kind of dependence upon one another, and be united together by their common interest" (*S* 69).

If he walked hesitantly among these Tory economists, he occasionally grew impatient with the inflexibility of mercantilists. At times he objected to their conservatism and greed as perversions of a theory that he approved. He belonged to a transitional era and warmed more to the proven resources of mercantile economics than to the novelty and risk of free trade. He was always on guard against ideas not yet tested in the market place. Furthermore, he had absorbed enough business psychology to condemn as impertinent any attempt to tamper with the system of well-regulated trade that accounted for his country's commercial euphoria.

England had earned her trading pre-eminence and with it—to paraphrase George Orwell—the right to be more equal than other nations. The trade of the world, Addison Whiggishly believed, existed for England's advantage, and he shared Sir Andrew's conviction that "the vineyards of France [are] our gardens; the spice-islands our hot-beds; the Persians our silk-weavers, and the Chinese our potters" (*S* 69). When in later works he turned from such lighthearted chauvinism to sober expression and statistics, he defended the principles of mercantilism that prevailed in the eighteenth century: the regulation of foreign trade; the protection of domestic manufacture by import duties; the aggressive use of protective tariffs against economic and political rivals; and most important, the establishment of a favorable balance of trade for England over all other nations.

Nowhere is he more the confirmed mercantilist than in *The Trial of Count Tariff,* an allegory with several collateral intentions. Politically it aimed to frustrate St. John's economic plan for England in 1713, which threatened to divide the Whigs by serving the merchant class a feast of trading opportunities at the expense of England's military allies, particularly the Dutch. The allegory, further, affirmed the tested dogmas of mercantile theory—world-wide export of British wool and a well-ordered trade—which have always been associated with Whiggism. Specifically, the allegory celebrated the parliamentary death of the free-trade articles, the eighth and ninth, of the Tory-effected Treaty of Navigation and Commerce between Great Britain and France. These articles had been submitted to the Commons for consideration on 14 May 1713. From that day through the eighteenth of June, when they were defeated by a scant nine votes, and then until the autumn elections, trade was "the greatest concern of the British nation, and the subject which now employs both the speculations of most men, and the pens of several writers."[24]

The Whigs inflated the Tory position on French trade into "a DOCTOR SACHEVERELL," to make as good use of it as the Tories had of the Sacheverell incident in February and March of 1709/10. As his contribution Addison sometime between 18 June and 28 June wrote *The Trial of Count Tariff,* which was published on the last day of the month.[25] He intended the pamphlet as propaganda for the Whigs whenever they needed it, and they did again in the election year of 1714. If it lived "no longer than the question that produced it," as Dr. Johnson was to say in his *Life of Addison,* the author had no illusions about its place in literary history. The Tories, fearing the effect of this resounding trumpet of Whiggish truculence and economics, ordered Defoe, then Harley's economic propagandist in the *Mercator,* to rebut it. On 20 August, nearly two months after the publication of *The Trial of Count Tariff,* Defoe produced the lengthy and scurrilous *Memoirs of Count Tariff,* in which he denounced the Addisonian hero Goodman Fact as a counterfeit, an impostor, and a pawn of "political falsehood."[26]

Addison's pamphlet is adroit. It does not speak openly of mercantile theory (that he would do elsewhere) but alludes compassionately to "weavers, clothiers, fullers, dyers, packers, calenders, setters, silk-men, spinners, dressers, whitsters, winders, mercers, throwsters, sugar-bakers, distillers, drapers, hosiers, planters, merchants, and fishermen" (*Trial,* pp. 267–68). These were the humble people, loyal Englishmen whose trades would be destroyed by the ratification of the commercial Treaty of Utrecht. No wonder they sobbed when they saw Goodman Fact, even as in their many petitions they bewailed the afflictions the eighth and ninth free-trade articles would bring to Britons.[27] They were the people who believed with Addison that there should be no economic appeasement of France and that every move to increase Gallic strength hastened British doom. Through obvious figuration the pamphlet darkly intimates that no one can escape the tragedy of Tory economics, neither squires nor their tenants, City manufacturers nor their laborers.

On the other hand, *The Trial of Count Tariff* glorifies the sound commercial principles of the Whigs. Goodman Fact, to use a biblical analogue, becomes a Whiggish angel of Bethesda walking for the first time in three years among "a great multitude of impotent folk, of blind, halt, withered, waiting for the moving of the water"; and indeed he stirred not the pool but the great oceans, and "whosoever then first after the troubling of the water stepped in was made whole of whatsoever disease he had." The English trading community is revitalized by the dynamic presence of Goodman Fact who, if less than an angel, is a walking illustration of the various maxims of mercantile theory. His English broadcloth suit advertised the British staple, wool. His "two or three little superfluities from Turkey, and other parts" indicated his acceptance of a well-regulated trade with nations that drained no bullion from the Bank of England (*Trial,* p. 267).[28] His bottle of neat port proclaimed, to all who would see, that the Portuguese trade, established by the Methuen Treaty of 1703, was a "vent" for British woolens and so "the most valuable branch of our trade; . . . the increase of which, of late years was mainly owing to the great quantities of wines that were imported from thence, and consumed in Great Britain, instead of French wines, by reason of high duties laid on the latter."[29] There is no economic radicalism evident in Goodman Fact's behavior. Whatever is prescribed by mercantile theory he accepts without question. Addison's earlier gestures of independence are suppressed by his hero, whose traditionalism silences any cry for economic innovation.

Even in the *Spectator,* where he sometimes flirted with concepts of unrestricted commerce, he broadcast with no sense of contradiction the mercantilist's demand for a "favorable balance of trade," a phrase allegedly coined in 1621 by Thomas Mun, refined by Misselden two years later, and supported by such disparate writers as Temple, Berkeley, and William Wood. For all its acceptance, it was semantically misleading. It did not pretend to argue for equipoise of exports and imports, but for a government-controlled flow of commerce in which output is greater than intake. In Addison's romantic translation, "Our English merchant converts the tin of his own country into gold, and . . . his wool [into] rubies. The Mahometans are clothed in our British manufacture, and the inhabitants of the frozen zone warmed with the fleeces of our sheep" (*S* 69).[30] These words prompt comfortable images: of the world's inhabitants—from pole to pole and from east to west—dressed in British wool; and of an endless one-way flow of bullion into the swollen bags and onto the "pyramids of guineas" owned by the English damsel known as Public Credit.

Addison also dealt with the idea of a favorable balance of trade in the *Freeholder,* using it there to applaud the Whig-sponsored Treaty of Commerce with Spain signed in December 1715. This piece of diplomacy succeeded the 1713 trade agreement between the two nations that had been attacked by the Whig Speaker of the Commons as "insidious and precarious." What sanctified the new document was that it restored to British merchants in the Anglo-Spanish trade the security of protective tariffs, bounties, and time-tested prohibitions. Addison seemingly rejoiced in its signing and underlined its importance by devoting a large portion of a *Freeholder* essay to a description of the treaty's technical provisions and efficacy. He must have known he was writing an essay so dull as to raise the protesting shade of Mr. Spectator, but dull or not, it gave him a vehicle for praising George I and the Whigs.[31] In the *Freeholder* the needs of party fought with and often conquered the demands of literature.

He discussed trade as a Whig journalist, popular essayist, allegorist, satirist, and economic historian. He discussed it with wit or with a deadly—indeed, deadening—insight into "gratias," percentages, cedulas, and the salt crises at La Tortuga. From these varied techniques emerges a justification of his country's commerce that flatters the national ego and is a Siren song of reason. Addison's ideas are not original, but the manner in which they are conveyed is uniquely his.

He emphasizes the moral values of trade—its humanity and tolerance—while adjusting them to the material good of English society. He moves either with urbane easiness or with a freeholder's heavy tread between the practical and the ideal. He rarely forgets divine sanction and always remembers that the "national commerce redounds more to the riches and prosperity of the public, than any other act of government" (*F* 41).

To write his rationale he joined with others—from Coke and Barbon to Tillotson, Defoe, and Kennett—who were convinced that their sceptered isle was designed by God for trade.[32] Today their view of divinity as economic planner may seem like an exercise in chop logic, but the idea that commerce enjoyed divine approval satisfied Addison, although in his customary fashion he added to it the weight of human obligation. With evangelical fervor he termed it sacrilege not to "make these blessings of Providence and advantages of nature turn to their proper account." Over and over again he used the truths of trading economics to teach social responsibility, even as in his ethic trade itself functioned on behalf of communal order. Offering employment to the poor who might otherwise become rebellious, it also allowed "many, who have no fixed property in the soil of our country, [to] make themselves masters of as considerable estates, as those who have the greatest portions of the land descending to them by inheritance" (*F* 42). The statement, despite its circuitous language, suggests vigorous optimism; it predicts fulfillment of the Addisonian dream in which merchant and squire are reconciled.[33]

When he closed his mind to the partnership of war and commerce (and like most men he often forgot ugliness), he posited trade as a means by which man's difficulties might be eased and his dreariness relieved. England, he admitted, was self-contained as long as she was content with "the bare necessaries of life"; but he wanted more for his countrymen than Spartan endurance. He therefore looked kindly on the traffic that brought items "convenient and ornamental" as well as utilitarian. The movement of such goods helped refine English crudity, even "barbarity," and served as an antidote to English provincialism. Half in earnest, half in jest, he gave himself—and by extension his countrymen—the title "citizen of the world" (*S* 69). In the *Spectator,* where he judged his compatriots with critical accuracy, he implied regret that British tolerance of human differences was compelled by the needs of foreign trade. But in the *Freeholder,* where he had less reason to be either critical or accurate, he heaped fulsome praise on a nation of Englishmen who through commerce had become "kind, benevolent, and open-hearted to their fellow-creatures" (*F* 42).[34]

In the Addisonian image trade seems to be personified as the Tutelary Spirit of Great Britain, a towering figure who holds an oversized cornucopia in one hand while a snowy dove flutters gracefully over the outstretched palm of the other. The inspiration for such a stereotype is plain enough in Addison's periodicals and pamphlets. In these same works he rounded out his mercantile rationale by borrowing from Barbon the premise that international commerce "doth not only bring plenty, but hath occasioned peace." However, the peace that Addison upheld in the *Freeholder* had little to do with the *Spectator*'s ideal of mutual good will and dependence among nations. In 1716 he saw trade as a surrogate for armed hostility; it avoided bloodshed and mutilation but not "the advantages of conquest." Without recourse to brute force and the wasteful expenditure of military goods, "without violence or injustice," it gained for England "the wealth of [her] neighbours in an honest way; and . . . [laid] the several nations of the world under a kind of contribution" (*F* 42).[35] The *Freeholder* paired trade and successful blackmail, a coupling that Addison spoke of openly as a tribute to English derring-do and initiative. In blessing this profitable union he suppressed his earlier scruples and the moral sensitivity that vibrantly informed the *Spectator.*

During the twentieth century Addison has suffered severe attack for exalting British commerce. It is true that he saw it as the source of England's power and prosperity, an undeniable good for which sacrifices must be made. It is true that he often eulogized trade, divorcing it in the *Freeholder* from material motivation and forgetting at times the many bloody wars fought for international markets. Even in the *Spectator,* where he conceded the inseparability of trade and profit, he strained for lyrical effect in describing the exchange of England's homely wool and tin for the glittering wealth of the Orient. But the critic who stops here lacks historical perspective and misunderstands Addison's relationship with his readers. For he lived in and reflected the values of a mercantile culture whose affluence he welcomed for himself and other men, but especially for the national treasury.

He wrote of trade, moreover, as a journalist who often addressed laymen ignorant of and hostile to commercial adventure. He tried to reach such die-hards as the fox hunter and his innkeeper, to move them sympathetically in the direction of his own commitment. Factual truth, bald statement, statistics, and even lighthearted descriptions would never have dented their armored prejudice. With little compunction, then, he made a nonintellectual appeal to those anachronistic Tories who could be depended on to respond instinctively and emotionally to sacrosanct platitudes. He therefore waved the flag and proclaimed the holiness of British tradition, he lured with the promise of island invincibility and cajoled with the image of easeful wealth. But at the same time he earnestly held that trade is more than private bank accounts and the national treasury, that it is a moral force capable of lightening man's physical burden even as it animates his spirit and sharpens his conscience.

CHAPTER FOUR

THE WAR OF ECONOMIC RIGHT

SIR William Temple once compared the international exchange of goods with its "element," the sea that "has a certain pitch above which it never rises in the highest tides, and begins to ebb as soon as ever it ceases to flow; and ever loses ground in one place, proportionable to what it gains in another." The metaphor was his way of stating that with only a fixed amount of world trade each nation had to compete without letup for its maximum share. Similarly Addison believed that if English trading initiative lost its tensity, the slack would be taken up by other countries. He was jealous of all competitors, suspicious that whatever enriched another country impoverished his own. But there was always the comforting converse when England was prosperously in the ascendant. He did not care whether the trade-poor country was an ally like Holland or a foe like France; what mattered was the game of beggar-my-neighbor played not for selfish, individual spoils but for an England humane and powerful among the trading nations of the world.[1]

Unlike the ebb and flow of the sea, the movement of England's foreign trade was controlled not by natural phenomena but by the will of men on the Exchange, in countinghouses, and in government offices. Addison saw his country's trade—foreordained, to be sure—as a human activity to which he should make an offering. Thus in his own voice as a Whig pamphleteer or in the masks of Mr. Spectator and the Freeholder, he cheered any effort, even that of war, that would speed the perpetual flow of British commerce to the ends of the earth. As a civilized man and mercantile economist he would have conceded that peace was both more desirable and lucrative than war, especially for a country as affluent as England. Peace and war, if he chose to believe Defoe's maxim, are determined by a simple rule of necessity: "Rich nations love peace and poor ones war; the reason is plain, the poor have less to fear from the war, and the rich more to lose by it, than other people." And like Defoe he would probably have subscribed to an unwritten codicil: the rich no more than the poor will admit satiety. Both Addison and Defoe knew that as each state struggled for its share of the world's limited trade and treasure, amicable competition yielded in time to military force; and wars for economic advantage became "a point of undisputed right."[2]

In the spirit of his generation Addison boldly approved trade wars, particularly the War of the Spanish Succession. Not that he was bloodthirsty or drawn to the redcoat and feather. On the contrary, he was saddened by the toll of conflict. One day, as Mr. Spectator's invisible companion on a walk through Westminster Abbey, he grieved that "the present war had filled the church with many of these uninhabited monuments, which had been erected to the memory of persons whose bodies were perhaps buried in the plains of Blenheim or in the bosom of the ocean" (*S* 26). This is of course conventional lamentation, adjustable to the sentiments of a wide range of readers. Still, it appeared on 30 March 1711 when the Whigs, in their desperate effort to maintain public support for the war, urged their adherents to speak only of glorious victory and not of death or destruction. It was not often that Addison disobeyed party authority, and his disobedience in this instance was slight. But within the brief limits of a single sentence he at least acknowledged the reality of war, the bloody deaths of real people lost forever to their country. His feelings, however, and even his lament in no way dissipated his conviction that individual sacrifices must be made in a war waged for the national good. A country engaged in hostilities to protect its trade, he insisted, was beyond reproach, for it was then "in a natural state of war" and its course of action obligatory (*War,* p. 241). He consequently opposed any premature cessation of hostilities. Whenever talk of peace threatened the prosecution of the war—whether in 1707, 1710, or even the armistice year 1713—he scorned the peacemakers, either directly or through innuendo.

Prompted by Whig dependence on merchant support, he stood guard against England's potential enemies, her trading rivals. France, always a favorite contender for the role of malefactor, was "the most implacable" and "dangerous [foe] of the British nation" (*War,* p. 241). Even in 1716, when England was nominally at peace, he reminded his readers that "in former ages it was the constant policy of France to raise and cherish intestine feuds and discords in the isle of Great Britain, that we might either fall a prey into their hands, or that they might prosecute their designs [their commercial aspirations] upon the continent with less interruption" (*F* 28). His hostility was not uniquely Whiggish and certainly not new; ever since the reign of Elizabeth, England and France had competed in a constricted trading world. Their relations became abrasive when a French prince—Louis XIV's grandson, Philip, duke of Anjou—seemed about to inherit the Spanish kingdom and its possessions in Europe, America, and the West Indies. With polished outrage Addison called up the specter of Louis XIV, who, having devoured Spain, was preparing for fresh orgies: "What will he do when the trade of the Levant lies at his mercy; when the whole kingdom of Spain is supplied with his manufactures, and the wealth of the Indies flows into his coffers; and, what is yet worse, when this additional strength must arise in all its particulars from a proportionable decay in the States that now make war upon him?" (*War,* p. 242).[3]

Addison made his first journalistic commitment to the Anglo-French struggle in *The Present State of the War,* which in November 1707 he tailored to fit Whig propaganda. The pamphlet form was useful, for it allowed him to draw on a tradition pursued for nearly two hundred years by Englishmen writing on matters political with what Johnson called "a happy temerity"; it also satisfied his need to compose rapidly for a maximum audience prepared to spend only a few pence for his opinions.[4] In a pamphlet he could speak *in propria persona* and be more detailed, serious, and finished than in a government-sponsored periodical. And free of open association with a party, he could treat a single theme with pervasive intimacy.

When he wrote *The Present State of the War,* he was a fledgling pamphleteer, experimenting with various tricks of his craft, alternating between fact and fervor, and working for different emotional effects. He threatened and placated, intending to alarm or to ease tension, to coerce or to wheedle. To support his own militant posture, he sounded a roll call of illustrious names: William III, Caesar, Boccalini, and Vauban. He also evoked "common sense" and the aims of a vaguely defined posterity. Eventually he became a much more skilled debater and a less obvious one, but in this early piece he was convincing because unlike most propagandists he believed his own propaganda.

And why not, since he had what he regarded as incontrovertible sanction? The organization of his pamphlet, its logic of cause and effect, is his own; the policy it espouses, however, was worked out in conjunction with Whig leaders in party councils. Yet cunningly he never mentions party, either Whig or Tory, except for a sly anti-Jacobite reference to the "number of friends and well-wishers, which, it is to be feared, [the French] have among us" (p. 241). The pamphlet purports only to set before open-minded English patriots, unsullied by factional affiliation, data that provide a rationale for the war and its augmentation. Indeed, for some nine thousand words it plays on a single theme: "Let it not therefore enter into the heart of any one that hath the least zeal for his religion, or love of liberty, that hath any regard either to the honour or safety of his country, or a well-wish for his friends or posterity, to think of a peace with France, till the Spanish monarchy be entirely torn from it, and the house of Bourbon disabled from ever giving the law to Europe" (pp. 244–45). His presentation is simple and affective, carrying as it does the implication that only a traitor looks to peace.

Addison began with an exhortation to all good Britons: the countryman desiring an impregnable England, safe from "the force of [French] fleets and armies"; the Protestant hoping to secure the Anglican church from rampant Catholicism; the liberal seeking to uphold the English constitution against French absolutism; and the anti-Jacobite imagining the Pretender behind every door and bed curtain. He welded this diversity with a compound image whose intellectual contradictions are submerged in their patriotic appeal. Thus he portrayed England as imperiled by the "animosities and aversions" of France but superior in wealth, power, and honor to the Gallic tyranny (p. 241). He portrayed France both as having "something in it so terrifying, that one does not care for setting it in its proper light" and as merely swollen and readily deflatable: "The French monarchy is already exhausted of its best and bravest subjects. The flower of the nation is consumed in its wars: the strength of their armies consists at present of such as have saved themselves by flight from some or other of the victorious confederates; and the only proper persons to recruit them are but the refuse of those who have been already picked out for the service" (pp. 244, 250). Tying together this montage technique of depiction are details, carefully and intelligently interspersed, that point to the ultimate triumph of English power. The despair present in restrained passages of doom is minimal; optimism is dominant.

From the first pages of his pamphlet Addison describes the war as a many-faceted struggle. "Our All," he says, "is at stake, and irretrievably lost, if we fail of success" (p. 242). But he compresses "All" into economic concern and interprets the war as a test of England's right to clothe the world in broadcloth and serge. His language plainly connotes and enforces his preoccupation; he speaks thus of *substance, treasures, coffers, bullion, merchandise, value, sums, money, trade, pounds sterling, wealth, commodity, estates, cash, commerce, riches, gold, silver, power, masters, advantages, exigencies, traffic, expence, success, computation, levies, business, funds, taxes, credit, expedient.* And "Great Britain," who appears at the end of the pamphlet, is transfigured by a Midaslike glow. She is not only "rich as she stands in comparison with other states, but is really so in her own intrinsic wealth. She had never more ships at sea, greater quantities of merchandise in her warehouses, larger receipts of customs, or more numerous commodities rising out of her manufactures than she has at present. In short, she sits in the midst of a mighty affluence of all the necessaries and conveniences of life" (p. 262).[5]

The structure of the pamphlet that emerges from this rhetorical scaffolding is not complicated. In its opening section Addison piles detail on detail and principle on principle to bring his readers to the conviction that ruin must follow an English defeat. He describes portentously the stream of endless wealth flowing from the Spanish West Indies into France, wealth that will make England's implacable foe the dominant force in Europe. He speaks of the "melancholy prospect" lying in wait for the "woollen manufacture [that] is the British strength, the staple commodity and proper growth of our country," of the decay of England's prosperous Levant trade, and of the destruction of her fleet. He is convinced that these hypothetical disasters will become realities if ever France should overcome Britain (pp. 243–44).

His prologue is foreboding, but soon he makes a manly statement of purpose, appealing for consensus while paradoxically setting down "a fixed rule" and "an inviolable maxim." In a tone both conciliatory and firm, he assumes that all Englishmen are with him and are agreed "never to lay down our arms against France, till we have utterly disjoined her from the Spanish monarchy" (p. 247). He moves from this bellicose avowal to a comforting comparison of the relative strengths of England and France, in which the former is superior in numbers of horse and men and in brilliance of military leadership. The mood of the essay then changes from the near despair of the first section to rising hope as Addison tests idea after idea for winning the war. He concludes exuberantly that "if we carry it on vigorously, we shall gain for ourselves and our posterity a long, a glorious and a lasting peace; but if we neglect so fair an opportunity, we may be willing to employ all our hands, and all our treasures, when it will be too late; and shall be tormented with one of the most melancholy reflexions of an afflicted heart, that it was once in our power to have made ourselves and our children happy" (p. 263). Readers who at this juncture of the war were almost as belligerent as he were readily persuaded that an enlarged conflict was desirable and inevitable. To induce this state of mind had been Addison's open aim throughout the pamphlet, whose subtitle is *and the Necessity of an Augmentation, Considered.*

There was halfhearted peace talk late in 1707, but it was drowned out by the voices of those who, like Addison, feared an insatiable France and her Jacobite allies in Scotland.[6] By the end of that year, when he wrote *The Present State of the War,* he spoke to and for a people who remained predominantly Whig and prowar. Still, there were strong reasons for peace in 1707. France's fleet had been almost destroyed and her troops routed from Italy and the Spanish Netherlands in 1706, thus fulfilling the military objectives of the 1701 Treaty of Grand Alliance. Despite this accomplishment, there was dissension among the allies, and they were unprepared in 1707 for the defeats at Almanza and Toulon, the raid of Villars into Germany, and Marlborough's stalemate in the Netherlands.

Of these setbacks only the failure at Almanza was politically critical, since it was there that the Spaniards had sworn allegiance to Philip V. Yet the meaning of Almanza went unperceived by most Englishmen, Addison among them. Had they been sensitive to Spanish pride they would have anticipated the futility of their own efforts and shortened the war by six years. But the bankruptcy of English diplomatic and military adventure, which is apparent today, was not recognized by many who still warmed themselves in the pleasing afterglow of Blenheim and Ramillies. Even if the populace had recognized the significance of Almanza, the Whig hierarchy would have rejected any peace offer as unworthy of English valor and destiny. For they wanted to continue an expansion of trade that their country was just beginning to enjoy, to impoverish English allies—especially Holland—through military expenditures, and to minimize France as a commercial rival on the Continent. They also wanted "the trade of the Levant . . . the whole kingdom of Spain . . . and the wealth of the Indies." These were the prospects in wait for England, whose "generous resolutions" and respect for pounds sterling would make her mistress of the commercial universe and fair-minded guardian of the world's wealth (p. 259).

It is no wonder then that Addison judged it prudent to throw aside all caution, "to cease all talk of peace," and to argue for intensified military engagement in Europe as a complement to overflowing abundance at home. He accepted military investments, whether of men or of treasure, as safe risks in terms of the financial gains attendant on victory: "It may be necessary," he said, "for a person languishing under an ill habit of body to lose several ounces of blood, notwithstanding it will weaken him for a time, in order to put a new ferment into the remaining mass, and draw into it fresh supplies" (p. 260).

Throughout *The Present State of the War* he speaks in many voices: as a doctor recommending therapy to a nation in uncertain health; as a nonpolitical person urging Whig policy because it is the right policy; and as a City man goading Englishmen to the excitement of economic daring. "We have been tugging a great while against the stream," he said, "and have almost weathered our point; a stretch or two more will do the work; but if instead of that we slacken our arms, and drop our oars, we shall be hurried back in a moment to the place from whence we first set out" (p. 248). This is frank propaganda, unoriginal but vigorous, designed to hold emotions at a martial pitch.

Addison's pamphlet, though successful in his own day, has not withstood the erosion of time, primarily because it lacks the moral idealism often present in the best political writing and that he himself attained later in certain *Freeholder* essays. But it satisfied the martial cravings of the English at a time when they were warlike, and it conveyed special information that made its readers feel like privileged participants in the intrigue of policy-making.

In December 1707 Addison's patron Lord Somers "reported from the Lords Committees" their unanimous opinion, incapable of realization, that "no peace can be honourable or safe, for Your Majesty or your allies, if Spain, the West Indies, or any part of the Spanish monarchy, be suffered to remain under the power of the House of Bourbon." The report concluded the parliamentary debate on Spain and for a time established government policy on the war. By a scant thirty days, and certainly not by chance, Addison anticipated Lord Somers's report, whose contents *The Present State of the War* summarized in the moral rhetoric of a "fixed rule, and an inviolable maxim" (p. 247).[7]

With a forthrightness unusual in a propagandist he extended the implications of this rule and maxim. He pointed out that England could no longer be satisfied merely to hold the line, to secure conquered territory; efforts must be redoubled, to "make the greatest push that we are able on our own side" (p. 254). He did not hesitate to recommend action whose results might be measurable in even heavier casualties than had so far been experienced: "We are indeed obliged by the present situation of our affairs to bring more troops into the field than we have yet done" (p. 257). He had in mind a recent and controversial scheme to improve the striking power of British armies by increased use of native conscripts who would lessen the need for expensive foreign mercenaries. Nor did he advocate recruitment as a mere "tongue-warrior" who would "run out of the engagement upon the first onset" (*F* 28). Unlike such a verbal strategist, Addison in 1707 was prepared to hazard significant personal stakes. For a wrong decision or even a false note could at that early stage of his career have lost him prestige, preferment, political reputation, and financial security.[8]

Several years later he was to reveal sensitivity to the hardships of war and his patriotic sympathy for those who suffered in it, but he never seems to have regarded war itself as a threat to civilization and moral order. His suggestion in *The Present State of the War* that England assume an aggressive military policy seems to take no more account of the men involved than if they were pins on a battle map. His objective was clear-cut and vigorously worded, without muddied language or euphemism. An almost biblical phrasing recalls a prophet demanding violence in the name of his cause: "The only means therefore for bringing France to our conditions, and what appears to me, in all human probability, a sure and infallible expedient, is to throw in multitudes upon them, and overpower them with numbers. . . . and in one summer overset the whole power of France" (p. 250).

Only his certainty that the war was just and the present sacrifice of men and fortune vital to England's future enabled him to forget that Prince Eugene had in that same year already lost ten thousand of the multitudes thrown against the French. Only Addison's optimism enabled him to believe that one summer or even "one pitched battle would determine the fate of the Spanish continent" (p. 263).[9] Still it is precisely this union of confidence and muscular righteousness that made him a competent polemicist, able to gauge and typify public sentiment in 1707. The waste of such competence on so questionable a cause may be deplored, but the burgeoning skill that was in less than ten years to achieve fulfillment in the *Freeholder* must be recognized.

Although Addison kept his enthusiasm for the war, others grew weary of it. By 1709 most Englishmen were exhausted and hungry after an unusually rigorous winter and depressed by the stalemated peace talks at The Hague.[10] They were ready to listen to Tory politicians and writers chanting of plowshares and pruning hooks. Alert to this alteration in national spirit, the Tories from 1709 to 1713 turned their propaganda against the militarists in the Bank of England and on the Exchange—the furious City men who wanted to silence talk of armistice. Neither Tory energy nor party treasury was spared, to win the peace on the hustings and in the press. Addison writhed under Tory attacks, which he was later to characterize as "false and fraudulent" (*Trial,* p. 268). He may have enjoyed the last word, but he smarted from the onset of this abusive paper war to its end. On 5 August 1710 he wrote to Joseph Keally that he began to "hear from all parts of England, that the people daily recover their senses" and that the tide of public opinion was moving in the direction of Whig policy and an energetically prosecuted war (*Letters,* p. 229). He clung to his illusion for three more years, and never with less reason than in the summer of 1710.

The day of the Tories arrived when, on 8 August of that year, Queen Anne dismissed Godolphin and authorized the formation of a moderate coalition government under Harley and St. John. The Whig ministry had been headed toward this disaster for several months, during which the marquis of Kent resigned in mid-April and the earl of Sunderland was dismissed on 14 June. Not even the Whig structure could withstand the mounting pressure of public disaffection; Queen Anne, in calling for new leadership and a general parliamentary election, acceded to the popular wish for peace. The Tories had long been rehearsing for their return to power. St. John, anticipating Godolphin's collapse, began the *Examiner* on 3 August as a weekly periodical for the dissemination of Tory opinions on peace and prosperity, and attacks on Whig villainy for arresting progress toward these goals. In the first dozen numbers of the *Examiner* St. John was joined by Atterbury, Prior, and Freind. Then—between 2 November 1710 and 14 June 1711—Swift assumed editorial responsibility.[11]

The journal spoke with militant abusiveness of peace; without subtlety or any concession to fair play, it pointed to the Whig "moneyed men" as avaricious republicans whose hands dripped with the gore of English troops fallen in needless battle. Even Tory-sponsored Defoe was dismayed by his party's virulence: "It would be happy for us all, if we could talk of peace with a little more of it in our tempers, that we could be at peace when we pretend to desire peace; it is to me the strangest thing in the world, that we are all falling together by the ears, and making war about peace." But in 1710 few would credit this, least of all loyal Whigs. On 14 September at the suggestion of Arthur Maynwaring, who "could not suffer [the *Examiner*'s] insolence to pass, without animadversion," Addison issued the *Whig Examiner* as a rebuttal to the Tory periodical. His entrance into openly factious journalism is a clue to the desperation of the Whig position. From the start he maintained that his paper was both defensive and righteous, designed "to give all persons a rehearing, who have suffered under any unjust sentence of the *Examiner*. As that author has hitherto proceeded, his paper would have been more properly entitled the *Executioner*. At least, his examination is like that which is made by the rack and wheel" (*WE* 1).[12]

In terms of his own metaphor, having been judged guilty of association with Steele and the *Tatler,* Addison became a victim of the Tory "rack and wheel." Only two days after Godolphin was deposed, *Examiner* 2 observed that the "Tories happen now to have other work upon their hands" than responding to their enemies. Nevertheless it reversed a commonly voiced Whig charge against the Tory press and hinted that the *Tatler* was a Jacobite organ issued in collusion with the French government. After a few weeks, as Tory assurance increased, the *Examiner* again assaulted the *Tatler,* this time for its pretentious wit, and linked it to the *Gazette,* declaring that the two papers "move together in an amicable way, hand in hand, and like the two kings in the Rehearsal, smell to the same nosegay."[13] And St. John's *Letter to the Examiner* ridiculed "the Censor of Great Britain who resembles the famous censor of Rome in nothing but espousing the cause of the vanquished."

Accusations like these embittered Addison. For himself, as for his party, he had to nullify them, and in the *Whig Examiner* he tried to bear down on the Tories with biting mockery. Despite its intention, the journal was tepid and flaccid where heat and fiber were needed. Its author could give it only a half-time interest because he was already engrossed in the *Tatler,* whose occasional neutrality was a promising departure from factionalism. And he looked forward to a new journal, perhaps to be called the *Spectator,* whose aim would be nonpartisan. He was, moreover, too fastidious for sustained name-calling and too shy for the dirty dealing of open political journalism. Only party loyalty and Whig need could have driven him to it.

Of the many causes underlying the debility of the *Whig Examiner,* none was more significant than its déjà vu quality; it could say little that had not been said before in pamphlet, broadside, and periodical. It bragged, for example, that England had "been taken care of" through the opening of new trading opportunities in Flanders, the Levant, Gibraltar, Minorca, and Naples; it predicted the "happy prospect" of renewed commerce with Spain (*WE* 4).[14] After *The Present State of the War* Addison seemed to suffer from intellectual stasis; there is hardly anything imaginative or bold in the outmoded slogan of the *Whig Examiner,* "No Peace without Spain," which he lifted from the earlier work. And once more he was indifferent to benefits for the allies in his Exchange-minded insinuation that England's new plenty was enhanced by a corresponding depletion of allied wealth. He and many others would have appreciated Gay's observation that the *Whig Examiner* was done "with so much fire and in so excellent a style, as put the Tories in no small pain for their favourite hero."[15] But something more than this kind of endorsement was needed to make the journal catch on. Its stale advocacy of war could not move many Englishmen tired of short rations, high taxes, slaughter, and "uninhabited monuments" (*S* 26). The arguments of Addison's journal, stripped of their learning and often-strained satire, primarily satisfied an audience of Whigs engaged in international commerce. They did not need to be convinced.

The *Whig Examiner* could not make headway or survive in a paper war with the *Examiner,* which raged against the opposition and justified its invective in a Juvenalian spirit of *nec pudor obstabit.* Not only did the Whig journal want the excitement of new ideas, it had the lackluster, defeatist tone of a failed cause. Addison must have sensed that banner waving and sentimental recollection of the good old days could not attract popular allegiance. Yet he defended the Whigs, their program, and their war as long as he could, even though this meant repeating worn-out maxims. His fatigue appears, for example, in his failure to mention the parliamentary election ordered by the queen for October. This is odd negligence for a periodical initiated in part to advance the Whig cause at the polls, especially in view of the parliamentary campaign that the *Examiner* had begun in late summer. "Can any thing," asked the Tory journal, "be more likely to intimidate France, and dissipate the vain hopes they have conceived from our divisions, than the unanimity and vigour of a new British Parliament, which meets with firm resolutions of pushing the war to the utmost? . . ."[16] The *Whig Examiner* did not answer this question or even raise counter-questions.

The Whig command recognized that Addison lacked the editorial belligerence necessary in a crisis year. Certainly he miscalculated the general cultural level of the times when he challenged the *Examiner*'s hacking satire with a mild defense of Dr. Garth's poetry, or that journal's surliness with a discourse on "high" and "low nonsense" (*WE* 4). And why should he have assumed that a reading public easily given to topical passions would become as indignant as he at the *Examiner*'s misuse of classical allusions, impropriety of speech, and mixed metaphors? Even his analysis of nonresistance and passive obedience in *Whig Examiner* 5 was defeated by its own erudition. What could it say to minds closed to almost everything but the promise of a long-cherished peace? The *Whig Examiner* as a journal of opinion was a failure; its words seemed hit-or-miss, inadequate to express Addison's convictions or to conceal his Whiggish desperation. He was therefore freed from his chore by the experienced Maynwaring, who understood the fruitlessness of an intellectualized response to the *Examiner.*[17]

A week before the last *Whig Examiner* appeared, Maynwaring issued the first number of the *Medley,* which succeeded Addison's periodical. Oldmixon, who was always on call to flay any member of the opposition, alive or dead, aided in this venture. For forty-five numbers over a period of ten months, from 5 October 1710 to 6 August 1711, the *Medley* dogged the Harley–St. John ministry, ridiculing by name members of the Tory cabinet and certain favorites like D'Avenant and Mrs. Masham. It stormed against what it called the political falsehoods of such Tory scribblers as the authors of the *Essay upon Credit* and *Faults on Both Sides* and the "insolent villains" of the *Examiner.* It excoriated Tory peace plans as acts of treason or downright lies. The *Medley,* which unabashedly declared itself an antidote to Tory poison, was as scurrilous as the opposition press, as passionate, and as inflammatory. In short, it satisfied all the expectations of effective—that is to say, rancorous—political journalism; and yet it could not alter public opinion. The paper failed, and a Tory peace, in spirit if not in fact, was achieved by 1711. For the next two years Addison wrote little about the war, although in a letter to Edward Wortley on 3 October 1711 he contemptuously said that his countrymen "talk of nothing but a peace" (*Letters,* p. 266).

When in 1713 peace became a fact at Utrecht, the few dissident voices would not have been heard above the sounds of public joy. Nor would they have been welcome. With celebrations being held all over the country, the Whigs abstained from counter-demonstrations, an inactivity that reflected caution and anxiety. Berkeley, who dined with several Whigs at Dr. Garth's house on the day peace was announced, found that "they had not the heart to speak one word against the peace. Indeed the spirit of the Whigs seems quite broken." It is true that by 7 July 1713 they still ignored the end of hostilities, even to boycotting the public thanksgiving at St. Paul's "for the safe and honourable peace." They were, however, more resilient than Berkeley supposed, for they had already begun to undermine the public's confidence in the peace treaties and the Tory journals that argued for them.[18]

Addison abetted this Whig subversion. For three years his political friends had been without power, and he had neither patron nor the fruits of patronage; for three years he had brooded over the fall of his *Whig Examiner* before the polemics of the *Examiner.*[19] In 1713, at the first moment when the odds appeared to be better than even for his party, he returned to do battle with the Tory periodical. His effort was frail, but heavy guns were not needed in a year when Whig victory loomed brightly. So in *The Trial of Count Tariff,* which summed up his loathing of the three long years of Tory control, the *Examiner* is personified as one "who had abused almost every man in England, that deserved well of his country." True to his own perversity, he first appears in the courtroom babbling uncouth insults and slanders against those who had disagreed with him. "He called Goodman Fact a liar, a seditious person, a traitor, and a rebel" (p. 271). In creating this portrait, Addison's aim was to exonerate not only himself but all Whigs who, scarred and broken by Tory invective, carried on the fight against the *Examiner* as "an endeavour set on foot to confound truth with falsehood, and to turn the whole history of the present times into a lie." Like Steele, whose words these are, Addison forgot his own gentility when he thought of this journal; indeed, he hated it as he hated no other opposition paper. Not even the *Plebeian,* personal in its nastiness, could provoke him to comparable fury.[20]

From September 1710 to February 1716 he sniped at the *Examiner.* In both the *Whig Examiner* and the *Freeholder* he likened its composite author to a mechanized character assassin, an executioner bent on the extirpation of those who "were of a contrary opinion to him" (*F* 19).[21] In *Tatler* 229 he employed a dual image for the *Examiner*'s "small wits and scribblers." They were "numberless vermin," mite-sized, filthy, and parasitic, who foreshadowed English destiny under a Harley–St. John ministry. Building upon this idea, he compared the Tory attacks on the *Tatler* to "ivy about an oak, which adorns the tree at the same time that it eats into it; or [to] a great man's equipage, that do honour to the person on whom they feed." Perhaps he took aesthetic comfort in the precision of the *Tatler*'s imagery, but it was not until 1713 that he could gloat at the memory of the *Examiner*'s threat to muzzle and emasculate the Whigs as a political entity. His *Tatler* was besieged, his *Whig Examiner* defeated, but he and his party endured and triumphed. It would have been surprising if, in retrospect, he had not regarded his suffering as glorious and his sacrifice as noble.

The year 1713 was one of bold promise for him. He struck out at the Tories, visibly tottering, with derision and—equally damaging—with silence. First, in *The Trial of Count Tariff,* he openly ridiculed the *Examiner,* but refused to discuss or even to mention the peace. In observing this silence, he accepted a tactic probably recommended to the party by Lord Somers. The Whig leader, said Swift, had advised his friends—and certainly Addison would be among them—not to oppose the treaty of peace that Anne seemed resolved to sign, but to "find fault with it after it was made." This, continued Swift, was thought by the Whigs to be "the safest as well as the most probable way of disgracing the promoters and advisers."[22] That Addison followed Somers's line of tacit disapproval is apparent in his *Guardian* 101, published on 7 July, on what he ironically called "the great day of thanksgiving for the peace." Beyond this reference, however, he said nothing about the occasion and neglected even to mention the service at St. Paul's. Instead he reminded his readers of England's new ally; without any attempt to conceal his animus he described the paradox of splendor and poverty in despotic France, where "every one sings, laughs, and starves." A week before, in *The Trial of Count Tariff,* he had challenged neither the English desire for peace nor the cessation of hostilities, although he undermined the commercial treaties of Utrecht as documents engineered by men who were at best ignorant of mercantile principles and at worst in the pay of England's foe.

Addison's discontent was inspired largely by concern over England's loss of precious metals and the diminution of public credit brought about by the supposedly abortive peace. Three years later, in 1716, he still lamented the passing of a "glorious and successful" war and an armistice that wantonly sold out a "long and wonderful series of victories" and deprived England of her rightful "fruits" (*F* 41, *F* 25). What he had in mind was a commercial harvest: the economic destruction of France, the financial depletion of the allies, and the consequent trading supremacy of England. But these fruits, he felt, had been lost through the collapse of national will and Tory degeneracy: "our patience failed us; we grew tired of our undertaking; and received terms from those, who were upon the point of giving us whatever we could have demanded of them" (*F* 25). Like a man betrayed, Addison was frustrated and embittered by the failure of determination and decline into the lassitude of fainting valor. The peace was infamous, he said—anticipating George I—because the commercial treaties of Utrecht, like the fraudulent truce, robbed England of her rightful advantage.[23]

At different times he condemned the peace as unnatural, a threat to English free institutions and, more broadly, "pernicious to the liberties of Europe."[24] Indeed he came to see it as an act of gross immorality, for he knew, although he could not say openly, that in negotiating peace England had deserted her allies in the field, sold military secrets to the French, and disregarded treaty commitments. He treated these sordid acts not as English defections but as the sins of the Tory high command—Harley, Moore, and St. John. He allegorized their culpability in *The Trial of Count Tariff* through minor symbolic details like the French clothing of the count (a composite of the secretaries of state and the chancellor of the exchequer) and the Spanish dress of Don Assiento. Each sartorial item proclaimed the ministers' allegiance to England's enemies. But such delicate censure did not satisfy Addison, who also has Goodman Fact accuse Tariff of maliciously concealing "several books, papers, and receipts" (p. 269). The charge symbolizes the lengthy, secret negotiations of the treaties of peace and commerce between the Tory ministry and France, negotiations that in fact violated the terms of the Grand Alliance and in Whig eyes surrendered British interest to the French.[25]

Addison's approach to the war is thoroughly partisan. This is not to call it either simplistic or selfishly one-sided, for it embraced not only the material values of City men but also, if to a lesser extent, the moral concerns of the Latitudinarian bishops and many of their clerics. Moreover, he never altered his position or flirted with the arguments of the Tories, who would have gladly purchased so authoritative and elegant a journalist. He consistently affirmed that the war was not only a natural conflict but a just one designed to secure England's treasury, territorial aspirations, constitution, religion, and freedom.

On the other hand, his essays on the war contributed to a conspiracy of omission worked out by the Whig policy makers and their writers. In them he ignored the facts that after 1709 many Englishmen desperately wanted peace, that the poor suffered from the war-effected rise in corn prices and the excise on malt, and that shopkeepers felt the pinch as money became scarce. Nor did he mention the plight of the squires, who bore as their special cross the weight of the land tax at its wartime rate of four shillings in the pound and who for eleven years watched those with large incomes but little landed property escape the burden of this same tax. He neglected, as well, to take into account certain other truths: that the Junto, for all its talk of peace, failed to achieve an armistice when it would have been easy to do so; that the Austrians did not make adequate contributions to the war; and that the Barrier Treaty, born out of Whig desperation for Dutch support, gave too much to Holland. In withholding these facts he obeyed the wishes of the Whig leaders but lost the opportunity to create a political journalism that would have lived far longer than the Junto itself.

PART II

ON THE HUSTINGS

CHAPTER FIVE

WHIGGISM

THE forbearance evident in Addison's judgment of social manners and commercial behavior also shaped his political thinking. Yet his capacity to live and let live should not be confused with imperfect conviction or timidity: it is not true, as one critic has charged, that "the man lacked guts."[1] On the contrary, in his political actions he steadfastly adhered to the liberalism designed by the Revolution Settlement for English freeholders in a trade-centered environment. It was, in fact, a liberalism formed by Protestant discipline, Whig ideology, and respect for constitutional authority resting on the supremacy of statute and common law. His political ethic therefore would restrain governmental control, royal prerogative, and the ambitions of statesmen within a legal framework; it would protect property, civil rights, and the claims of conscience. Like Addison himself, it was sternly rational, not yet marked by the subjective doubt and enthusiasm for innovation that were to become part of the liberal ideal in the nineteenth century.

What is remarkable is that his political thinking, created within Whig councils, should have been idealistic at all. He was so much a party man that Mrs. Manley—a Tory Xantippe—scolded, "Politics and sordid interest . . . have carried him out of the road of Helicon, snatched him from the embraces of the Muses." Warming to her Tory metaphors, she saw him as one who "could cease to be himself; could degenerate his godlike soul, and prostitute that inborn genius, all those noble accomplishments of his, for gold; could turn away his eyes from the delicious gardens of Parnassus, of which he was already in possession, to tread the wandering maze of [political] business."[2]

She underestimated the profundity of his Whig allegiance and oversimplified the reasons for his party dedication. To a degree it was prompted by a desire for security, legitimate employment, and even for gold. But this drive was quickly fulfilled, for his rise was meteoric. In 1704 his name was still on the rolls of Magdalen College as a fellow. Largely through the efforts of Halifax he soon occupied the chair of the late John Locke as a commissioner of appeal in excise at £200 a year. By the summer of 1705 he had become a secretary in the office of Sir Charles Hedges, then the second secretary of state. Even when Sir Charles was replaced by the powerful Sunderland in 1706, Addison himself was untouched. In a letter to Emanuel Scrope Howe dated 3 December 1706 he blandly described the series of shifts: "My Lord Sunderland was appointed to succeed Sir Charles Hedges as secretary of state in the Southern Province. His Lordship has Mr. Hopkins for one of his undersecretaries, Mr. Tucker being out of that place. Mr. Swinford the first clerk is likewise displaced which are all the changes His Lordship has made in this office" (*Letters,* p. 63). With no visible sign of disturbance over what was after all a commonplace of English political life, he immediately took up his work with equal efficiency for the new secretary. His material well-being was further assured in 1709; his brother Gulston, who had been president of the East India Company, died, leaving Addison a rich man. But financial independence did not alter his relations with the Whigs. The desire for gold, in short, was far from being the only or even a primary stimulus of his loyalty.

With a constancy rare in his age he joined the Whigs, took his appointed place in their hierarchy, worked with tactful diligence in party councils and as an administrator in government posts, and fulfilled his obligation almost until the day he died. Such steadfastness was ordered by his belief in the sound principles of Whiggism: respect for mixed government and for a moderate church whose prelates worked for the glory of God and country within the constitutional framework of the state. His Whig ties were further matured by the claims of friendship. He never forgot his political benefactors; nor did he ever engage in the treachery so often taken for granted in power politics. For example, he was undeniably repelled by the immorality of the earl of Wharton. Yet he never spoke publicly against him although it was fashionable and safe to do so after the earl's death in 1715. He remained silent because of the kindness shown him by Wharton when, in 1709 and 1710, the two men served together in Ireland. Addison's Whiggism, grounded in principle and camaraderie, reflects his suspicion of all things Tory and his need for political commitment.

So intense is this commitment that it becomes his introduction to *Spectator* 162, an essay on the bookish theme of human mutability.[3]

"Nothing," he said, "that is not a real crime makes a man appear so contemptible and little in the eyes of the world as inconstancy, especially when it regards religion or party." When Addison wrote this essay, he had already lived through a year of Tory triumph under the Harley–St. John ministry and had reconciled himself to losses and frustrations. It may indeed be that the opening sentences of the essay were intended to discourage Tory cajolery. They may also have been inspired by bitterness, for Addison undoubtedly thought that men like Swift had betrayed his friendship, deserted the Whig cause, and sold out to the Tory interest.

At the beginning of the essay Addison observed that "though a man perhaps does but his duty in changing his side, he not only makes himself hated by those he left, but is seldom heartily esteemed by those he comes over to." He himself, however, wished to avoid the recriminations of society and never renounced either party or church affiliation. Unlike Steele in his *Letter to the Earl of O——d, concerning the Bill of Peerage,* Addison escaped the dilemma of the apostate. Nor was this mere good fortune. To forestall even the suspicion of shifted loyalty during the bleak days of the Harley–St. John regime, he preferred to give up "an employment rather than hold it under the Tories, which by a little compliance he might have done." In this respect he again differed from his friend Steele, whose reputation for generous integrity is paradoxically more secure in the twentieth century than Addison's. The mercurial captain may not have been above making a deal with Harley in the autumn of 1710; he may indeed have been willing to give up the *Tatler,* whose party slant had become more and more obvious. In any case, at a time when Whig affiliation was the brand of the political pariah, Steele kept his £300-a-year commissionership in the Stamp Office.[4]

Addison, for his part, early pledged himself to the wishes and patronage of Somers, Halifax, and Wharton, three leaders of the Junto who gave the Whig party most of its driving force and organization. Admission in 1703 to the Kit-Cat Club strengthened his party faith and assurance that the Revolution had in fact been a glorious one. The club was dominated by the Junto, an oddly assorted group of men who stayed together because they shared political values and a desire for power. Their strong loyalty to one another made its impact on Addison, who adopted every Whig cause and friendship as his own. In spectatorial days he was to become more critical of

Whig decisions and quarrels, but during those early years and again after the late spring of 1713 his allegiance was beyond question.

His devotion to party made him respect its ministries. He wanted nothing to detract from their parliamentary freedom or power even if both had to be maintained at the expense of others. Thus in a letter to Henry Newton dated 31 December 1708 he spoke disdainfully of the "remarkable" attempt to introduce into the Commons voting by ballot. The attempt, he continued with some relief, "was thrown out, but, but by nine voices, and might have proved very fatal to all ministries had it succeeded" (*Letters,* p. 123). Neither time nor circumstance was to diminish his regard for ministerial authority. Hence he was incapable of joining the Walpole-Townshend dissidents, who between 1717 and 1719 tried to seize party control from Stanhope and Sunderland. His friendship with Stanhope (which probably began when they met in Holland in 1703) and with the imperious Sunderland forbade such a step.[5] Unwilling to remain neutral, he undertook between 19 March and 2 April 1719 the *Old Whig* in support of the ministry's peerage bill and his party's policy makers against the Walpole insurgents. This periodical—far more personal and vindictive than most of his political writing—was so hortatory that party leaders used it to direct the legislative thought of indecisive Whigs. Thus "a certain great man," probably Charles Powlett, duke of Bolton, recommended the *Old Whig* to the vacillating Lord Chancellor Midleton in the hope that Addison's journal would succeed where other efforts had failed and obtain Midleton's backing for both the peerage bill and the ministry.[6]

In 1708, many years before the peerage-bill quarrel, Addison had gone to Parliament briefly as a Whig member for Lostwithiel. From that time, whenever he was involved in an election, he campaigned earnestly. On 14 October 1710, for instance, he wrote to Joshua Dawson, "I have been very busy upon my election which I carried without opposition" (*Letters,* p. 242). Only two days earlier Swift with less reserve commented that while the Tories were claiming parliamentary seats at a ratio "among new members six to one," Addison had won his easily. And Swift added, "I believe if he had a mind to be chosen king, he would hardly be refused."[7] His election victories are not easily explained, for his genius as an essayist—his capacity for persuasive, wide-ranging articulation—was not carried onto the hustings. He was like his own Mr. Spectator, a shy man who dreaded to address large audiences or to promise in pounds and pay, if at all, in pence.

Introspection was a political liability and diffidence a barrier to performing on the floor of the Commons with oratorical dash. At times he sat in the House virtually tongue-tied with "silly sheepishness" (so his cousin Budgell said). There is an apocryphal story that once during his early parliamentary days he rose to speak to an issue, lamely beginning: "Mr. Speaker, I conceive. . . ." Then, with all eyes fixed upon him, he began to stammer. Again, "Mr. Speaker, I conceive. . . ." Once more he tried. Losing the pathetic remnants of his confidence and his argument, he sat down. Upon this silent rout, a Tory member rose and bowed to the House: "The three miscarriages which we have witnessed on the part of a writer known for his fertility proves beyond all doubt the feebleness of the cause he wishes to defend." The witticism, according to this legend, aroused the Commons to laughter, and whatever oratorical ambition Addison may have had vanished in humiliation.[8]

However exaggerated the anecdote, its essence at least can be substantiated. In March 1714, for example, when he defended Steele against Tory charges of sedition, he prepared many of the closely reasoned arguments that his friend used during the trial. Yet Addison himself refrained from speaking publicly, not because he feared open association with the author of *The Crisis* and the *Englishman* but because he was uncertain of his ability to face a large audience. After 1715 he would every now and then break his silence in Parliament to declare the king's pleasure on various matters of state, but even on such formal occasions those who heard him must have sensed his constraint, his "trembling and concern" (*S* 231). He wrote three *Spectator* essays on the subject of public speaking, as though understanding might defeat embarrassment. In one paper he learnedly compared the classical and British styles of rhetorical gesture, conceding that he [as Mr. Spectator] was "a dumb man, and therefore . . . a very improper person to give rules for oratory" (*S* 407). On the whole, he seemed resigned to his reticence though he sought ways to vindicate it. In an essay of tortured logic, he described silence not as mere speechlessness but as "mute eloquence," befitting modesty, deference to one's audience, and ethical fortitude (*S* 231). In another essay he gently mocked Mr. Spectator's hesitance to disturb fifty years of nontalking but implied that all too frequently the gift of tongues was hollow, a studied "wrangle and dispute for exercise" (*S* 556).[9]

He played his role behind the parliamentary scenes, where he could aid colleagues, like the flamboyant Steele, who were obvious Tory targets. And as a strategist in the wings he could calculate the outcome of parliamentary struggles. In June 1717, for instance, the Walpole-Townshend group was able to bring to the floor of Parliament a test motion that accused Lord Cadogan of embezzlement. Appalled by Walpole's temerity, Addison voted against the motion, his decision determined by the merits of the case and his hostility to insurgence. In a little-known letter to the earl of Stair, he described the significance of the vote:

> Yesterday we look upon to have been the decisive day of this session. Both parties made their utmost efforts and summoned all their friends that could be got together from every quarter of the nation. . . . the whole body of the Tories were there, and not a single man among them voted for us. . . . All the Prince's Court was against us, and 78 Whigs, among whom several in places. But upon the division we were 204 to 194. As this was the utmost effort of all parties united against the present interest, I believe it is not hard to guess which of the sides is likely to grow the strongest for it. Those who lost the day are amazed at their ill success, and wonder from whence such a body could be drawn together against 'em, for it was their own and the common opinion of the town that they would carry it by 50 or 60 voices. But they could not have fallen on any other man that could have so well bestirred himself in his defence, though at the same time none appeared in it who, I believe, would not be ready to promote his Majesty's service with the utmost zeal and diligence in all other points, as I believe several of those who appeared against his lordship will do for the future.

The letter reveals Addison's delight in a ministerial victory to which he contributed; it reveals further his political astuteness, his ability to identify a trial of strength for what it was and to predict the parliamentary future for the next few years. And most significant, it emphasizes his desire to minimize differences between the two Whig factions in the hope of effecting a truce, if not a lasting peace.[10]

However active in backstage service, he did not feel that it sufficiently offset his oratorical paralysis. Beyond personal obedience to the Whig command, therefore, he proved his fidelity by supporting discipline as an instrument of party unity. On 31 December 1708, after certain Whig members of the Commons had left for Covent Garden during a debate and so contributed unwittingly to a party defeat, he told Henry Newton approvingly, "These gentlemen . . . have been so reproached by their party for this piece of negligence, that it will have a good effect upon 'em for the remaining part of the Parliament" (*Letters,* p. 124). Several years later he boasted of his own perfect voting record: "I do not remember," he wrote to Delafaye on 18 June 1715, "that since I have been in the House I have separated from my friends in a single vote" (*Letters,* p. 343). His open pride records devotion to what he considered a just and farsighted program joining "an honest party of men" (*F* 29).

Rarely and only under the most stringent circumstances was he guilty—the word would be his—of a failure to support party aims in and outside of Parliament. He refused, for example, to take part in the debate concerning Henry Sacheverell. Doubtless he would have found it awkward to explain that he had disqualified himself because of a conflict of interest. On the one hand, he would not compound the difficulties of "dearest Harry," with whom he had shared rooms at Magdalen and to whom he had dedicated *An Account of the Greatest English Poets.* Furthermore, Sacheverell's bail was provided by Vice-Chancellor Lancaster of Oxford, who as college bursar had befriended Addison in his student days. On the other hand, he could not compromise his loyalty to Lord Wharton, one of the Whig principals who demanded Sacheverell's trial before the Lords. In the early months of 1710, during the most heated debate of the decade, Addison therefore remained silent.[11]

In effect, he subordinated his abhorrence of Sacheverell's High Church principles to sympathy for a friend who had never done him any harm. A comparable situation arose in 1715 when the duke of Ormonde was about to be made a scapegoat. The Whigs had agreed in June to impeach the duke, St. John's pawn, for high treason, and Addison was troubled: "I have great difficulties with myself in relation to the duke of Ormonde," he told Delafaye. "When I was of the University of which he is Chancellor I was favored with his countenance and encouragement. When he succeeded My Lord Wharton in Ireland he resisted many solicitations which were made for the place that I have ever since enjoyed in that kingdom." Because of such indebtedness Addison declared, "I shall never pardon myself if

I give a vote that may have a tendency to the taking off his head, . . ." He assessed his dilemma honestly but resolved it deviously. To placate both his party and Ormonde, with no disadvantage to himself, he voted neither for nor against the impeachment but was "absent as by accident" when the votes were counted (*Letters,* p. 343).[12]

For many years grateful Whig officials repaid his loyalty with minor government positions. His dedication to the party's interests won him a climactic reward when, on the night of 15 April 1717, he accepted the secretaryship of state for the Southern Department. He had reason to consider the ministerial appointment an opportunity for service rather than a political plum. Not only from his own earlier experiences but from Cicero and especially the Whig protomartyr Algernon Sidney he learned that "government is not instituted for the good of the governor, but of the governed; and power is not an advantage, but a burden."[13] Among the heavy cares of office, as he forewarned himself less than a year before assuming the new post, was the abusive ingratitude that any public servant had to expect from perverse "multitudes" as well as from jealous rivals, "so that the most perfect administration, conducted by the most consummate wisdom and probity, must unavoidably produce opposition, enmity, and defamation." Even before he took office, then, he was disabused of any glamour that might be attached to official service: "The condition of a minister of state," he declared on 4 June 1716, "is only suited to persons, who, out of a love to their king and country, desire rather to be useful to the public than easy to themselves" (*F* 48).[14]

He appears to have accepted his ministerial office because he could not ignore the insistent pleas of his party. The withdrawal of Walpole and his disciples left a creaky Whig machine; there were so few candidates for cabinet places that Stanhope begged nominees to set aside private interests and expose themselves to "any trouble or hazard" for the welfare of their party and country. Addison's term of office was marked by trouble, hazard, and an illness that became critical. George Tilson wrote in December 1717 to Lord Polwarth: "Mr. Secretary Addison lies extremely ill, and the doctors seemed to have given him over. . . . his recovery is very uncertain." Until 13 March 1718, nevertheless, when he was replaced by James Craggs, he held a secretariat that was distasteful and used up his waning time and energy.[15]

A major contribution to the Whig cause was the organizational talent that, on the death of Arthur Maynwaring in November 1712, made him director of party propaganda. He recruited, advised, wined, and in a few cases even housed such writers as Eustace Budgell, Thomas Burnet, Laurence Eusden, Thomas Tickell, Ambrose Philips, Edward Young, Digby Cotes, and Edmund Smith. He was soon the acknowledged link between Whig propagandists and the party leaders. The association between Addison and many of his writers seems to have been a relaxed one: "He used to breakfast with one or other of them at his lodgings in St. James's Place, dine at taverns with them, then to Button's, and then to some tavern again for supper and the evening. And this was then the usual round of his life." Despite such good fellowship, he was demanding of his writers—whom he also rewarded appropriately. His authority to dispense favors was so familiar that Swift, though he withheld his lampoon until 1730, mocked him as the man who

> ... wisely left the Muse's hill,
> To business shaped the poet's quill.
> Let all his barren laurels fade,
> Took up himself the courtier's trade,
> And, grown a minister of state,
> Saw poets at his levee wait.[16]

Swift sneered with decanal righteousness, but Addison took up his task as a moral obligation as well as a party duty. He never minimized its importance, for he knew that voters in county constituencies and also in the large boroughs had increased during his lifetime in both numbers and political awareness. To win over these voters to the Whig side, he searched constantly for writers with a gift of persuasion. Few were too obscure or too renowned for his civilities as long as they might be useful to the party. One author with journalistic potentiality whom he may have solicited was Gay, who wrote to Addison in December 1713: "I cannot neglect this occasion of returning you my thanks for the benefits you have done me and I beg you to believe that I have such a just sense of them, if you even could think of doing more for me, you could not engage me further to you, for 'tis impossible to owe you more love and gratitude than I do already." Clearly, also, Addison never abandoned his ambition to renew Pope's services to the Whig party. Indeed, his well-known attempts at a reconciliation with the poet prompted the ungenerous Thomas Burnet to remark of his employer that "Addison and the rest of that riming gang have dropped their resentment against the lordlike man. . . . It has very often made me smile at the pitiful soul of the man when I have seen Addison caressing Pope, whom at the same time he hates worse than Beelzebub and by whom he has been more than once lampooned."[17]

Of political necessity Addison catered to hack and artist. His ability to work with party writers enabled him to assign the right pamphleteer to the right cause. He probably used Burnet's second-rate talents to harass the opposition with diatribes, which were more irritating than harmful, and recruited Laurence Eusden to fawn upon the mighty and powerful. But when a program needed the journalistic skill of rational debaters, he abandoned the Burnets and Eusdens and drew on men of restraint and sounder intellect, who served him gladly.[18]

The 1719 peerage-bill controversy was the most cerebral of the century's paper wars, one that encouraged journalists to fight, as Charles Mordaunt said, like gentlemen "without ill manners or violence . . . or priestly contention."[19] By then Addison was already mortally sick. But when he realized that Walpole, who could dip freely into the Prince of Wales's purse, was prepared to make a *cause célèbre* of the bill, he marshaled the prominister writers as pamphleteers along with himself. For the first few days of the war he was like a general caught off guard. He could not immediately cope with the speed and thrust of the opposition press, which on 14 March brought out Walpole's *Thoughts of a Member of the Lower House* and the first number of Steele's *Plebeian*. Retaliation became mandatory; the need was for any kind of counterassault as long as it was fast. Within four days—on 18 March—he commissioned and saw published the first pamphlet in defense of the bill, the anonymous *Some Considerations Humbly Offered, Relating to the Peerage of Great Britain*. It was so inadequate a response that Addison began on 19 March to issue the *Old Whig;* he also had Viscount Molesworth on the same day answer Walpole with *A Letter from a Member of the House of Commons to a Gentleman without Doors* and from 21 March to 14 April confront Steele's *Plebeian* with the *Patrician*. While Walpole bought writers of the stature of Trenchard, Steele, and Eustace Budgell, Addison assembled an even more impressive force: Robert Molesworth; John Asgill; Charles Mordaunt, earl of Peterborough; and Richard West.[20] When he was no longer strong enough to participate actively, he goaded them to greater militancy against the dissident utterances of Walpole's writers.

As long as Addison's physical resources allowed, he used his own literary gift to promote Whig policy. From the *Poem to His Majesty* in 1695 to the *Old Whig,* he steadily advertised his party's program. He spent his talent perhaps too generously, sacrificing a part of it to political toxin. Like the very party writers whom he scorned, he recognized in *Spectator* 567 "the secret virtue of an innuendo" and sometimes descended to epithets used by every journalist, whether Whig or Tory: "faction, Frenchman, papist, plunderer . . . scribbler, liar, rogue, rascal, knave, and villain." Later in *Freeholder* 1 he spoke with contempt of the "Grub Street patriot" whose "passion for liberty . . . arises only from his apprehensions of gaol." But throughout his career he turned out party literature, knowing that whenever he espoused a good cause he was likely to be stigmatized as a scribbler who merely mouthed doctrines of freedom.

He preached such Whig shibboleths as religious toleration of all Protestant sects, continuing war with France, Scottish union, and the Hanoverian succession. He interpreted the principles of the Revolution as Whig principles that promised men of good will the rewards of order, liberty, and riches. Though he insisted on the pre-eminence of his party, he was nonetheless ready to affiliate with a coalition government or with individual Tories, if such coexistence was likely to insure domestic tranquility. When partisan fury menaced the good of England, he usually sought to assuage its anger and cool its heat. To his dismay, however, he unwittingly achieved an opposite effect in 1713 when he presented *Cato.* From the opening night Addison's enemies insisted that the play was politically symbolic, the creation of an agent of Whig factionalism. The charges were so unfounded in the opinion of the Tory high command that, John Gay reported, "my Lord Oxford, Lord Chancellor and the Speaker of the House of Commons have bespoke the box on the stage for next Saturday" [25 April]. The trio had every reason for such confidence since at least one of them had already read the play in its manuscript state. Nevertheless, the abuse continued, and Addison remained silent. Not until three years later, on 16 April 1716, did he attempt to vindicate himself publicly. It was his wish, he wrote, "that everything should be banished the stage which has a tendency to exasperate men's minds, and inflame that party rage which makes us such a miserable and divided people" (*F* 34). In the light of this statement it is hard to believe that the intention of *Cato* had been inflammatory.[21]

Even in *The Trial of Count Tariff,* Addison's spiteful polemical pamphlet, he was capable of acknowledging a debt to a Tory, Sir Thomas Hanmer—the "gentleman of Suffolk who did [Goodman Fact] signal service" (p. 269). He remembered that Sir Thomas voted against the eighth and ninth articles of the commercial treaty of Utrecht as his repudiation of a pro-French trend in government policy; this must have been his "signal service" to the Whig cause. A week later Hanmer was again a disciplined Tory, eager to re-establish his loyalty by moving on 23 June that Her Majesty be thanked "for what she has done in the Treaty of Commerce with France, by laying so good a foundation for the interests of her people in trade."[22] The motion irritated most Whigs, who saw their victory of 18 June being dissipated in Tory double talk and duplicity. But Addison, who would not give way to peevish anger, merely observed that Sir Thomas had done the Whigs a favor at a time of crisis; the pamphlet admitted the debt.

Moreover, in 1713—a year of anticipation for the Whigs and desperation for the Tories—Addison urged restraint on both parties. One way to accomplish this, he agreed with Lord Halifax and Harley, was to consult moderate Tories in policy decisions and even appoint them to office in the Whig government whose formation was expected after the queen's death. In the same year he was embarrassed by Steele, whose firebrand journalism had brought about his expulsion from the Commons. "I am in a thousand troubles for poor Dick," Addison wrote on 12 October to John Hughes, "and wish that his zeal for the public may not be ruinous to himself; but he has sent me word that he is determined to go on, and that any advice I can give him in this particular, will have no weight with him" (*Letters,* p. 280). Steele's political enthusiasms baffled Addison, whose sense of decorum was violated by the captain's dash and vehemence.[23]

The rage of faction promised to disarrange further Addison's world: party violence appeared to be the birthright of every Englishman, and no one felt secure against the danger. Anne herself, who feared both Whigs and Tories as contentious "bugbears," wrote to

Marlborough: "I can never be convinced that Christianity requires me, nor that it can be for my service to put myself entirely into the hands of any one party." And Pope echoed the queen when he complained to Caryll that "this miserable age is so sunk between animosities of party and those of religion, that I begin to fear most men have politics enough to make the best scheme of government a bad one, through their extremity of violence, and faith enough to hinder their salvation. I hope, for my part, never to have more of either than is consistent with common justice and charity. . . . I am ambitious of nothing but the good opinion of all good men on both sides, . . ." Such impartiality as Pope's did not suit Addison. He wanted to avoid party cabals when he could, to judge political controversy with reason rather than emotion, and even to work with Tories who were receptive to co-operation between parties. But he would go no further in his concessions. He was comfortable within the sheltering limits of party designation. On 27 February 1707/8, three days after the Commons ended its investigation of the conduct of the war in Spain —an inquiry that saw the crossing of party lines—Addison wrote to Lord Halifax in the spirit of one who had survived a time of upheaval: "We look upon the debate of last Tuesday . . . as that which has fixed all men in their proper parties and thoroughly established the present ministry" (*Letters,* pp. 94–95).[24]

His Whig loyalties, however, did not dissipate his desire for freedom of thought and association within the party. In *The Trial of Count Tariff,* for example, by showing Goodman Fact, the symbol of Whiggism, as he moves intimately among the people who support him, Addison, in advance of his time, emphasized the value of consultation between party leaders and their followers. He wished to bring them closer together not merely through the sociability of the Kit-Cat and Hanover clubs but also through the exchange of ideas and the relaxation of arbitrary discipline. In certain political essays of the *Spectator* and even the *Freeholder,* he suggested that the reform of party structure was intrinsically important. But it was also an extrinsic necessity, for to promote a reasonable exchange between Whigs and Tories would guarantee the smooth operation of the parliamentary system. He would therefore not join Defoe or anyone else in bemoaning the "iniquity of the times," which made men use "the unhappy names of distinction, by which our state differences are kept up, and which serve the contending parties to spit fire and brimstone at one another with." Addison tried not to extinguish the "fire and brimstone," only to dampen them, not to suppress "state differences," but to order them so that through rational debate they would serve a free people. Further, he knew that since the reign of William III parliamentary competition demanded government by party. He seldom fought the practical realities of politics, especially when the realities—in this case the existence of rich and powerful factions—meant the widespread distribution of "interest" (patronage) and "service" (employment).[25]

For these reasons he could not be a mere onlooker while Whig collided with Tory. By June 1713, as the Whigs approached the victory feast, he fully expected to be a guest at the banquet table. He might make a token gesture of disinterest, but he had waited so long for preferment that his mind could not be closed to imminent political rewards. He therefore concerned himself only perfunctorily with the *Guardian* and the renewed *Spectator;* after June 1713 his contributions to both give the impression of time-marking handiwork—as indeed they were. But still he was uneasy about his total reliance on Whig fortunes. Late in the autumn of 1713—on 2 November—he endorsed Pope's resolution to stay "out of the fray." He reminded his friend of earlier advice not to "content yourself with one half of the nation for your admirers when you might command them all" (*Letters,* p. 281). Characteristically Addison avoided overt revelation of his feelings, but the sense of regret is inescapably close to the surface. The time for regret was past, however, and he could no more back away from the political arena than could any other Whig who had decided to stand or fall with his party.

Perhaps in writing to Pope he uneasily recalled that *The Trial of Count Tariff* had been designed to persuade the "one half of the nation" who were not yet his party's admirers. In that work the heroic Goodman Fact symbolizes not only the perfection of Whig principles but all loyal party members who are substantial, levelheaded, candid, devoted to mercantile interests, and dedicated to the prosperity of all Englishmen. They are men of plain talk who use no "art, rhetoric, or circumlocution." They are like Fact himself, who "cuts down the finest orator, and destroys the best-contrived argument, as soon as ever he gets himself to be heard" (p. 267). Contrasted with Goodman Fact and the Whigs is Count Tariff, Addison's objectification of the party of treason, the Tories, who would sacrifice English affluence to Frenchmen and the Jacobite gentry. Tariff's title is associated in English minds with the French court, his name with impersonal statistics. His double-dealing is figured in his Gallic volubility and dandyish clothing—"a fine brocade waistcoat, curiously embroidered with flower-de-luces. . . . a broad-brimmed hat, . . . silver-clocked stockings," and a French shoulder-knot (p. 269). He stands for an oppressive party that would stifle dissent and gag all opposition with the specious legalism of *scandalum magnatum.*

There is nothing subtle, moderate, or conciliatory about these two allegorical figures. Addison created Goodman Fact to exorcise the count's Toryism and destroy the image of the Harley–St. John ministry. But he never created their like again. Not even the *Freeholder* fox hunter and his publican duplicated the simplistic depictions and political distortions of *The Trial of Count Tariff.* In more characteristic writings, Addison reminded his Whig and Tory readers that they were first of all pledged to defend England's constitution and church. In both conversation and journalism he pleaded for "moderation in parties." He did not conceal his annoyance with anyone who was "too much of a party-man," especially "his dear friend Steele."[26] He courageously laid bare not only the evils and dangers of party extremism but also its follies, even in the middle of political battles. His was a rational courage, which only occasionally faltered under party pressure or, less often, degenerated into flag-waving Whiggish bombast.

He did not find the inanities of partisanship difficult to describe in the pages of the *Spectator.* From the point of view of four Indian kings, for instance, he jovially satirized the shallowness of political belligerence, its distortions, and its myths:

"The queen of the country appointed two men to attend us, . . . But we soon perceived these two were great enemies to one another, and did not always agree in the same story. We could make a shift to gather out of one of them, that this island was very much infested with a monstrous kind of animals, in the shape of men, called Whigs; and he often told us, that he hoped we should meet with none of them in our way, for that if we did, they would be apt to knock us down for being kings.

"Our other interpreter used to talk very much of a kind of animal called a Tory, that was as great a monster as the Whig, and would treat us as ill for being foreigners. These two creatures, it seems, are born with a secret antipathy to one another, and engage when they meet as naturally as the

> elephant and the rhinoceros. But as we saw none of either of these species, we are apt to think that our guides deceived us with misrepresentations and fictions, and amused us with an account of such monsters as are not really in their country." [*S* 50]

But in the *Freeholder,* where gentle wit was a luxury he could not readily afford, he wryly described the eccentricity of English politics, which gave children a factional education. They "no sooner begin to speak, but whig and tory are the first words they learn. They are taught, in their infancy, to hate one half of the nation; and contract all the virulence and passion of a party before they come to the use of their reason" (*F* 53). Obviously Addison's irony has stiffened between the *Spectator* and the *Freeholder.* In the latter the phrase *virulence and passion* indicates the seriousness with which he viewed meaningless party rages and his fear that their anarchical poison would spread through England, whose liberty and plenty depended on order.[27]

The phrase in fact summarizes once more his support of the truism that, as Sir William Temple put it, from the "fire of faction" rise up "popular commotions, and at last seditions," which in their turn succeed "either in setting up some tyranny at home, or bringing in some conquest from abroad." Addison first set forth a like idea in the *Spectator,* asserting that "a furious party spirit" ultimately "exerts itself in civil war and blood-shed; and when it is under its greatest restraints naturally breaks out in falsehood, detraction, calumny, and a partial administration of justice" (*S* 125).[28] In the mask of Mr. Spectator he anticipated the Jacobite rebellion of 1715, but as the Freeholder he abstained from the gloating that usually accompanies fulfilled prophecies and tried instead to heal the wounds of civil war. Actually, his plea for "moderation in parties" was a test of his literary ability to handle varying moods and tones. If in certain *Spectator* essays he presented his case for political temperance with good-natured humor and delicate satire, in other essays in that journal he expressed his anger starkly toward all party fanatics, Whig or Tory, who sow dissension with "feuds and animosities that extinguish religion, deface government, and make a nation miserable" (*S* 16). In the *Freeholder* he abandoned any appearance of impartiality and functioned as a Whig evangelist bent on conversion; but he preached his text—moderation in parties—calmly and, in at least two significant essays, analytically.

Freeholder 31, one of the essays, is the exegesis of a political issue so explosive that it could well have toppled the Whig ministry or weakened it to the point of dissolution. Like many other numbers of the journal, it is directed to a problem caused by the rebellion, in this case the judgment to be imposed upon the sixteen hundred prisoners taken during the uprising. Coffeehouse politicians struck magisterial postures and debated whether the rebels should be punished with gibbet and axe or pardoned as a token of royal clemency. The matter was further clouded by the publicity given to the seven Jacobite lords captured at Preston and ordered to stand trial. Aware of the sympathy that these men evoked, the government had them tried by parliamentary impeachment. In this way the king and his ministers were spared the onus of judgment, while their power in both houses assured a decision to their liking. Such a procedure, moreover, alterable only by parliamentary act, absolved the king from having to grant or refuse a reprieve. On 19 January 1715/16, six of the seven impeached lords, "the Earls of Derwentwater, Nithsdale, and Carnwath, the Viscount Kenmure, and the Lords Widdrington and Nairne, pleaded guilty to the Articles of Impeachment against them." Their trial was quickly over, and all were condemned to death, as many commoners had been for their part in the rebellion.[29] Reaction set in immediately. Among the High Church Tories there was a consensus recommending pardon not only for the six noblemen but for all other insurgents. Among the Whigs, already fractured by internal differences, there was only widespread disagreement.

Steele thus became the Whig spokesman for clemency and Walpole the party's advocate of relentless prosecution. Both men concentrated on the condemned lords as a test case for determining the fate of all other rebels. On 2 March, in the government's *St. James's Post,* a four-column allegory, ostensibly an account of the proceedings of the Diet of Poland, described the lords' trial in terms so close to Walpole's prejudices that he must have written the piece himself or stood at the author's elbow. In an uneven mixture of stylistic cleverness, moral vindictiveness, and learning, the essay makes its points. First it abuses the six "rebels and parricides [who] aggravated their guilt by . . . sullen silence, and prevaricating answers." Then it hacks roughly at those who disagree with Walpole, especially Steele. Turning an elaborately erudite pun on *chalybean steel* against the latter, the allegory calls him "Cavaliero Risko Chalybeski," "a common prostitute" in the role of a "public censor." He is made to appear a captious, frustrated critic of the ministry, who has "exhausted the common topics of clemency and mercy." In an open *Letter* [to Spencer Compton, Speaker of the Commons] *concerning the Condemned Lords,* Steele was so intent on defending himself against such cruel gibes that he almost forgot the Jacobite noblemen, and his statement of moral principle appears anticlimactic: "I never talked of mercy and clemency," he said, "but for the sake of my king and country, in whose behalf I dare to say, that to be afraid to forgive, is as low as to be afraid to punish; and that all noble geniuses in the art of government have less owed their safety to punishment and terror, than grace and magnanimity."[30]

This fracas generated so much noise that most Whigs, and even the two major participants, seem to have ignored the fact that on 23 February the earl of Nithsdale was allowed to escape, that on the next day the earl of Derwentwater and Viscount Kenmure were beheaded on Tower Hill, and that the remaining three were indefinitely reprieved. Party followers, mesmerized by the Walpole-Steele feud, failed to realize that many Englishmen were reading the pamphlet in which Atterbury piously repudiated the Jacobite conspiracy while defending royal clemency for all who participated in it.[31] But Addison, who had a knack of being at the center of things, was among those who read and reflected upon the Tory's argument.

He may not have recognized Atterbury as its author since the pamphlet was unsigned. On the other hand, he surely identified it as the expression of a High Church minority, particularly of its clergy, who were using the legal judgment against the condemned lords to attack the uncertain Whig ministry and the unpopular new king. Because their plight was desperate, they abandoned restraint and decorum, haranguing their congregations and resorting to any device that might arouse compassion for the condemned lords who, they said, were guilty only of romantic idealism. So strident was the High Church attack that it provoked those on the other side, whether moderate Tory or Whig, to fight back in letters to newspapers. One such letter appeared in the *Flying-Post* for 3–6 March 1715/16:

SIR,

On the Sunday which preceded the execution of the lords, a great many clergymen within the city prayed in a more particular manner for the lords condemned. I leave it to any indifferent party, to consider whether this were a prayer of charity, or an expression of their inclination to the cause for which those rebels were condemned, and of their disaffection to the king and government.... The lords are condemned for rising in arms, in favour of the Pretender; hence that concern and tenderness for their condition! Had it been usual for these ministers to have commended the condemned criminals to God, in their prayers, the practice had been laudable, and full of charity, and no man living could have refused to join in such a prayer. But when the congregations, by their starting, listening, and a new attention testify that this is all innovation unusual, and unheard of before, what can we think but that the purpose of these men was to commend these lords to the compassion of the crowd? ...

Had Addison seen this letter, he would have approved it, for he took the same stand in *Freeholder* 31, printed on Friday, 6 April. The longest essay in the periodical, it discussed the punishment due the condemned lords and all the others who had participated in the rebellion. Unlike the letter writer of the *Flying-Post,* he did not attack the High Church clergy as a whole; either as individuals or as a group, they presented too large a target for him and were in fact too respectable. Nor did he mention the dispute between Walpole and Steele. They were Whigs and therefore honorable men who erred because their positions were extreme. He addressed himself only to the persuasive, unknown pamphleteer who had synthesized the High Church position in *An Argument to Prove the Affections of the People of England to Be the Best Security of Government.* And contrary to a cardinal rule of the experienced polemicist, Addison replied seriously, point by point, to the pamphleteer's assertions. The result was a triumph.

Without any preamble, he isolated the incendiary purpose of the pamphlet, "to stir up our compassion towards the rebels, and our indignation against the government." Once that was done, he openly challenged the author of *An Argument,* calling his cadenced pulpit oratory and emotional rhetoric "studied confusion" and his "matter" spurious reasoning. These weaknesses Addison countered with his own "perspicuity" and the familiar message of moderation. He moved from fact to fact and principle to principle with a serious deliberation designed to establish objectivity. Categorically, he took up his opponent's proofs to point out the contradictions caused by the definitions on which they were constructed. "His whole argument," said Addison, "turns upon this single consideration; Whether the king should exert mercy or justice towards those who have openly appeared in the present rebellion? By mercy he means a general pardon; by justice, a general punishment: so that he supposes no other method practicable in this juncture, than either the forgiving all, or the executing all." Addison confounded this naïve thinking with his own sophisticated logic, more particularly his program that, unlike the unnamed pamphleteer's, was intended "to temper justice with mercy; and, according to the different circumstances that aggravate or alleviate the guilt of the offenders, to restrain the force of the laws, or to let them take their proper course."

With this assertion he reconciled government policy to the biblical concept of justice and recalled the obligation of the British monarch, whose coronation oath required him to "execute 'justice in mercy,' that is, to mix them in his administration, and not to exercise either of them to the total exclusion of the other" (*F* 31). Thus while adroitly invoking scriptural authority for the government's position —and his own—Addison also condoned the ministry's treatment of the captured rebels. Because he had access to privileged information available only to the friends of Stanhope, he knew, for instance, that a large number of noble prisoners found it easy to escape or to obtain a quiet reprieve and that most of the rebellious commoners were not executed but sent to "serve in the Plantations for the term of seven years from the time of their arrival there."[32] He did not parade his knowledge, but its implicit presence allowed him to dismiss as caprice all proposed action except that of the government. His private information, in short, allowed him to render sinister or sentimental Atterbury's and Steele's recommendation of full clemency and to expose the cruelty of Walpole's demand for harsh punishment. Addison's call for temperate retribution was successful because it sounded a middle, common-sense note for people who were tired of and frightened by revolutionary hysteria.

From a desire for party moderation he sometimes tried to conciliate extreme differences not only among members of his own party but between Whigs and Tories. He functioned as a vigorous peacemaker when he once asked both parties to look behind the clichés and see themselves for what they were. In *Freeholder* 29, published on Good Friday in 1716, he reviewed Whig deficiencies, especially those of the unnamed but easily identifiable earl of Wharton whose secretary and protégé he had been. Unable to surrender partisanship completely, Addison indicated that for every Whig inadequacy there was a still greater Tory failure. Nonetheless, he criticized his own party for indifference to the established church, republican leanings, Rabelaisian social behavior, and self-seeking intrigues. He was in part urged on by moral purpose when he asked for a Whig renaissance, a rededication of the party to the liberal ideal and to "a laudable freedom of thought" that transcends the sectarian and promotes an "extensive view of the public good."[33]

But he also had in *Freeholder* 29 the pragmatic purpose of reducing the frictions among those in the highest echelons of the Whig hierarchy, frictions that affected the whole party. He was aware, for example, of the rivalry between Sunderland and Townshend, Somerset's disappointment at being removed from his post as master of the horse, and Marlborough's displeasure because he had been deprived of power and confidence. Therefore, when Addison asked his party to engage in a stern reappraisal of itself, he hoped that in the process his fellow Whigs would recall the years between 1703 and 1705 and between 1710 and 1713; then, without either advantage or power, they had been united.

He asked Whig leaders to remember that their followers were free men entitled to participate in policy discussions. More emphatically he asked rank-and-file members, whether they were country Whigs, court Whigs, or disciples of the late Junto, to remember that they were a party of "honest and prudent" men. He urged each to uphold conviction and principle, to surrender only "a doubtful opinion to the concurring judgment of those whom he believes to be well-intentioned to their country, and who have better opportunities of looking into all its most complicated interests." The climax of *Freeholder* 29 and the fulfillment of its rhetorical purpose is Addison's argument for unanimity, that the party at peace with itself is "of infinitely greater consequence than the same party aiming at the same end by different views: as a large diamond is of a thousand times greater value whilst it remains entire, than when it is cut into a multitude of smaller stones, notwithstanding they may each of them be very curiously set, and are all of the same water." Whether he was conscious of its effect or not, his metaphor provides a tangible, pounds-and-shillings justification for party tranquility. It is almost as if he said to his fellow Whigs, "Let us not by petty squabbles throw away the spoils for which we have been waiting these many years; let us in truth be a civilized party and not a barbaric tribe."

Although he demanded self-scrutiny from the Whigs (and even more from the Tories), he could not have been hopeful that many on either side would heed his cry. Party violence had already subverted the moral habits of the mind and had indeed imposed restraints upon "a laudable freedom of thought." It had elevated to power an incalculable number of secret agents later characterized by Swift as "the most accursed, and prostitute, and abandoned race, that God ever permitted to plague mankind."[34] Addison was incapable of Swift's explosive rhetoric but in a mordant *Guardian* essay matched his disgust. He visualized the master spy as a bloodthirsty lion, ferreting out secrets "that cut off heads, hang, draw, and quarter, or end in the ruin of the person who becomes his prey." This animal compounds its cruelty by using jackals, "who are his retailers of intelligence, and bring him in materials for his report" (*G* 71). Not even the political necessities that spawned them mitigated Addison's loathing of political informers.

He first used the same animal imagery in *Spectator* 343 (on the transmigration of the soul), where he also exploited the seventeenth-century pseudozoological notion that the jackal precedes the king-beast to rout out quarry for the kill on which both feed. The meaning of the jackal—a scavenging subordinate, a minor spy—in Addison's metaphor is simple and conventional. That of the lion is somewhat less expected, because the lion is shorn of his symbolic regality and removed from his honored place in the British coat of arms. To support his leonine metaphor, Addison alludes briefly in *Guardian* 71 to the Venetian statues of lions whose gaping mouths are utilized for the deposit of "private intelligence. . . . The informer is concealed, it is the lion that tells everything." Then, more elaborately, he relates the questionable, probably familiar, and amusing story of Sir Francis Walsingham's barber, a member of the Elizabethan statesman's ubiquitous spy-ring, "whose surname was Lion." By eponymous extension, according to Addison, master spies from that time on were known as lions.[35]

The beast fable in *Guardian* 71 allowed him to question political aspirations that relied for their fulfillment on secrecy, double-dealing, and connivance. The conspiratorial tactics of secret agents, he admitted ironically, had become indispensable deceptions in English public life; but that did not oblige him to like spies: "Hangmen and executioners are necessary in a state, and so may the animal I have been here mentioning; but how despicable is the wretch that takes on him so vile an employment." In his emphasis on the lion's predatory furtiveness, Addison is very close to the psalmist who warned that an evil man is like "a lion in his covert; he lurks that he may seize the poor, he seizes the poor when he draws him into his net."[36] Building, as he often did, on a biblical comparison while making an appropriate connection with Augustan values, Addison anathematized the political spy as a "creature hated both by God and man, and regarded with the utmost contempt, even by such as make use of him."

The jackal-lion figure was useful because it was literary; it isolated for discussion a detestable subject and yet avoided direct political confrontation. Through it Addison could insulate reproach in parable, treating informers as "noxious" animals, "beasts of prey," that "with mouths gaping in a most enormous manner" roared, lurked, and "infested" the town. As an artistic device it was arresting; it asked the reader "to unriddle this paradox"; it brought a hint of scriptural fiat to the repudiation of a base secular activity. In this way Addison managed to secure a maximum response to his essay, always the goal of a popular journalist.[37]

Although he concentrated his attack on the political spy in *Guardian* 71, he carried on his war against the party writer in a number of essays that varied in point of view. Addison often implied a similarity between the two in origin and characteristics. Both, he claimed, were produced by the gluttonous demands of party ambition, both were morally corrupt, and both were available for the practice of party lying. Although Addison was himself a master polemicist, he dissociated his compositions from those of journalistic hirelings, whom he despised but whom after 1712 he sponsored. He could rationalize such a dissociation because, unlike a mere salaried scribbler, he wrote about his party's program in the spirit of one who believed in it and had helped formulate it. He admired journalists who, like himself, were able without libelous "satire and ridicule" to "explain to the people the reasonableness" of the Revolution principle and "to justify the conduct of those who act in conformity" to it (*F* 19). No doubt the standards by which he rated excellence in political journalism were fixed by his own talent, personality, and Whiggism. During a time of journalistic invective, ribaldry, and slanderous distortion, however, his standards reflect a laudable respect for news writing and commentary as a form of intelligent moral action.

But before he had organized his own corps of political writers or written *The Trial of Count Tariff,* he was not sanguine about those of either side who wrote to escape debtor's prison. He castigated them as "zealots of parties," "sons of calumny and defamation," "dark, undermining vermin," and murderers and assassins. He saw them as the ultimate in depravity, "a scandal to government, and a reproach to human nature" (*S* 124, *S* 451). Party writers were natural targets in his day, but the moral intensity of his judgment is unusual. Not content to excoriate those who scribbled away their small talents, he extended his reproach to their patrons and readers.[38] By implying a parallel with the concept of accessory guilt, he argued that to approve a misdeed, in this case to sanction a writer's lies, is to abet a criminal act. He hoped by frightening the buyer to eliminate the purveyor.

On 7 August 1712, in *Spectator* 451, Addison concerned himself with the dual problem of the intellectual perversion of the party writer and the hypocrisy of readers avid for his libels. "There is nothing," he began, "so scandalous to a government, and detestable in the eyes of all good men, as defamatory papers and pamphlets; but at the same time there is nothing so difficult to tame, as a satirical author." His indignation mounted as he developed this theme. Then he took the attack one step further to enlist his readers' moral sense—their honor and prudence—in repudiating the practice itself. Using Bayle and Cicero as his authorities, he stated forthrightly: "We may therefore conclude that those who are pleased with reading defamatory libels, so far as to approve the authors and dispersers of them, are as guilty as if they had composed them; for if they do not write such libels themselves, it is because they have not the talent of writing, or because they will run no hazard." His was an adamant belief that self-knowledge and self-engagement were the touchstones of any moral reconstruction, whether it concerned the idols, the embryos, or the readers who sated themselves with political falsehoods.

So he spoke and thought in the late summer of 1712. But after Arthur Maynwaring's death in November, Addison assumed tighter control of Whig journalists. Since he now organized their assignments, fed them their information and point of view, and paid for their services, he necessarily placed less distance between party writers and himself. He could no longer afford the superiority that comes from detachment. At the back of his mind must also have been the nagging admission that scurrilous and inflammatory political journalism was the adjunct of unbridled party competition. They were unpleasant realities, but realities that had nonetheless to be endured and moderated to serve salutary ends for both party and nation. By December 1715 and the inception of the *Freeholder,* his feeling for party authorship took on an ambivalence that arose directly from the insatiable demands of crisis and expedience. Now a committed Whig journalist, he not only recommended governmental censorship to silence those who were critical of the ministry but praised others whose efforts—candid, impartial, and obviously Whig—had "a more particular tendency to the good of their country, and of the present age, than any other compositions whatsoever" (*F* 40).[39]

Addison had first looked upon all party writers with a mixture of aloof contempt and moral indignation. Within a short time, however, he came to accept them as inescapable evils in a government ordered by the consent of a politically conscious electorate. Ultimately he gave up any pretense of objectivity. Political journalists, if Whig, were usually worthy of endorsement; but if Tory, they were mere hacks who should be muzzled for the good of the community. His literary treatment of those who wrote for party was a compromising one that altered with the times and his duties. Yet in his early periodicals he never excused the evils perpetrated by the Grub Street tribe. And from the beginning of his journalistic career to its end he never minimized the distortions and innuendoes propagated by party enthusiasts, whether they were Whigs like Steele, Tories like Swift, or shuttlers like Defoe.

Indeed, Addison protested repeatedly in his journals that extremism nullified the good that partisanship could foster. Through such protest he set forth implicitly his own idealized standards as the measure of political morality. Partisanship was acceptable to him but only in a context of temperate, orderly endeavor that contributed to the public good. To politicize worthily, Addison suggested, an individual must be the steward of "something venerable, holy, and inviolable"—justice that leaves men "wholly intent on the equity of a cause, without being diverted or prejudiced by objects foreign to it"

(*G* 99). He must, as well, exercise constancy, a "virtuous resolution and firmness of mind," that would invite trust in the steadfastness of his judgments and authority (*F* 25). And, finally, he must inspire faith in the primacy of the greatest good for the greatest number in order that men may learn to subordinate the one to the many, the clique to society, the party to the nation. This was patriotism, "the most sublime and extensive of all social virtues" (*F* 5).[40]

CHAPTER SIX

THE STRUCTURE OF GOVERNMENT

DESPITE administrative distractions and exposure to factional chicanery, Addison always enjoyed theorizing about the nature of government. Indeed, the more involved he became in Whig schemes and schisms, the more he tried with middling success to separate his concept of polity from the day-to-day compromises of office and party service. His politics had to accommodate an often mean reality; but his values, while disposed to utility, idealized man's spirit and natural worth. As was true of much of his intellectual activity, he formulated a philosophy of politics eclectically. He drew on a succession of influential thinkers from the Roman Stoics to Locke who, in the tradition of rational liberalism, defined the state as an organism that liberates individual benevolence, works for the public good, and secures for its constituents peace, safety, and happiness. At another level of derivation, he was indebted to a variety of contemporary principles imbued in his generation with the authority of Whig approval. Virtually maxims, if not clichés, these were pragmatized by the Revolution of 1688–89 with the presumed sanction of Locke's *Two Treatises of Government.* For the next quarter of a century they were severely tried by the ever-present but suppressed Jacobitism that erupted into civil war in 1715.

Warmth was not characteristic of Addison; nevertheless, in a controlled way he was responsive to human desire. In his search for political truth and the confirmation of civil rights, he looked to the nebulous law of nature described in the rhetoric of Cicero, the theological dialectic of the Scholastics, and the prolix Anglicanism of "judicious" Hooker. He paid special attention to the increasingly secular interpretations of the seventeenth century when men like Grotius and Pufendorf, Cumberland and Culverwel, invoked natural law to unite the Protestant community. From these four men he learned that natural law originated in divine will and in human reason whose possession makes all men equal: it therefore exalted conscience as the ultimate test of public and private performance. And if at times the protean conclusions of these philosophers bewildered him, he could find them simplified and popularized in the sermon literature of such liberal moralists as Samuel Parker, John Wilkins, Henry More, John Tillotson, Benjamin Whichcote, Isaac Barrow, and Edward Stillingfleet.[1]

All his sources, from Cicero to the Latitudinarians, saw the law of nature as the antecedent and basis of civil institutions, and as universal in its application because it originated in God's design. All agreed that natural law was the measure of human activity, whose common denominator was reason. To Grotius it was simply "right reason, showing the moral deformity, or moral necessity there is in any act, by either its complying, or disagreeing with human nature itself, and consequently that such an act is either forbid, or commanded by God the author of nature." As Addison pondered this statement and others like it, he concluded that the law of nature is a vague code of things to do and not to do, a set of unformulated principles that drive man to desire good and shun evil. But he would not have long concerned himself with an effort merely to define natural law, even if this were possible. What was important to him was the law's accommodation of rationality to moral behavior and social responsibility: "If, in the several districts and divisions of the world, men would thus study the welfare of those respective communities, to which their power of doing good is limited, the whole race of reasonable creatures would be happy, as far as the benefits of society can make them so. At least, we find so many blessings naturally flowing from this noble principle, that in proportion as it prevails, every nation becomes a prosperous and flourishing people" (*F* 5). Rejecting the materialism of Hobbes, Addison identified the law of nature as the perfect expression of altruistic self-love or benevolent private interest. He accepted it as a proclamation of equality and dignity, an assertion that each person as an integer of society warrants the respect of his fellows.[2]

From his sources, which stressed moral affirmation, he derived the assumption that natural law overreaches time and space. It was, said Pufendorf, the "law universal and perpetual; the former, in regard that it binds the whole body of the human race, the latter, because it is not subject to change." Always constant, it predicated the political values that Addison revered: unity, order, and continuum. It underlay his vision of a lasting social structure in which men knew that the well-being of each was part of the well-being of all. But he hesitated to make a mystique of the state or its structure, especially in journals designed for popular consumption. His object was to translate the idea of natural law into terminology readily within the grasp of his readers.

The familiar word *justice* was his synonym for *natural law,* and in his essays he treated the concept with simple, instructive clarity. In *Spectator* 243 it was one of "the good qualities that render us beneficial to each other." To make this good quality impressive, he traced it to its source in deity and extracted reverential implications; yet he flattered his readers with confidence in their capacity to employ it. "As to be perfectly just is an attribute in the divine nature," he said in *Guardian* 99, "to be so to the utmost of our abilities is the glory of a man." Beyond prejudice, time, and change stands the luminous truth of justice, the principle that secures the rights intrinsic to the law of nature. Earlier in his career, in *Tatler* 100, Addison devised an allegory to press home the practical implications of the concept. Justice, as he personified it, guarantees rightful ownership—"titles and claims to riches and estates." It also guarantees the right of recognition to "persons of the greatest merit, abilities, and perfection." From the abortive *Whig Examiner* to the unfinished *Old Whig,* he described justice not as an abstraction but as a working tool, useful for social order. It gave him hope that men as moral creatures would respect the explicitly codified rights of others and that the rights implicit in natural law would be assured by the legal structure of the state.[3]

His discussions of justice helped reduce the vagueness and mystery of natural law by placing it in the solid context of daily life. More significantly, they gave his audience cause for optimism, for everyone likes to know he has rights defined and protected by a legal code, a frame of government to reward the good and punish the evil. But while Addison dwelt on the benefits of justice, he warned that for each benefit there is a corresponding obligation. Human rights, he insisted, do not flow toward the individual smoothly and inevitably; they become his only if he is prepared to give as well as receive. Justice, which began in the exercise of private conscience and extended to communal action, could never be divorced from social duty.

Yet at times external events brought the public conscience to the forefront of Addison's attention. During the "tumults and commotions" of 1715–16 he became pessimistic over the failure of corporate good will, fearing that the English government would be as much eroded by selfish neutrality as by rebellion. Too many people, in his opinion, sought safe aloofness. Justice, he was sure, forbade passivity, because no man could will his conscience into his brother's keeping. On the contrary, justice required total commitment. Like Cicero, he fervently believed that to evade choice was itself to make a choice; more than that, such evasion was a perverse, cowardly act of injustice. For these reasons Addison in 1715–16 condemned those "who profess a state of neutrality in times of public danger"; he berated them for disinterest, which, heedless of justice, ignores responsibility to God and the good of society. "The safety of the whole," he again echoed Cicero, "requires our joint endeavours. When this is at stake, the indifferent are not properly a part of the community; or rather are like dead limbs, which are an encumbrance to the body, instead of being of use to it" (*F* 13).[4] In his practical mind justice, like the law of nature itself, was spirit and fact, virtue and juridical function, thought and action. It sustained the good, superior to parochial consequence; but it also fought for the Hanoverian succession against the Jacobite revolt.

For the most part Addison hewed to a line of political inquiry formulated by Locke; and like the older man, he would not concede a meaningful division between speculation and application. Locke, with certain changes, both continued and extended the Western tradition of natural law, so that there was no conflict between his work and the other sources read with respect by Addison. Whenever Addison cited Locke, who had the status of a Whig demigod, he indirectly attested to the wisdom of his party. There were between the putative philosopher of the Revolution and the essayist, further, a near contemporaneity and an affinity confirmed by shared beliefs. Both, for instance, rejected utopias and adhered to a state that they postulated as a confederation of men who wanted primarily to realize themselves as human beings.

Although Locke had borrowed much from earlier interpreters of natural law, he went beyond them to correlate it with innate rights and duties. He insisted therefore that reason "teaches all mankind who will but consult it, that being all equal and independent, no one ought to harm another in his life, health, liberty or possessions." As the creations of "one omnipotent and infinitely wise Maker," men may not assume any authority which destroys the works of God or of His rational creatures. "Everyone, as he is bound to preserve himself, and not to quit his station willfully; so by the like reason when his own preservation comes not in competition, ought he, as much as he can, to preserve the rest of mankind, . . ."[5]

Similarly, Addison argued that all men are naturally free, equal, and their own masters in the rank assigned them by divine wisdom. He agreed that, subject only to the law of nature in the beginning, men consent to the formation of political states as a safeguard of their lives, independence, and property. Finally, he asserted that each individual, even while subordinating himself to government, limits its prerogatives in order to insure his "civil liberties, as the natural rights of mankind" (*F* 2). Addison's definition of civilized society is Lockean. At its center is the image of man who no longer acts like a furtive savage but moves among his fellows openly and unarmed because he assumes that others will not, unprovoked, harm or attack him. The definition thus springs from a sensitivity to man's yearning for freedom and safety and his consequent willingness to live among other men in peace and with good will.[6]

Addison was concerned with a complex liberalism. It originated in the law of nature and extended to the idea of government as a contractual partnership between the governed and governing. For all its intricacy his political theory was dominated by the single purpose of defending the gains achieved by the Revolution. He ignored the forceful Tory support of the events of 1688–89, choosing instead to interpret them as a triumph of Whig policy and courage. The Revolution, as he looked back on it, meant many things, among them the promise of a new stability to replace that lost in the fanaticism of the Protectorate and under the rule of James II. Like others of his time, moreover—from Defoe to many Latitudinarians—he credited the limited monarchies of Anne and George I to the Revolution, which had secured the independence of Parliament from the Crown. He therefore joined with those who, like Bishop Kennett, celebrated the newly won integrity of the legislative body by praising the Revolution Settlement as "the best foundation, the whole frame of our government." What most heartened him were signs that the struggle in 1688–89 precluded reunion with Rome and government without consent, that it nullified phrases like *passive obedience, nonresist-*

ance, and *hereditary right.* But in spite of his cheerful conviction during the first decade of the century, these slogans were more persistent than he suspected, especially between 1710 and 1716. Whenever they became popular, as at the beginning and end of this six-year period, he denounced them as "ensnaring terms" intended to delude with their "mild, gentle, and meek-spirited sound"; they were "supple and insinuating" lies, unrelatable ideas both "absurd" and "unnatural" (*WE* 5).[7]

The stability he wished for his country was not to be achieved until the onset of Walpole's hegemony, soon after his own death. But in his lifetime his devotion to the ideal of an orderly society increased as he reacted to the mounting confusion of a nation whose political slogans warred with English constitutionalism and whose church, torn between its bishops and its lower clergy, was a center of factional controversy. During most of his life England was turbid with discontent and insecurity. Within twenty-eight years after Charles II's return to the throne, a Stuart once more fled English soil, and his crown was given to William. Twenty-five years later the reign of Anne ended without any certainty that the Protestant succession, made mandatory by law, was secure. His was an age of tension climaxed in the beginning years of Hanoverian rule by rebellion, which Addison castigated as "one of the most heinous crimes which it is in the power of man to commit" (*F* 12). The national church was no more stable than the government in this half century, nor could it be since its fortunes were tied to those of the state. Having barely survived the Puritan interregnum, the church was shaken again by Charles's apostate leanings and James's open affiliation with Rome. When William and Mary came to the throne, the Anglican establishment, already weakened by lip-service faith, had to support a government that many clergymen viewed as illegal and a menace to the inseparability of church and state.

Through all this turmoil Addison moved with caution prompted by instinct as well as prudence. There is little evidence of ill temper or rancor in his journalism; on the contrary, it usually reveals in its assertions as well as in its tone a calm good will toward the problems of party and government. Where there were anger and zeal Addison recommended discriminating forbearance; where there was unwholesome division he applied the leaven of soft words. He tried to subdue party extremists by gentle laughter and to stir political neutrals into action by rational persuasion and classical precedent. To those who cried for order at any authoritarian price, he exposed tyranny's denial of civil liberty. To those who advocated a church secure from restlessness and change, he pointed out the danger of "implicit faith," which would smother the authority of conscience and cause persecution for the sake of conformity. Outbursts of rage or spiteful indignation, then, are startling in Addison because they are so rare. What his contemporaries learned to expect from him was control, and he often steadied them with his reasonableness and good humor.

He subordinated his interest in natural law to a concern for the civil and political community, whose development was measurable in time and whose efficacy was liable to empirical tests. Yet it was natural law that gave him the values for his politico-moral creed and the language for its expression. He defined *state* as an entity to which its members assented by tacit contract and by which they were therefore provided with the benefits of communal organization. To support this definition, he went again to the commentators on polity who described the workings of natural law; from them he borrowed the doctrine of consent as the foundation of a well-compacted government, one that avoided the polarities of absolutism and mob-subverted democracy.

According to Cicero a commonwealth was "the property of a people . . . in large numbers associated in an agreement with respect to justice and a partnership for the common good." Except for some tentative explorations by Hooker and a few republicans in Cromwell's regime, the doctrine of consent had been neglected for centuries. During and after the Restoration, interest in the concept increased; it was, for example, analyzed by Temple and late in the century invested with the romantic drama of Sidney's execution. But its pragmatic significance was clarified for Addison by Locke's assertion that "the liberty of man, in society, is to be under no legislative power, but that established by consent, in the commonwealth, nor under the dominion of any will, or restraint of any law, but what the legislature shall enact, according to the trust put in it." In other words, the state and its law belong to the people, the state's prerogatives being confined to the legislature properly balanced by the three estates. Governmental power must conform to majority will.[8]

Addison distilled from his sources the theoretical elements that could best be translated into the context of a state directed by party government and threatened by rebellion. He stressed the goal of public safety sought after by "civil government," which is "an institution, whereby we are all confederated together for our mutual defence and security" (*F* 13). The word *confederated* suggests both Cicero's ideas of association, agreement, and partnership; and Locke's of contract, volition, and formal affirmation. Addison's ideal government, synonymous with England's constitutional monarchy, was established by consent and projected through law, which "makes an innocent man, though of the lowest rank, a match for the mightiest of his fellow-subjects." Majestic in its power and liberating in its effects, the law is seen by Addison as a leveler that allows man "to control the insolence or injustice of any private oppressor" (*F* 12). It recognizes no distinctions among men and so gives each his freedom—specifically, his right to dignity and self-assertion.[9]

Addison's respect for the law merged with his regard for the House of Commons as the instrument through which all freeholders gave their "consent to every law which passes" (*F* 1). He saw them as but one step removed from being their own lawgivers and therefore like Aristotle's subjects of "approved virtue," who knew "how to rule and how to obey."[10] This was both the privilege and duty of a free Englishman, who, Addison wrote, was expected "to stand up in the defence of those laws, which are in some degree of his own making." In *Freeholder* 1, where he sounded this call for social responsibility, he wrote with satisfaction that under the English constitution "the bulk of the people virtually give their approbation to every thing they are bound to obey, and prescribe to themselves those rules by which they are to walk." Here, as earlier in *Spectator* 287, Addison celebrated the status of free men; and in doing so, he reiterated Locke's premise that the majority has an absolute right to represent the consent of the whole. As a somber acknowledgment of the threatening events of 1715, he affirmed that the well-being of the people depended on the subordination of their singular identities not to the mob but to the corporate will, to the "bulk" of the state.[11]

He was faithful to a viable tradition, which recognized the state as an evolving entity, the result of centuries of trial and error. In the course of time the diverse and even jealous elements that comprised the structure of the state acquired a common purpose. The harmony of this contractual partnership was maintained by the equal distribution of duties and rewards among its three social orders. The same tradition, moreover, taught that behind every political scene and controversy was a struggle for power. Not that he thought power was in itself evil. He took account of its natural basis in consent, which enabled men to emerge from a state of nature and create government as the benevolent trustee of their voluntarily surrendered rights. But Addison like many of his contemporaries realized that freedom, the breath of English liberalism, could be endangered by the power that legitimately inhered in government. His political assumptions therefore were finely centered between the need to protect liberty and the need to restrict power without endangering the state.

He proceeded from the not wholly accurate maxim that an Englishman's liberty was a birthright inherited from Saxon ancestors and that it had been so designated in an ancient constitution, which sought to safeguard the human desire for freedom, property, and life. Along with most of his readers he understood by *constitution* not a written document but a design of government and a catalogue of rights unalterable by ordinary law. Whatever difficulty he had in defining the term, there was no doubt in his mind that it operated for the common good. This it accomplished when it balanced and checked the major classes of society, and when it separated them into "the regal, the noble, and the plebeian; because the whole community is cast under these several heads, and has not in it a single member who is without his representative in the legislature of such a constitution" (*OW* 1). With this statement he voiced his confidence in "mixed government" as it had been hypothesized by Aristotle, "the greatest philosopher" of antiquity, by Polybius, "the most impartial historian," and by Cicero, "the most consummate statesman" (*F* 51).[12]

For Addison this concept became political fact not with Charles's begrudging "Answer to the Nineteen Propositions" on 21 June 1642 but with the reign of William III. In the *Spectator,* the *Freeholder,* and the *Old Whig* he declared his admiration for both the idea and the reality of mixed government as an antidote to absolutism and as a liberty-preserving force. Yet the vigor of his approval is curious, for few in his generation questioned the efficacy of mixed government as the basis of British constitutionalism. Those who spoke of Britain's "frame" or "scheme" or "system" or "combination of powers" held that it was nicely balanced "between the extremes of too much liberty, and too much power; the several parts of it having a proper check upon each other." This image of balance, described by Atterbury in 1701, was congenial to many shades of opinion before and after that year. Thus Steele, who was politically at odds with the bishop, justified it for England, while Algernon Sidney, who often rose above national bias, had categorized the "best governments of the world" as those "composed of monarchy, aristocracy, and democracy."[13]

Such unanimity seemed to make the theory inviolable; nonetheless, most Englishmen recognized that the symmetry of their constitution could be maintained only through vigilance. The threat to its balance, and hence to its guarantee of liberty, came most commonly from the royal prerogative, because few men driven by a desire for preferment would withstand either the blandishments or the natural weight and authority of the Crown. For Addison and every other Whig this had been axiomatic since 1711, when Anne created twelve new peerages to promote the peace efforts of her Tory ministry. The problem posed by the wanton use of the prerogative continued to be acute. In 1713, for instance, Steele, agitated by rumors that six additional peerages might be created as an aid to the embattled Harley–St. John regime, declared that "the whole constitution is in danger" if the arbitrary creation of occasional peers "is not prevented by some future law." Six years later Stanhope and Sunderland attempted to provide such a law when on 28 February 1718/19 they had the duke of Somerset bring to the Lords a special committee's resolutions for the reform of the peerage. The chief of these were "that the number of English peers should not be enlarged beyond six above the present number, which upon failure of male issue might be supplied by new creations; that instead of the 16 elective peers in Scotland, 25 be made hereditary on the part of the kingdom, whose number, upon failure of male heirs, should be supplied by some other Scotch peers." These resolutions, seconded by the duke of Argyll, became the basis of the so-called peerage bill, which was introduced into the House of Lords on 14 March. With this measure the ministry hoped to curtail the newly begun aggrandizement of the Commons at the expense of the Lords and to stabilize the still dominant but weakening upper house essentially as it was in 1719 by fixing its membership at 235.[14]

Addison undertook to promote the bill in the *Old Whig,* a periodical that represents only a minor achievement in Addisonian journalism, if it is that. During a time of constitutional crisis, its title gave it an aura of tradition by suggesting an association with the substantial country Whigs and even with the Whiggish patriarchs of William III's time who had distrusted the court and wished to diminish the influence of the Crown. For all the cleverness of title, however, Addison's authorship of the journal was as unexpected as his wholehearted participation in the peerage-bill controversy.

His feeling for the cause of mixed government was so strong that he ignored his illness and his usual party role as peacemaker between Whig factions. That his involvement was as much emotional as rational is apparent in his loss of perception and even political shrewdness. On another occasion he would have seen that in exchange for the verbal promise of constitutional symmetry the bill made the position of the hereditary lords impregnable; for in hamstringing the monarch by restricting his authority to create new peers, the bill took away the most formidable check on the power of the entrenched lords. Whether through confusion or mistaken fidelity to the ministry, Addison advocated a law that would have effected just what it wanted to prevent. It would have given the upper house an exorbitant oligarchical power to inhibit the rights of king and people alike and would have been a disaster for constitutionalism as it was conceived in Addison's generation. The oratory of Steele and Walpole, however, was so rousing that the measure was defeated by a substantial margin of ninety-two votes after an all-day parliamentary session on 8 December. But Addison never knew the outcome. When the votes were counted, he had already been dead for six months.

His advocacy of the peerage bill was a repayment to the ministry for past favors, as well as a gesture in defense of British liberty. That it proved mistaken in no way impugns his suspicion of power and of its aggressive tendency to encroach on the natural and legal boundaries of what is free. He believed that tyranny, which he feared and loathed, sprang from power wrongly used. He equated tyrant and absolute monarch, interchanging these epithets to describe the ruler who contradicted reason and invalidated natural rights. Unlimited power, Addison said in *Freeholder* 10, "naturally tends to make a man a bad sovereign, who might possibly have been a good one, had he been invested with an authority . . . circumscribed by laws." On the day before the anniversary of the death of Charles I "the blessed martyr"—a day usurped by the Tories as a political memorial —he cynically dismissed the absolutists and High Churchmen who "tell us we ought to make our governments on earth like that in heaven, which . . . is altogether monarchical and unlimited. Was man like his Creator in goodness and justice, I should be for following this great model; but where goodness and justice are not essential to the ruler, I would by no means put myself into his hands to be disposed of according to his particular will and pleasure" (*S* 287).[15]

Because of the success of the Revolution, Addison had long regarded despotism as an indigenously Gallic evil, which could never be transplanted to his native soil. But events after 1710 diminished his assurance. The Tory victory in that year and then the visible illness of Anne were warnings of stormy days to come. By 1713 he joined those who insisted that Jacobites had captured the Tory party and were conspiring toward a tyrannical take-over. George Berkeley, for example, remarked on 23 February 1712/13 that "Mr. Addison and Mr. Steele (and so far as I can find, the rest of that party) seem entirely persuaded there is a [Tory] design for bringing in the Pretender." The despotic tenets of Jacobitism—"unlimited power and indefeasible right," as Addison saw them—threatened British liberalism and promised to void the hard-won gains of 1688–89. He was anxious lest Jacobitism, implemented by Tory respectability and wealth, impose an absolutist government on England. For, as he knew, after the 1713 election about one hundred members of the Commons were committed to the Pretender, at least half of them were active in the St. John faction, and early in 1714 over eighty Tories attended a single meeting of the Jacobite Club. However, ignoring evidence of anti-Jacobite activity among Tories as influential as Hanmer, for example, Addison systematically used his anxiety to construct what was to become a dominant plank in the Whig platform between 1713 and 1716, the association of Toryism, Jacobitism, and the suppression of British liberty. So successful was this propaganda that the Tories were put on the defensive and even the followers of James III made a feeble effort at refutation. Thus a spokesman for the Pretender scored as Whig lies the statement that "the King would certainly make all [Englishmen] slaves; because being educated in France, he has been used to the maxims of arbitrary government, and those are so natural to be liked by young monarchs, that he will . . . transcribe the French tyranny into the British constitution."[16]

Few Englishmen were persuaded, least of all Addison, and when in June 1713 he read of the celebrations in Scotland honoring the Pretender, any doubts he may have had of the potency of Jacobite menace were resolved. While some of his more sanguine contemporaries still referred to the Jacobites as "the sinking party," he dismissed their optimism as self-delusion. Certainly his fears were supported by the reward of £100,000 offered by the Lords in September 1714 for the arrest of the Pretender; and these same fears were aggravated by the first of the king's proclamations in November for suppressing riots "of the discontented party, who had already begun to throw off the mask."[17]

On 20 July 1715 George I announced that "such a spirit of rebellion has discovered itself, as leaves no room to doubt, but these disorders are set on foot and encouraged by persons disaffected to my government, in expectation of being supported from abroad." Lord Mar, on 6 September, unfurled the rebel flag at Braemar. Four months later, on 21 January 1715/16, George I reluctantly announced that the Pretender was in Scotland. But Addison did not wait for that admission to act against the rebellion, as every loyal subject must, "in a manner suitable to his station and abilities" (*F* 55). He acted through the journal created the previous December and named for freeholders, who by their numerical strength could swing county elections and hence influence parliamentary majorities. In it he set about to convince all good Britons, as well as those deluded people who strove for neutrality, that James III on the throne of Great Britain would be a tyrant and his subjects "obliged in conscience to be slaves" (*F* 10).[18]

It was probably his most satisfying venture in political journalism because it permitted him to fulfill philosophical conviction and Whig need. Although the Pretender had been in Scotland less than two months before fleeing on 4 February, Addison continued his journal until 29 June 1716. For five months he warned of the Pretender's imminence, having learned as long ago as 1708 that parliamentary elections could be influenced by the half-lie, which when spoken with enough certainty will be accepted as truth.[19] His intention therefore in scattered numbers of the *Freeholder* was to exploit fear of Stuart restoration in an attempt to secure victory at the polls for the Whigs, long identified as Jacobitism's foe.

Addison also continued the journal to frustrate what the Whigs labeled Tory "artifices and insinuation . . . by which it is intended to reflect on His Majesty's conduct and stigmatize such of his servants as were most active in carrying on the late war against France, and in pursuing the measures found necessary for suppressing the rebellion."[20] In number after number he justified honest faction, preempted George I as the titular head of the Whigs, and emphasized the royal virtues that reflected favorably on the principles of the Revolution, which were of course Whig principles. He used the *Freeholder,* then, as a vehicle to rewrite the history of the Whig Diaspora from 1710 to 1713, reclaiming his party's honor, which had been traduced by Tory calumnies, and celebrating once-defamed leaders like the late Lord Somers.[21]

Finally, the journal was prolonged in a futile effort to moderate reaction to the widening conflict between George I and the Prince of Wales. It was no secret that the prince was encouraging the Tories materially in order to counter his father's Whig sympathies. And Addison, who anticipated the ill effects of the prince's conduct, feared that "the Whigs in general are become so uneasy and divided, that should things continue upon the present foot, the prospect for the next session of Parliament would be but melancholy." The party, after its long-awaited return to control, was being split by the royal quarrel as well as by a scramble for power within its own ranks. The *Freeholder* reminded the Whigs of their lean years and preached cohesion as a guarantee of continued affluence. It tried to bring concord within the royal family by praising the Prince of Wales for virtues that he shared with his father, and Princess Caroline for "behaviour by which she has so much endeared herself to His Majesty" (*F* 21).[22]

For all its party bias, the *Freeholder* forthrightly recorded Addison's hostility to political absolutism, his respect for an Englishman's "legal claim to liberty and property," and his insistence on constitutional rule for a free people. He tried to commit each of his readers to his own dedication to liberty by reciting in a simple catechism the need for vigilance in order to keep freedom responsible and tyranny at bay. The journal was admittedly an organ of propaganda, sponsored and paid for by affluent Whigs.[23] Still, its consummately skillful editor blended political philosophy, ethics, and the demands of party ambition to recommend liberal truths contingent on the stamina of the community and the integrity of its members.

If in this journalistic effort Addison never betrayed his liberalism, he was sometimes forced to qualify it in the interests of party service. He believed, for example, that civil rights were the sacrosanct inheritance of every Englishman and that as such they had constitutional authority, which could not be changed or set aside by ordinary legislation. In *Freeholder* 16, however, he reversed himself, justifying the curtailment of a basic civil liberty when he felt that the public good depended on restraint. On 20 July 1715 the king announced the existence of open rebellion in Great Britain, and the next day Parliament presented a bill for a six-month suspension of habeas corpus, which was enacted on 23 July after only two days of debate. Most Britons, stunned by news of the rebellion, did not react to the temporary annulment. But when on 10 January 1715/16 Parliament offered yet another bill "for continuing the act to impower His Majesty to secure and detain suspected persons," Lord Harcourt, Lord Trevor, the duke of Buckingham, and the earl of Abingdon dissented in the upper house, as did William Shippen in the lower.[24] Protests continued even after the renewal of the suspension on 21 January and increased in volume after the Pretender's flight on 4 February.

Addison published *Freeholder* 16 on 13 February to mollify the growing antiministerial sentiment that the renewal provoked. When he prepared the essay, he probably worked closely with Stanhope, who had carried the Whig defense of the suspension onto the floor of Parliament less than a month before; however, no hint of such collaboration appears in the essay to expose its bias. Calling forth the logic of Cicero and Locke, Addison expatiated on the rule of national self-preservation:

> When, therefore, any law does not conduce to this great end, but on the contrary, in some extraordinary and unnatural junctures, the very observation of it would endanger the community, that law ought to be laid asleep for such a time, by the proper authority. Thus the very intention of our Habeas Corpus act, namely, the preservation of the liberties of the subject, absolutely requires that act to be now suspended, since the confinement of dangerous and suspected persons, who might strengthen this rebellion, and spread a civil war through all parts of this kingdom, secures to us our civil rights, and everything that can be valuable to a free people.[25]

It seems obvious now that he wished to free his essay from partisan taint. Its arguments were drawn, he claimed, "from the first principles of government, which, as they are of no party, but assented to by every reasonable man, carry the greater weight with them, and are accommodated to the notions of all [his] readers."

He constructed a façade of objectivity for his defense, but he seems to have sensed its propagandistic inadequacy. For this reason, perhaps, he introduced two rhetorical tricks. He asserted, first of all, that since complaints against the suspension of habeas corpus were stirred up by "malicious and artful enemies" of British security, those who questioned the suspension were either Jacobite dupes or traitors. Secondly, he played on popular deference to classical politics by pointing out that the Roman constitution permitted temporary dictatorship during an emergency.[26] Historical precedent therefore sanctioned England's revocation of a constitutional guarantee.

From the vantage point of more than two hundred years, this essay stands out as the *Freeholder*'s most obvious example of special pleading. Its persuasiveness depends almost as much on what it omits as on what it includes. Addison fails, for instance, to acknowledge the flight of the Pretender or to mention the signs of Jacobite disintegration, which were so conspicuous that the English government rescinded the order for German mercenaries to augment the standing army. Surely Addison was as well informed as the Edinburgh newswriter who on 14 February, a day after the publication of *Freeholder* 16, wrote that "The rebellion is now looked on as quite over, and a few days longer will . . . leave this country entirely in peace. His Grace the Duke of Argyll having distributed the troops into the proper places for that end, is expected here tomorrow or next day in his way to London: as is likewise the Earl of Sunderland, and some others soon after."[27] Not only did Addison conceal these facts but he exaggerated the Stuart threat, hoping through intimidation to justify the continued suspension of habeas corpus.

Freeholder 16 fails even to take passing notice of the dangers implicit in the suspension. By referring to the Roman constitution, Addison gave his essay a learned air. But this was simply throwing dust in his readers' eyes, for no amount of classical theory or precedent could make these dangers less real. To counter the argument that the suspension "invaded the most valuable rights of English subjects, encouraged malicious informations, and gave a handle to those in power to oppress innocent persons," he fell back on evasion. "How mildly and equitably this power has been used," he pointed out, and how judiciously had the king regulated himself—not "by any private jealousies or suspicions, but by those evidences and informations he has received." Several years later, when Swift applied the same test of constitutionality to the same suspension of habeas corpus, he protested against laying aside "any law upon which the liberty of the most innocent persons depended." And while, undeniably, he spoke with hindsight and not for publication, he went on to declare "it better that ten guilty men should escape, than one innocent suffer," and to denounce as a violation of biblical justice the very law Addison defended.[28]

Freeholder 16 may be singled out as an example of Addison's readiness to subordinate a principle of British liberty to Whig service or narrow national interest. As a political journalist, however, his purpose was pragmatic and his method rhetorical. Many of his decisions were indeed governed by "expediency and reasonableness," for he perceived that the ideal sometimes must be compromised for the sake of survival, even if this meant that certain freedoms were temporarily abrogated. Pliancy like Addison's has long been acceptable in civilized societies that assume responsibility for communal safety during crises.

The omissions in *Freeholder* 16 were occasioned in part by political necessity and in part by the oratorical dicta of Cicero and Quintilian. Both rhetoricians, whose authority was unquestioned in the eighteenth century, held that information contrary to an orator's argument must be concealed and that occasionally public good required him to exaggerate or perhaps even to deny truth. In this essay, Addison intended to advance a dual, interrelated good: the strengthening of the Whig cause at a time when it was harassed by hostile criticism and the attainment of stability in a country threatened by revolution. He therefore argued for a measure that, if repressive, might enforce order among a people who in the universities, in remote villages, and on London streets had shown themselves ready for mob action. Refusing to be lulled by signs of a new peace, he maintained that desperate times called for desperate legislation. He went even further to imply that any rhetorical means, even those of concealment and distortion, were justifiable if they contributed to the end of rebellion and the security of the legally constituted (Whig) government.

Addison's desire for Whig power and national stability also

prompted his support of the Septennial Act of 1716. This legislation, by abrogating the Triennial Act, postponed until 1722 the general election scheduled for 1718, and thus prolonged the Whig House of Commons. By his advocacy of the Septennial Act, Addison assumed a complex task. He had to bury the historical fact that the Whigs, fearful of Tory influence on William III's government between 1690 and 1694, had fought hard and successfully for the earlier act which made mandatory a short Parliament. Further, he had to anticipate the grumblings of his contemporaries; according to Gibbon's account: "The First Parliament of George the First had been chosen (1715) for three years: the term had elapsed, the trust was expired; and the four additional years (1718–1722), during which they continued to sit, were derived not from the people, but from themselves; from the strong measure of the Septennial Bill, which can only be paralleled by *il serar di consiglio* of Venetian history."[29]

He wasted no time on a counterargument to such thinking, since there was none. Instead he drew his rationale largely from the preamble to the Septennial Act itself. This charged that the triennial clause of William III's legislation "hath proved very grievous and burdensome, by occasioning . . . more violent and lasting heats and animosities among the subjects of this realm, than was ever known before the said clause was enacted; and the said provision, if it should continue, may probably at this juncture, when a restless and popish faction are designing and endeavouring to renew the rebellion within the kingdom and an invasion from abroad be destructive to the peace and security of the government." Like the author of the preamble (probably Walpole), Addison justified the act on the assumption that it would bring order to a country torn by rebellion and would forestall the agitation that inevitably preceded a general election. His defense contains a typical Addisonian mixture of ideal and practical. He realized that the passage of the bill lengthened the duration of Whig power, and that was all to the good. He also acknowledged that such legislation had necessarily to make his countrymen "not only a more safe, a more flourishing, and a more happy, but also a more virtuous people" (*F* 37). In this instance he was more right than wrong, as history was to show. Years later Gibbon himself had to admit that "the Septennial Act, so vicious in its origin, has been sanctioned by time, experience, and the national consent. Its first operation secured the House of Hanover on the throne, and its permanent influence maintains the peace and stability of government."[30]

The *Freeholder* is the summation of Addison's political journalism. In its methods and tone, contents and spirit, it exhibits an urbanity that is more reminiscent of the *Spectator* than either the contentious *Present State of the War* or the *Whig Examiner*. Its logic and rational exposition well-seasoned with Whig pieties, his serial painted the horror of *unnatural* rebellion and gently courted the plotters back to the fold of constitutional government. Toward those of his countrymen who remained true to the Stuarts, Addison was conciliatory but not sentimental; he was in fact very much like Cicero, who during the Catiline conspiracy invited the rebels to return to the authorized state. Only slightly less generous than the Roman, Addison wished to "incorporate" the Jacobites into the British "community," so that all Britons, loyalists and rebels alike, might partake of the freedom that was their due (*F* 19).[31]

The journal was the product of Addison's obligation to party and country; it also fulfilled a creative need. Ever since 1712 he had been aware that his destiny, tied to knockabout Whig action, would allow him little time for serious composition. He felt pressed to seize whatever opportunity offered itself, and the *Freeholder* was just such an opportunity. He regarded it as a worthy effort in which each essay, polished and complete, was a general statement "upon government, but with a view to the present situation of affairs in Great Britain." By universalizing the local and immediate he hoped for fame beyond the reach of most political writers of his day. Consequently, he wrote about the foundations on which the state must be erected—the principles of natural law and the doctrine of consent; he proved their assimilation into the British constitution and the near subversion of that noble frame. But his vision in the *Freeholder* did not end with isolated theory. Because all political action is performed by men, he had to confront head-on the issues of life in the organized community, to discuss the relationship of ethics to politics, and to confirm the immorality of rebellion and the morality of liberal government. He discussed all these matters in the pages of the *Freeholder*, sometimes objectively, sometimes Whiggishly, but almost always with an absence of "that mixture of violence and passion, which so often creeps into the works of political writers" (*F* 55).

He had a sense of mission when he wrote the *Freeholder*. Indeed, it is his dedication that gave the journal its tone of high seriousness. Yet he was sufficiently professional to appreciate the need for leavening in a sustained work of political writing. He gracefully admitted that he catered to popular taste by brightening the often dull materials of polity with witty analogies of incident and character:

Our nation are such lovers of mirth and humour, that it is impossible for detached papers, which come out on stated days, either to have a general run, or long continuance, if they are not diversified, and enlivened from time to time, with subjects and thoughts accommodated to this taste, which so prevails among our countrymen. No periodical author, who always maintains his gravity, and does not sometimes sacrifice to the graces, must expect to keep in vogue for any considerable time. Political speculations in particular, however just and important, are of so dry and austere a nature, that they will not go down with the public without frequent seasonings of this kind. The work may be well performed, but will never take, if it is not set off with proper scenes and decorations. A mere politician is but a dull companion, and, if he is always wise, is in great danger of being tiresome or ridiculous. [*F* 45]

The "proper scenes and decorations" in the *Freeholder* took the form of obvious satirical wit. It was employed in the creation of stock political types, in the portraits of the Tory fox hunter, his innkeeper, and the highland seer known as Second-Sighted Sawney. It animated the many essays dealing with High Church ladies, "stateswomen" whose stays are "ready to burst with sedition" (*F* 26). It enlivened the irony with which Addison exposed the "absurdity and inconsistence" implicit in the "political faith of a malcontent" (*F* 14). His satire is often bold, but he never attacked an individual or derived malicious pleasure from the suffering of the miserable and innocent. He was contemptuous of such scurrility, which he thought had no more effect than being "burnt in the hand with a cold iron." The *Freeholder,* whether grave or mirthful, never departed from Addison's standards of "decency and good manners" (*F* 55).[32]

CHAPTER SEVEN

CIVIL LIBERTIES AND NATURAL RIGHTS

ADDISON'S political philosophy idealizes "civil liberties, as the natural rights of mankind" (*F* 2). It asserts the equation between those freedoms innately man's and those guaranteed by the state. By making the free individual the center of his ideological spectrum, the journalist exhibits a "tincture of humanity" too strong to be blotted out by a tendency toward aloofness or Catonian rectitude. Neither is present in his expression of "tenderness and concern . . . for the good and happiness of mankind" (*T* 117). At the same time the equation reflects a dominant social attitude of the century; it points to an ideal of government that provides for human freedom within the impersonal structure of the state. Long debated, this ideal gained legal authority within forty years after Addison's death when Blackstone argued that "civil liberty, rightly understood, consists in protecting the rights of individuals by the united force of society."[1] Both men claimed the inseparability of natural and civil rights. Both predicated a social order secured through three interrelated truths: first, that natural liberty or freedom of will is the source of consent necessary for the formation of the state; second, that men bind themselves to lawful government in order to protect their natural rights; and third, that civil liberty is so firmly hammered into the British constitution that to deny the former is to dissolve the latter.

Addison adapted his thesis to the proposition that reason and equality are the ne plus ultra of liberty. Concomitantly, the first two are innate conditions, and the third is their social or civil extension. Liberty, in other words, begins with reason, whose "dictates . . . are the same through the whole species"—another way of saying that all men are born equal because all men are born with reason (*F* 6). In Addison's syllogistic process, when a group of equally endowed men gather for mutual benefit, they are exempt from the subjection of one to another. "This," he declared earlier in *Spectator* 287, "is what may properly be called liberty." Understandably, he correlates his conclusion with respect for enlightened British government. It is proper, he thus concedes, to limit liberty through the "order and economy of government," which is bound by contractual agreement to secure "public peace and tranquillity."[2]

For the initial assumptions of his argument—those concerned with human equality—he had the precedents of such men as Cicero, Hooker, Pufendorf, and even Burnet, Molyneux, and Locke. Like them, he respected the theory; but in his writings he subordinated the idea. He concentrated instead on its practical operation in the English state. Yet to foster the illusion that he too could rise above the mundane, he used metaphor as well as plain prose. He likened liberty to a beautiful goddess whose "every glance . . . cast a track of light where it fell, that revived the spring, and made all things smile about her. My heart grew cheerful at the sight of her, and as she looked upon me, I found a certain confidence growing in me, and such an inward resolution as I never felt before that time" (*T* 161).[3] As prosopopoeia, the figure takes a familiar route. But if the radiant creature turns up no literary surprises along the way, she does throw Addison's optimism into relief. That is to say, she suggests his happy talent for reconciling different qualities, in this case those of the real and the ideal. He implies that Liberty, which harmonizes them because she is an accommodating spirit, is friendly to man even among the restraints of civil discipline. By allowing all men regardless of station the opportunity and obligation of moral choice, she anticipates an afterlife, when through divine judgment all inequalities will be righted.

He wanted maximum liberty for all those whom he vaguely defined as responsible members of the state. Such freedom would help individuals tranquilize their pain and frustration and would reduce instability within the political structure. He was convinced that the uneven enjoyment of liberty "only aggravates the misfortune of those who are deprived of it, by setting before them a disagreeable subject of comparison" (*S* 287). Though the conclusion was not uniquely his, he had the evidence of his eyes and intelligence to support it: as a young traveler he had observed "petty" but liberal St. Marino, which continued to survive as a constitutional republic for "thirteen hundred years, while all the other states of Italy have several times changed their masters and forms of government" (*Re-*

marks, p. 73). Over the years, no matter how embroiled he became in party affairs, he axiomatically held that a free society, except in times of immediate peril, requires maximum individual liberty and minimum public authority. The lasting state serves rather than enslaves its people.[4]

For Addison, as for many of his countrymen, freedom was an operable ideal that involved codependent, inseparable pairings: theory and practicality, individual identity and social cohesion. The right of self-assertion he took to be as inviolable as the right of property. One was not complete without the other, just as a mathematical equation is incomplete until at least two quantities are understood to have an equal function. "Liberty and property," he said in 1710 in *Whig Examiner* 5, are similarly interrelated as "the birthright of the English nation," and so he wrote again in *Freeholder* 1 in 1715. Their oneness was a doctrine he derived from Locke, who in the *Treatises* had categorized the end of government as the preservation of property. Both men argued that government was inadequate if it assumed no larger obligation than to insure property in its finite, tangible sense. Both argued that in the name of property the state had to guard and dignify human existence, protect all subjects against tyrannical "incursions," and honor—constitutionally as well as legally—mankind's natural independence. Only when all these conditions were met was the right of property itself fulfilled.

Addison was often capable of sustaining Locke's interpretation of the right of property. But there were other occasions when, diverted by the materialism of his comfortable class, he joined self-interested contemporaries for whom property consisted of estates, investments, and trading opportunities, the protection of which were "the Alpha and Omega, the original and end of government."[5] In this commercial spirit he opened the *Freeholder* with a paean to property, which he now reduced from liberty into mere "possession." Ingenuously candid, he admitted that the journal's title captured the dynamism of a "happy tribe of men" and suggested the substance in which he and they most gloried. But his eulogy of property did not end in a sun-drenched vision of hedged fields or sentimental delight in England's "little cabbage-garden[s]." With unusual ruthlessness, he looked in 1719 on property or wealth as a source of plebeian invincibility. As the Old Whig he considered it an instrument by which "the commons of England" could solidify their "due strength" against noble and king, "for, of all maxims, none is more uncontested than that power follows property" (*OW* 1). He borrowed this maxim from James Harrington but adjusted it to his own awareness of a submerged class rivalry, particularly of a middle station contesting entrenched hereditary privilege and seeking a dominant place in English life.[6]

From 1688 onward most Whigs celebrated the natural right of property as a civil liberty. "It is the happiness of an Englishman," said Steele, "that his property is fenced about with laws and privileges, into which no power can make an incursion, except it is encouraged by his own stupidity or cowardice." However the term *property* was interpreted, the right itself was as unalterable as that of "inborn freedom." And the obligation to defend both—liberty and property—was as absolute as the obligation to defend life itself. So Addison argued in justifying the use of force against any arbitrary restriction on private ownership. He therefore applauded the desire of free men in any age or place "to rescue themselves from the most violent and illegal oppressions; to throw off a tyranny that makes property precarious, and life painful; to preserve their laws and their religion to themselves and their posterity." For reasons like these, he accepted revolution as the necessary solution "when no other means are left for the security of everything that is dear and valuable to reasonable creatures" (*F* 12).[7]

His outlook was neither radical nor original. It mirrored both acceptable theory and the values fixed by the events of 1688–89. The Revolution Settlement was a live volcano that periodically erupted into hot debate. There were those who believed its solution had solved nothing. Some fretful opponents, indeed, impugned the revolutionary thesis of freedom as a mere appeal for a return to naturalistic disorder. Charles Leslie, for example, said: "The restraint of government is the true liberty and freedom of the people; and that foolish notion of liberty, which is generally thought to consist in being free from the lash of government, as schoolboys from their master, proves only a liberty to destroy one another." Addison and his party derided this and comparable statements because they were confident of the Revolution's popular appeal. They scorned as anachronistic the cries of such as Leslie or Hickes for unreserved obedience to a divinely appointed monarch. The Whigs, however, had grown sleek and sleepy all too soon on their power, solidified only in 1707 and 1708. Within a short time they made the fatal mistake of misreading the signs of the age: they gambled on their ability to silence the reactionary slogans of passive obedience and nonresistance. To do so, they sought the public reprimand of Sacheverell, "a pragmatical insignificant man" who preached the necessity of submission in "a nonsensical harangue" at St. Paul's on 5 November 1709. These epithets capture the disdain of moderate Tories for the High Churchman Sacheverell, whom the Whigs were quick to use as a "handle" confirming the Revolution Settlement.[8]

During the impeachment proceedings the Whigs aligned themselves behind a common argument: that English laws, rights, duties, and privileges were applicable to all men, king as well as commoner, and that Englishmen had to protect those laws, by force if necessary, against all encroachments. The Revolution, illustrating these truths, had been a justifiable resistance against a despot contemptuous of the law. Several years later, echoing the Whig position during the Sacheverell impeachment, Addison said that the struggle had been provoked by a sovereign—James II—who "was flattered by a set of men into a persuasion, that the regal authority was unlimited and uncircumscribed," and who therefore repudiated English law as "but a dead letter" (*F* 2). The successful outcome of the Revolution, according to the Whigs in 1710, revitalized English law and outmoded the principles of passive obedience and nonresistance.[9] In that year their rationale for the Revolution Settlement did not play upon emotions, but neither was it in tune with the temper of most Englishmen who were tired of war and of Whigs and their causes. Under the clever influence of St. John's journalists Sacheverell emerged as a romantic hero in clerical armor fighting a Low Church cabal to restore a Presbyterian republic. The Whigs were taken aback by angry street mobs who chose to lionize this "pragmatical insignificant man" and by viragoes shrieking in defense of his cause.

The Sacheverell incident was a contretemps for the ministry, which in 1710 won the battle and lost the war. Within a few months of the impeachment the ministerial battlements began to crumble, whereupon the Whigs refused to discuss at length the notions made glamorous by Sacheverell or to attack him further. It was too late for reticence, but they had no choice. Addison tried to remain obedient to party strategy even when the fall of the Godolphin ministry in September 1710 made it ineffective. In the first four numbers of the

Whig Examiner, which began in that month, he ignored the concepts of passivity and submission and flippantly dismissed Sacheverell as having "hit the sublime in nonsense" (*WE* 4). But shortly before 12 October, when the fifth and last number appeared, he had to accept his failure as a political journalist. The experience was a chastening one, but he found solace in his temporary liberation from party discipline. He wrote the final *Whig Examiner* not as a man taking dictation but as one who belongs to himself. For the first time in the journal, he expatiated upon the evils thought to be implicit in the "dangerous tenets" of passive obedience and nonresistance; and he condemned them without the sarcasm and fanciful wit of the previous numbers.[10]

The Whigs brooded on Sacheverell for four years, until the accession of George I. Then they were again willing to discuss freely passive obedience and nonresistance, doctrines that they had always associated with absolutism and whose reappearance in 1714 frightened most Britons. Within a year, when the earl of Mar hoisted the Jacobite standard, these "dangerous tenets" were so emotionally charged that they were converted into catchwords and even to be accused of endorsing them was political death. Addison, finally able to unleash his animosity, made propaganda out of this reversal by tartly blaming the Tories for the poisonous spread of principles that were contained only by his party's foresight. Even more damagingly, he asserted that the debate over them during the Jacobite rebellion was "not in reality between Whigs and Tories, but between Loyalists and Rebels. Our country is not now divided into two parties, who propose the same end by different means; but into such as would preserve and such as would destroy it" (*F* 13).[11] This was unusually vicious propaganda for him. He had borrowed its method from the *Examiner* but had worked out its substance in collaboration with the Whig leadership. He helped turn the wheel full circle. Only a few years before, his party had been blackened as the party of treason by opposition journalists; in the winter and spring of 1715–16, he and others could repay the Tories with the same malice.

He was every inch the party man when he attributed the notions of passive obedience and nonresistance solely to the Tories or, to what was more incriminating, a Tory-Jacobite conspiracy. Political controversies are notoriously ungenerous, and he was disinclined to draw sympathetic attention to the reality that many Tories, far from being intransigent even during the Sacheverell trial, conceded the "necessity and legality of resistance in some extraordinary cases." As one who doggedly followed the thinking of the opposition, Addison knew this, just as he knew that among the Tories there were "many gentlemen ... who though they may have a more than needful concern for the monarchy and the established church [were] yet zealous for the supporting Her Majesty's title and the Hanover succession, and [did] sincerely approve the Revolution-principles, and abhor the slavish doctrine of unlimited passive obedience."[12] He chose to pass lightly over such evidence or to conceal it, stretching simple truth until it was politically useful for the Whigs.

The statesman-politician author of the *Freeholder* was placed in an ambiguous position. He had long advertised himself as a foe of unlimited obedience and as an exponent of the right of revolution. In 1715 his convictions had not changed, but his world was shaken by Jacobite revolt. As a consequence he found it necessary to denounce in authoritarian language conservative Britons who remained actively loyal to the native house of Stuart and to exact their obedience to the alien Hanoverians. He was thereby emphasizing as forcefully as he could a distinction between lawful resistance and conspiratorial revolt. The differentiation was not his but a cliché of contemporary political moderation, whether Whig or Tory. According to Defoe, for instance,

> There is . . . a true distinction to be made between a rebellion and a civil war; the first is notorious, when subjects take up arms against lawful governors lawfully governing; but when a prince violates the established laws of the nation, raises taxes by his own authority contrary to the known rules of the constitution, invades the liberties of his subjects by illegal imprisonments, unjust prosecutions, and other grievous oppressions, and persists in such arbitrary acts of government for a course of years; if a people can find no other means to preserve their most valuable interests, but by having recourse to the last remedy, and shall take up arms to compel such a prince to restore their rights, and reform his ill government; . . . grave and impartial historians have not thought fit to treat this way of opposing the unlawful usurpation of princes with the odious name of rebellion.[13]

Except for slight alterations in terminology Defoe's statement could well have appeared in the *Freeholder*. For Addison, like others, drew an analogy between the Jacobite uprising and the conspiracy of Catiline, and labeled both *unnatural* rebellions. If the Roman was a usurper of inherent rights—and history had so marked him—then the Pretender must be equally guilty of tyrannical usurpation. Both men, Addison insisted, deserved indictment for conspiring to annul their responsibility to man and deity. Both contravened the "ends and benefits of government, by raising a power in opposition to that authority which has been established among a people for their mutual welfare and defence." Even further, they were satanically disobedient and ungrateful; they were "big with rapine, sacrilege, and murder," as they defamed "the sovereign ruler of the universe [who] is affronted by a breach of allegiance to those whom he has set over us." Addison's aversion to *unnatural* rebellion trapped him into using the language one might expect of a Leslie or any other apologist of divine right: he described the subversion of Catiline or the Pretender as a blasphemous attack on God's choice of a "supreme magistrate," and on His scheme "for the preserving of order and justice" among men (*F* 12).

Yet, in spite of statements like these, triggered by the excitement of the moment, Addison respected the Glorious Revolution as a Whig struggle warranted by the need to restrain monarchical oppression and renew civil rights. Five years before the outbreak of the Jacobite rebellion he upheld the "doctrine of self-preservation" on the grounds that a people could legally "resist a tyrant, and take up arms in defence of their lives and liberties" (*WE* 5). During the rebellion itself, which he had sworn to help put down, he boldly restated the right of revolution: ". . . the duties of protection and allegiance are reciprocal; and as the safety of a community is the ultimate end and design of government, when this, instead of being preserved, is manifestly destroyed, civil societies are excusable before God and man, if they endeavour to recover themselves out of so miserable a condition. For in such a case government becomes an evil instead of a blessing, and is not at all preferable to a state of anarchy and mutual independence" (*F* 12).[14] Natural law taught him that if the state fails to respect the dignity and liberty of those who consented to its formation, then righteous men within its borders have no alternative but to sever all bonds of loyalty with what is no longer a government but a tyranny. In compositions ranging from *A Poem to His Majesty* and *The Campaign* to the *Old Whig*, Addison asserted the truth of this conclusion.

He was therefore stoutly partial to all Englishmen "bred with an aversion to everything that tends to bring [them] under a subjection to the arbitrary will of another." He cut across class lines to praise ordinary freeholders, noble Nassau, and self-made Somers for having "stood up manfully against the invasions of civil liberty" (*F* 1). Exhortations like these, though uttered without radical intention, reminded rulers and legislators alike that Englishmen would not endure arbitrary restraints for long. At the same time Addison soberly held that revolution—destructive of peace and property, hospitable to "anarchy and mutual independence"—was justifiable only as a last resort. Human fallibility, he acknowledged, would produce minor errors or injustices in government; but these had to be borne. Even more serious inadequacies in the administration of government were to be suffered as long as there was hope of legal amendment. In short, although he always hedged the right of resistance, he saw in the right itself a weapon to frustrate tyranny.[15]

In all his comments on human rights he exalted the free spirit of man as the guide to moral purpose and action. Not least among the liberties identifiable with man's independent self was that of conscience. From the apolitical Cambridge Platonists through Locke and the partisan Burnet, all "looked on liberty of conscience as one of the rights of human nature, antecedent to society, which no man could give up, because it was not in his power." On the other side of the coin, to be sure, were the views of such men as Dr. Sherlock, for whom liberty of conscience was a mere "pretence," a euphemistic cover for anarchical selfishness. But such suspicion was atypical during and after the Restoration, when almost everyone at least professed to favor toleration. There was no risk in making the declaration since it was readily qualified. As one anonymous pamphleteer wrote, liberty of conscience "is a right of mankind never to be invaded, till such thoughts lead men to act in such a manner, as undermines the order of the world, and under a pretence of religion discovers a design upon secular authority."[16] With its hearty, reversible generalities, the statement suggested certain pertinent conditions that would have made it palatable to a good many Augustans. It recognized that England's political frame was inseparable from mild-mannered Anglicanism. It implied as well fearful recollection of the Puritan interlude, when a group of men in the name of God and righteousness imprisoned Parliament and beheaded the king.

The passage in 1689 of the Toleration Act gave qualified legal status to liberty of conscience and seeded already fertile ground for a new controversy, which would be cultivated by faction early in the eighteenth century. By 1703 or possibly the year before, a full-blown debate over toleration was responsible for the coinage of two new political labels: *High Church* as a synonym for Tory and *Low Church* for Whig.[17] Thus the Tories, while ostensibly defending the principle of toleration, painted a dark image of Jack Presbyter, whose rights had to be circumscribed for the safety of the Anglican community. Conversely, the Whig establishment, whose tolerance did not extend to "papist Jacobites," argued for the political and Protestant orthodoxy of the dissenters and until 1711 resisted any infringement of their liberties.

In effect, support of the Toleration Act unaltered by further restrictions became as well-hewn a plank in the Whig platform as the Revolution Settlement, the denial of the Pretender, and "no Peace without Spain." Addison accepted it willingly along with the rest of the platform. He looked on toleration as a practical measure that did not assume equality of faith or even the admission that one Protestant sect was as good as another in providing salvation. He was sure that the ideal of Christianity was fulfilled in Anglicanism; but he was equally sure that the dissenters, ridiculous and mistaken as he took them to be, in no way threatened English stability. Thus he put up with them as useful men of substance who strengthened the Protestant struggle against Catholicism, brought numbers and wealth to the Whig organization, and, as merchants and traders, contributed to British prosperity. For these many reasons he condemned Tory hostility to the dissenters as "intemperate zeal, bigotry and persecution" (*S* 399). Three years earlier, during the near frenzy of the Sacheverell impeachment, he derided as nonsensical the High Churchman's charge, as reported by Bishop Wake, that he "is a false-brother with relation to God, religion, or the Church, who defends toleration, and liberty of conscience."[18]

Addison, always worldly in his toleration, believed that piety, regardless of sect, helped to preserve civil society. Cicero, Polybius, and their Christian disciple Charron taught him that religion elicits compliance and so restrains man's impulse toward anarchy. This Stoic conclusion was amplified by his practical contemporaries who, after equating religion with trinitarian Protestantism (preferably of the

Anglican variety), turned the catechism to the service of the status quo. The consequence of such thinking was a marriage of religious means and secular ends, a sanctification of the national treasure and the public credit. Not only did piety "lead to heaven and a blessed state hereafter," as D'Avenant wrote, but it was "the best way of securing to a people in general prosperity, peace, safety, power in this present world." This mélange of substance and spirit was made orthodox by such Latitudinarians as South and Tillotson, whose ideas Addison respected and repeated.[19]

He himself resorted to the same mixture when he warned that no government could endure, much less prosper, which did "not encourage and propagate religion and morality among all its particular members." He advised further that "justice, temperance, humility, and almost every other moral virtue, do not only derive the blessings of Providence upon those who exercise them, but are the natural means for acquiring the public prosperity" (*F* 29). Half-admonitory and half-pleading, Addison's remarks are coarsened occasionally by materialism, as, for example, when he supported England's war for commercial sovereignty. At other times, however, his remarks are softened and refined by an idealization of communal service; this, he said, is a moral obligation, for only in voluntary sacrifice is the human soul liberated to create a society of content and happiness. His capacity for sustaining opposed views is no more surprising than that of any man of good will in an age of expedience; for conscience may genuinely strain toward social altruism, even while the pressures of an era dictate compromise.

If Addison's scruples made for inner conflict, he did not allow them to dominate his writing. On the contrary, he asserted often and with evangelical fervor that religious morality is basic to the political and economic system of any durable state. He particularized this idea in several ways. In one instance he argued for limited toleration, knowing that religious peace contributed to harmony within his country and party. He was therefore ready to extend the hand of friendship to the various Protestant sects in Britain. He knew too, from the example of mercantile Holland, that toleration, as Locke had said, "may tend to the advancement of trade and commerce"; Addison, therefore, urged concessions to initiative and to nonconformity in its many forms. Ultimately his own liberalism urged his defense of toleration. He probably remembered that the dissenters had subscribed to thirty-six of the Thirty-nine Articles; hence he could dismiss as circumstantials those ritualistic practices that divided the Protestant community. As positive evidence of unity, on the other hand, he underscored those values held in common by English Protestants: a single reform heritage, respect for the authority of conscience, and dread of Catholicism.[20]

As long as the Whigs could withstand Tory pressure for antidissent legislation—specifically, the occasional conformity bills of 1702, 1703, and 1704—Addison had no dilemmas to resolve. But the Whigs, who after years of ascendancy were the minority party in 1711, wanted to continue the War of the Spanish Succession, whatever the cost. Early in December Halifax therefore met with Harley and Somers at the latter's house, where the two Whigs may have agreed to accept an occasional conformity bill in exchange for Tory support of the war.[21] The parliamentary lists are not available, but Addison, who delighted in his perfect voting record and his loyalty to Halifax and Somers, would have voted with his party on behalf of a repressive measure toward which he had been hostile. He may have rationalized the need for a propitiatory gesture, the rightness of sacrificing the lesser to the greater good, but partisan interest would in any case have stifled his usual tolerance and driven him into an uncharitable act.

On 2 October 1711, only two months before the passage of the Occasional Conformity Act, he had attacked the religious fury of "the most zealous for orthodoxy," who would be the first to push and vote for such a measure (*S* 185). On 8 January 1711/12, a few weeks after the bill became law, he mockingly allowed Sir Roger to acclaim the effectiveness of "the late Act of Parliament for securing the Church of England, . . . for that a rigid dissenter, who chanced to dine at his house on Christmas day, had been observed to eat very plentifully of his plum porridge" (*S* 269). The old Tory had deluded himself into believing that legislation could put the dissenter on the road to orthodoxy, a mistake Addison made but once. Through his gentle ridicule of Sir Roger's belief in the efficacy of "plum porridge," he suggested that the act was designed only for harassment and had no validity, either moral or practical.[22]

He must also have been offended by the Tory-sponsored Schism Act of 15 June 1714, which denied religious freedom and education to dissenters. And this time his revulsion would have carried the stamp of party mandate, for toleration was again dictated by the Whig leadership and the act was contested by his close associates Wharton, Sunderland, Townshend, Somers, and Halifax. The Tories justified their statute as they had several times in the past with warnings that the church was in danger. Addison had always dismissed this particular Tory alarm as fraudulent and would continue to do so. It was, he said even before 1714, a deliberate ruse perpetrated by members of a vocal faction, "persons who make use of religion to promote their cause, not of their cause to promote religion" (*S* 243).[23] Thereafter he consistently treated it as a political gesture designed to promote party fortunes. His analysis, while oversimple, was nonetheless more right than wrong.

Not only did he write about the value of toleration, but as a political leader he used legislative channels to restore the rights of dissenters, most of whom happened to be Whigs. In May 1715, he was a member of a parliamentary committee that successfully sponsored "An Act that the Solemn Affirmation and Declaration of the People Called Quakers Shall Be Accepted, instead of an Oath in the Usual Form." Two years later, in the spring of 1717, he and other members of the Stanhope ministry met with groups eager to amend legally the inequities endured by dissenters since 1711. For this he and the ministry were calumniated with the Tory label of "Jack Presbyter" and dogged as subversives by the Walpole-Townshend dissidents, who were in strange league with High Churchmen. But Addison and his political friends prevailed in their limited fight against bigotry. They were led by Stanhope, who (with no less political acumen than moral stamina) established "the equity, justice, reasonableness and advantage, of restoring dissenters to their natural rights; and of easing them of those stigmatizing and oppressive laws, that had been made against them in turbulent times, and obtained by indirect methods, for no other reason, than because they ever showed their zealous and firm adherence to the Revolution and Protestant Succession."[24] The ministry by January 1718/19 secured the repeal of both the Occasional Conformity and Schism acts of Anne's reign. The reversal must have exhilarated the ailing Addison because it was a victory for the Old Whigs and the practical enforcement of his long-cherished hope that the various Protestant sects could coexist harmoniously.

Whenever he spoke in favor of toleration he was supported by

Whig pamphleteers, who likewise denounced bigotry and recommended brotherhood; almost all of their arguments, because they emanated from the same party source, were also his. He advanced one, however, which was not often repeated by the Grub Street political hirelings. He stated that the persecution of men for "conscience sake" was an act of wanton cruelty and division. Besides embittering the victims "with hatred, indignation, and all the vehemence of resentment, and ensnaring them to profess what they do not believe; we cut them off from the pleasures and advantages of society, afflict their bodies, distress their fortunes, hurt their reputations, ruin their families, make their lives painful, or put an end to them" (*S* 459).[25] In his running battle with the Occasional Conformity Act, he observed seven months after its passage that religious persecution fails to secure its goals, because it is unable to effect either belief or virtue. At best it might exact superficial conformity but to what end, he demanded, since forced worship was an abomination in the sight of God and a denial of the Protestant heritage with its call to responsible freedom.

While he condemned as both immoral and impractical the persecution of any religious group, he would extend toleration to none outside the Anglican community but trinitarian Protestants. He never suggested that the Toleration Act be rewritten to grant even qualified civil acceptance to Catholics or that the Test Act of 1673 be abrogated. Yet, like Locke's in the preceding generation and Steele's in his own day, his anti-Catholicism was political rather than theological. All three men feared that "popery," as a disciplined ecclesiastical organization, was dedicated to the ruin of England's national church, constitution, free institutions, and prosperity. They gave their fear the pseudo validity of a historical context. Addison, for example, traced what he called a germinal Catholic menace back to the time of Charles II, who, for all his Roman leanings, "was too wise to own himself a Roman Catholic. . . . or to imagine it practicable for an avowed Popish prince to govern a Protestant people. His brother tried the experiment and every one knows the success of it" (*F* 43). Most Englishmen—for Addison's was a representative voice—saw the Catholic bogey translated during the reign of James II into a despotic reality, a tyranny foiled only by divine mercy and the Glorious Revolution. Having survived the peril once, they hesitated to forget it, especially when tension between England and Catholic

France became acute. Anti-Catholicism became an official way of English life by 1701 with the passage of the Act of Settlement. Then early in 1702 Parliament, though still Tory-dominated, passed a bill of attainder against the Pretender and voted the dying William forty thousand soldiers and as many sailors for the coming struggle against France.[26]

Circumstances like these became the basis of public quasi reasoning, a dubious impetus for identifying Catholicism with absolute rule. Popery, slavery, and the French interest Addison took to be interrelated conditions. Where there was one, the other two were sure to follow, bringing with them misery for a people who had been deprived of their civil liberties. His vigorous prose was an effective vehicle for establishing the synonymy of the three terms, whether he relied on expository language to make his point, or, less frequently, on imaginative devices. In *Freeholder* 27 he personified passive obedience, the familiar symptom of tyranny, as "an old-fashioned figure in a steeple-crowned hat . . . a cunning old gypsy." This is a clever piece of rhetoric, for it compresses the triad of fears within a seemingly mild description. The quaint gypsy-figure with her miterlike headpiece suggests the lawlessness, poverty, and repressive superstitions that he associated with the pretentious and anachronistic governments of France and the Vatican.[27]

The greatest spur to his anti-Catholicism, however, was a dread of the Pretender and his supporters. By 1713 he saw all Catholics as Jacobites conspiring to place a Catholic on a throne declared Protestant by parliamentary act. Nor was he eccentric in his fear. The hysteria that ran like a plague through England in 1715 and 1716 and in the years immediately before the rebellion is reflected by many proclamations and laws against Papists and Nonjurors. Addison's anxiety was an echo of national bias to which, ironically, he added. But as a worried witness to his prejudice, he sought to restrain its emotionalism with prudence and practical logic.

England's sovereign, he said again and again in the *Freeholder,* must be a Protestant able to serve as titular head of the country's church and eager to guarantee his subjects' constitutional freedom. It is absurd, horrifying, and senseless, he told his readers, to suppose "the quiet of a nation can arise from an establishment, in which the king would be of one communion, and the people of another" (*F* 43). Living in the midst of the Jacobite rebellion, or in anticipation of it, he deemed such quiet a good whose continuance was the first law of sound polity; he could not in either reason or conscience recommend the extension of religious equality to those who sought to disorder his nation. He was not the man to arm those he called his country's enemies with weapons from the national arsenal.[28]

Addison's political thought concentrated on man, whose intelligence had formulated the state to lighten the burdens of individual existence in the community. At the same time he acknowledged that the universe, the social order, man, and his achievements all depended on the benevolence of God, who was himself harmony and the source of harmony for a groping humanity. A scheme based upon such premises indicates that Addison thought of politics not as a science or activity distinct from other human relations but as an organic part of the entire spiritual and social scheme. He therefore dedicated himself to preserving not a fossilized order but a constitutional government determined by moral law, a government that used its achievements for the benefit of man and the glory of God. As essayist and party pamphleteer, Whig and statesman, he set forth a political program that was optimistic but not millennial, benevolent but not sentimental. Above all, it was realistic, taking careful measure of man, who is perfectible but not perfect.

Addison's social values were fixed by a revolution. The government to which he gave his loyalty and energy was born of this philosophical conflict in 1688 and 1689. He supported a new government, one still without the patina of time and tradition. Although dismissed by many High Churchmen and gentry as radical and even blasphemous, the young government was lodged in a hereditary monarchy and peerage, and in a representative body holding its right of office by the grant of a restricted electorate. Its structure and function were expressed in a constitution that Addison gladly and eloquently defended. His political position, in its own time and place, summarized the goals of Whig liberalism and a Revolution whose glorious principles introduced into England conditions and procedures far more conducive to freedom than those in the other monarchies of Europe. Theoretician and activist, Addison navigated dexterously between pure idealism and a less-than-pure reality. Occasionally he sailed into the political winds; much more frequently he sailed with them, but in either case he moved with a sense of Whig mission and public responsibility.

PART III

IN THE PULPIT

CHAPTER EIGHT

CHURCH AND PARTY

NO activity affecting man's welfare was out of bounds for Addison's journalistic curiosity. He wrote with easy authority of class ambition and responsibility, war and peace, commerce and manufacture, political theory and party organization. But he underlined religious belief, whose proper exercise he concluded was fundamental to human well-being. His inquiry after truth centered on these disparate matters, which he related to those acts and intentions consistent with man's ability to live peacefully on earth and to look hopefully toward eternity. Ideal social conduct, to Addison, was that of any temperate man devoted to heaven—merchant, soldier, politician, or statesman—who moved among his fellows in trust and good will.[1]

His was a discreet liberalism because he knew that any ideal is liable to corruption. Experience had taught him that class demarcation, although aimed at social order, often set large groups of people against one another in jealousy and fear. And trade, which should effect a nation's prosperity, sometimes provided leverage for exploitation. Even government, designed to secure "public peace and tranquillity," could be weakened by tyranny or shaken by the convulsions of unnatural rebellion. Piety, too, which should fortify man against the peril and anguish of his condition, often degenerated into atheism, lip-service devotion, or fanaticism.

Few English shortcomings escaped Addison's censure, and his aim always was to suggest correction. If he was offended by breaches of social propriety, he was disgusted by religious failings. From the *Tatler* to the *Freeholder* he sought reasons for the failure of piety, for the human folly that tarnished the "shining instances of virtue and morality" in early English Protestantism. He discovered one answer in his country's proliferation of sectarian opinion, to him a sign of spiritual collapse and the result of "cant and hypocrisy" (*F* 37). Perhaps too readily he attributed this profusion of sects to the Puritan interregnum, which in his view had corrupted the liberty of the Reformation into license. With this politically shaded judgment, he could allow no place for thinking that—like Milton's, for example—applauded religious diversity as a triumph of individual conscience and proof that the Reformation lived on.[2]

The years that divided the Protestantism of the two men account for Addison's coolness toward what he and his age labeled dissent. These were years of spiritual shift from the hyperreligiosity of Cromwell's world to the licentiousness of the Restoration and then to the supposed mean of Augustan Anglicanism. In those three generations the Puritan multiplicity of sects was discredited by the Anglican notion that religious plenty confused but did not replenish the spirit. John Scott, for instance, commented on the correspondence between plenitude and nothingness: "How many woeful examples have we of persons who had once a great deal of zeal for and satisfaction in religion, that upon their causeless defection from the church's communion have run from sect to sect, and from one extravagant opinion to another, till being at last convinced of the cheats and impostures of them all, they have discarded religion itself, and made their last resort into atheism and infidelity." The Anglican's cure for so paradoxical a cause of disbelief was a blinkered recommendation of the ritual and piety of the Church of England. That his cure, discouraging inquiry, subverted the church's rational foundation did not seem to disturb him.[3]

Nor did it worry Addison. He too deplored atheism as a refuge for the unwary who, sampling theological opinions and finding none to their taste, fell from spiritual excess into spiritual poverty. But the end of multiform Protestantism was not as simple for him as for Scott. Unlike the priest, he confronted the fact that some seekers became exhausted by too many samples and sought calm in the certainty of an infallible church. They turned to Catholicism, which was as threatening as atheism to the individual's salvation and the nation's political health. When he described these shoppers for divine truth, he alternated between pity and irritation, never quite understanding what he regarded as a betrayal of their destiny. Ultimately, however, his denunciation of sectarian division went beyond regard for the individual and the unity of church and state to a half-articulated fear that Protestantism, riddled by controversy, would no longer be a source of humane and virtuous life. This life promoted "justice, charity, munificence . . . the good qualities that render us beneficial to each other" (*S* 243). This life was the goal of reformed Christianity. To achieve anything less was to fail in religious duty and—what was almost as important to him—in civility.

He was sensitive to Protestantism's seemingly endless capacity to splinter. But in addition he was disquieted by the presence of non-Protestant groups in a country which by majority choice and legislation exalted its Reformation heritage. The depth of his unease is sounded in *Tatler* 257, an allegory whose dominant symbol is a waxwork show "carried up and down in Germany, which represents all the religions in Great Britain." Thus he gave an ingenious literary turn to a well-known spectacle: itinerant exhibits, many featuring lifelike religious figures, had long been popular in Germany and elsewhere on the Continent. Probably Addison had seen similar shows during his European tour of 1699–1703. His own "principal" effigies personified Anglicans, Catholics, Presbyterians, Jews, deists, Anabaptists, and Quakers. The meaning of the first three figures and Addison's preference are easy to decode, since he wrote to swell the membership of the national church and so to bolster the state's stability. The matron—cheerful, scrubbed, and dignified—is Anglicanism; the superannuated strumpet—a "tawdry composition of ribbons, silks, and jewels"—is Catholicism; the self-righteous frump is dissent. Only a dull Anglican could fail to see the deficiencies of Catholicism and Presbytery when set beside the wholesomeness of his own church; only a derelict Anglican could fail to make the correct spiritual choice.

The primary intention of the allegory is plain; as its author stated: "The design of the workman was so well expressed in the dumb show before us, that it was not hard for an Englishman to comprehend the meaning of it." But on a secondary level the allegory contends with a controversial issue, the religious changes effected by time. Neither the first in his century nor the last to comment on these alterations, Addison followed Swift and anticipated Gibbon. Like them, he interpreted England's religious condition with historical perspective. Through his waxwork figures he appeared to reject any assumption that faith is bestowed by God on a waiting multitude who preserve its purity without taint or change. The essay shows Addison's reluctance to substitute myth for fact. In the mask of a "friend" he described the seven dolls, each with its peculiar claim to God's truth, and implied that devotion is susceptible to division and even error. "Notwithstanding that the pliancy of the matter in which the images are wrought, makes it capable of being moulded into all shapes and figures, my friend . . . did not think it possible for it to be twisted and tortured into so many screwed faces and wry features as appeared in several of the figures that composed the show."

This generalization opens the description of the waxwork, but Addison smoothed its abrasive quality with his "friend's" glowing reaction to the Anglican doll: "I found my heart touched with so much love and reverence at the sight of her, that the tears ran down my face as I looked upon her; and still the more I looked upon her, the more my heart was melted with the sentiments of filial tenderness and duty." Addison achieved in this essay a triumph of discretion and politesse characteristic of his successful popular journalism. His view of religious mutation does not differ substantively from that of either Swift or Gibbon; yet he presents it so as to exalt rather than question the values and practices of Anglicanism. He would never have created a symbol like Swift's Martin, whose action is a reproach to the church for losing the purity of primitive Christianity: "Martin laid the first hand; at one twitch brought off a large handful of points, and with a second pull, stripped away ten dozen yards of fringe. But when he had gone thus far, he demurred a while: He knew very well, there yet remained a great deal more to be done; however, the first heat being over, his violence began to cool, and he resolved to proceed more moderately in the rest of the work. . . ." Nor would Addison, like Gibbon, have pronounced it the duty of the historian to "discover the inevitable mixture of error and corruption which [religion] contracted in a long residence upon earth, among a weak and degenerate race of beings."[4]

This realization made Gibbon melancholy and Swift indignant; but Addison suffered neither reaction, reassured by the thought that while Christianity was no longer primitive, many of its early values still endured in the Church of England. That compromise was good enough for him; he had never demanded perfection in a human institution. As an exercise in apologetics, therefore, he offered his portrait of the matron in the waxwork, she whose dress symbolized not only the Elizabethan Settlement of 1559 but also the garb of the Anglican clergy, particularly its bishops:

The middle figure, which immediately attracted the eyes of the whole company, and was much bigger than the rest, was formed like a matron,

> dressed in the habit of an elderly woman of quality in Queen Elizabeth's days. The most remarkable parts of her dress, were the beaver with the steeple crown, the scarf that was darker than sable, and the lawn apron that was whiter than ermine. Her gown was of the richest black velvet, and just upon her heart studded with large diamonds of an inestimable value, disposed in the form of a cross. She bore an inexpressible cheerfulness and dignity in her aspect; and though she seemed in years, appeared with so much spirit and vivacity, as gave her at the same time an air of old age and immortality.

Obviously this lady offered her admirers many advantages: sanctified age kept youthful by the pursuit of truth; pleasantness that spread good will among all her believers; discipline, organization, richness, and texture unspoiled by superstition and spiritual restraint; hallowed tradition that adjusted the good of primitive Christianity to a sensible modernity. Far from judging this last characteristic a weakness, Addison hailed it as a strength, for only through a historical sense could the church translate the lessons of Jesus into Augustan idiom or ease the inner pressures of the times. For these reasons he had no quarrel with the church: personified in "the middle figure" and imbued with a sense of the mean, she glowed with the radiant health of rational belief and practical morality.

A stereotype of the age was the contrast between what Simon Patrick called the "virtuous mediocrity" of the Church of England and "the meretricious gaudiness" of the Church of Rome. From the Restoration on through their rancorous climax in *A Tale of a Tub,* anti-Catholic charges of vulgar display and duplicity had been commonplaces of national intolerance. Addison subscribed to this prejudice with vigor and over the years added to it in a variety of ways. The waxen figure of the strumpet objectified his aversion to the proud sensuality of "popery." She was "so covered with ornaments, that her face, her body, and her hands, were almost entirely hid under them." Not only was she a caricature of artificiality, she was disfigured by superstition and rampant materialism: "Her garments had a thousand colours in them, and were embroidered with crosses in gold, silver, and silk: she had nothing on, so much as a glove or a slipper, which was not marked with this figure."[5]

Addison's satirical attack on Catholicism is more restrained than Swift's relentless parody in *A Tale of a Tub,* which had appeared six years earlier. In intellectual detail if not in tone, however, their disaffection is similar. It is apparent, for example, that Lord Peter's "three old high-crowned hats" have become the doll's three-storied coiffure, a pejorative emblem for the vanity implicit in the papal triple crown. Furthermore, the luxurious fabrics and gaudy ornamentation symbolized for Addison as well as for Swift the irrelevant ritual and venality they attributed to the Roman church. Both imposed on their personifications the extravagant lineaments of a fetish figure; they both scored Catholicism for having made a mockery of Christianity's simple piety.

But the waxen sculpture is far less intricate than the portrait of Peter. The details of Addison's figure were ordered essentially by a single premise, denial of the Catholic dogma that the rule of faith rests not only on Scripture but on oral apostolic tradition as well. Because he believed that Holy Writ contained all things necessary to revelation, he condemned Catholicism for refusing unique authority to the Bible, for founding many of its rituals on human error, and for spawning new dogma. He drew on Latitudinarian literature, particularly Tillotson's, to pile up evidence for his attack. Repeatedly, the clergyman's sermons proved to Addison that in the name of tradition Catholicism made numerous accretions to faith, "which were either directly contrary to the doctrine of Christianity, or too apparently destructive of a good life."[6]

To elaborate on this, Addison had his pliable doll sit cross-legged, a mark of immodesty typifying his view of Roman vulgarity. Her posture is also a parody of Catholic ritualism and a reminder that superstition can distort the structure of Christian belief. Still it must have occurred to him that parody might be misinterpreted. On 20 October 1711, eleven months after he first paraded his waxwork before a *Tatler* audience, he scoffed directly at Roman Catholic forms:

> If an absurd dress or behaviour be introduced in the world, it will soon be found out and discarded: On the contrary, a habit or ceremony, though never so ridiculous, which has taken sanctuary in the church, sticks in it for ever. A Gothic bishop, perhaps, thought it proper to repeat such a form in such particular shoes or slippers. Another fancied it would be very decent if such a part of public devotions were performed with a mitre on his head, and a crosier in his hand. To this a brother Vandal, as wise as the others, adds an antic dress, which he conceived would allude very aptly to such and such mysteries, till by degrees the whole office has degenerated into an empty show. [*S* 201]

Two weeks later he returned to the subject and intensified his attack by stressing the perversity of "superfluous ceremonies," which he had earlier mocked as merely absurd. Triviality turned into a duty, he said from his journalistic pulpit, "renders religion more burdensome and difficult than it is in its own nature, betrays many into sins of omission which they could not otherwise be guilty of, and fixes the minds of the vulgar to the shadowy unessential points, instead of the more weighty and more important matters of the law" (*S* 213). Ultimately, he condemned Catholic ritualism as a source of spiritual deformity and immoral conduct.

Why, he continued in his assault, did a multitude of believers accept absurdities? Once more he found an answer in the Latitudinarians. Prelates like Hoadly, Stillingfleet, and Tillotson accused the Catholic faithful of being spoon-fed from infancy on the "notion of authority and infallibility" and victimized by "spiritual tyranny, which commands and terrifies mankind into an open profession of anything." Undoubtedly he also remembered Locke's claim that despotism of any kind is accompanied by persecution, that "the inventions of men in religion need the force and helps of men to support them." Addison hesitated to discuss concepts like infallibility, implicit faith, and spiritual tyranny, which had little concrete meaning for most Englishmen. To give these abstractions immediacy, he added to his waxwork gallery a golem, a monstrous agent of tyranny called Persecution, which he used to represent the cruelty of Catholic harassment. Mindless, Persecution "moved by secret springs towards a great heap of dead bodies that lay piled upon one another." He could have had few doubts about public reaction to so gory a personification.[7]

Addison voiced the bias of his age when he made Catholicism the villain of the waxwork show. His susceptibility to bias is again evident in his portrayal of Presbytery. This separatist creature sat to the left "of the venerable matron" Anglicanism, whom she resembled as closely as though she were a sister. The figure of Presbytery is a milder caricature than that of Catholicism, for Addison wished to placate Whig and mercantile interests friendly to dissent. And he believed that the dissenters, while still a source of irritation to the Anglican establishment, could no longer subvert it. At worst, through fervor, they might attract a few others into their company. This he sought to forestall by using the technique first devised by the Whig bishops, who after 1688 portrayed dissenters as fumbling, half-mad anarchists to be derided rather than feared or hated. While Presbytery bore vestiges of Protestant beauty, "there was something . . . sickly and splenetic" about her; her face "was drawn up into a peevish figure, soured with discontent, and overcast with melancholy."

Value judgments implicit in the personification are contained in the words "discontent" and "melancholy." Presbytery tried to conceal her inadequacies from herself and others behind a mask of grim zeal. But her deception failed because she lacked conviction, and she presented a disgruntled face to the world. Four years later in the *Freeholder,* which wooed dissent as a bulwark against Jacobite insurrection, Addison did not mitigate his contempt for zeal as a form of self-deception. In that journal he represented zeal as a snow-lady with a bandage over her eyes, as one who disguises religious coldness with feigned passion. His scorn for such duplicity could not be restrained even by the pressure of political expedience. He therefore responded to the dictates of his conscience, formed by secular and biblical authority. He had the lesson of Locke that affectation "is always offensive: because we naturally hate whatever is counterfeit; and condemn those, who have nothing better to recommend themselves by." From Scripture he had learned that affectation is an insult to God as the source of infinite truth.[8]

Presbytery's melancholy was as distasteful as her discontent, from which it was inseparable in origin and manifestation. A pathetic form of dotage, melancholy betrayed its victims into religious enthusiasm. The "devout melancholist," he would have agreed with Stillingfleet, can be forced by illness to "embrace the issues of his imagination for the impressions of the Divine Spirit." Or, to use Dryden's chiasmus, "The text inspires not them; but they the text inspire."[9] The dissenters were accused by the national church of being madmen who substituted the diseased fancies of ego and passion for the word of God and the order of ecclesiastical authority. Within the Anglican community there was no disagreement over the diagnosis, only over the ailment's seriousness and its cure. The Whig bishops acknowledged the threat of dissenting lunacy—a threat as much political as religious—but played it down; the High Churchmen magnified it and passed their own fears on to their parishioners.[10]

Addison's urbane rhetoric reinforces the impression of a man of intellect who tempers emotion with civility. "We should," he said, "be particularly careful to keep our reason as cool as possible, and to guard ourselves in all parts of life against the influence of passion, imagination, and constitution." He may speak of the dissenter as one "that is crazed" or of Catholicism as "one huge overgrown body of childish and idle superstitions," but the final effect is moderate, not heated (*S* 201).

Dissenters and Catholics were fair game for many Anglicans in Addison's day, but they generally were stalked with such ferocity that by contrast his attack seems restrained. When Swift attacks zeal he does so with a chopping violence. He does not stop with the descriptive statement, "Martin's patience put Jack in a rage"; he casts aside civility to dramatize Jack's religious radicalism as maniacal fury. Addison's displeasure with dissent—and displeasure is all he can muster—is muted. But both men used dissent as a fixed point from which they moved to a larger war against hypocrisy. Again Swift's method was violent, compulsive in its intention to shock: "Last week I saw a woman flayed, and you will hardly believe how much it altered her person for the worse." As he strode among the charlatans and tricksters, the frauds and manipulators, he released his hostility in extremes. "The sublime and refined point of felicity," he concluded, is "the possession of being well deceived; the serene peaceful state of being a fool among knaves." Addison was not blind to the presence of fools and knaves, but he enjoyed none of Swift's outraged delight in knowing them everywhere about him. He diagnosed them for what they were—sick people in dominoes—and was therefore more interested in curing than castigating.[11]

He knew also that neither dissent nor Catholicism could be made to bear full responsibility for the decline in English piety. He admitted that Anglican strength was being sapped by communicants who went through the ritual of worship in an impious manner—like the gentry whom the Whig bishops scolded for not removing their hats in the drafty house of God or kneeling on his cold floors, and for whiling away the services in dreams of fox hunts or Tory strategy. Gilbert Burnet, for example, preached against the upper stations who found "it a modish thing, that looks like wit and spirit, to laugh at religion and virtue."[12] Such a statement, which singled out a social class, would have disturbed Addison. It smacked too much of factionalism and of enmity between Whig bishops and parishioners who often supported the High Church clergy. In his own desire to restore Anglican vigor, he tried to avoid party thinking or innuendo. He was successful in this during the quiet years of the *Tatler* and the *Spectator,* less so during the tumultuous months of the *Freeholder.*

When he criticized the vapid faith of many Anglicans, he referred to no one class but to each man who prided himself on being "well-bred." Such a man, said Addison wryly, reveals a religious "bashfulness" that obliges him "to conceal any serious sentiment of this nature, and very often to appear a greater libertine than he is, that he may keep himself in countenance among the men of mode." Addison was piqued when modesty, designed to serve "prudence and religion," was subverted for the sake of fashion. Behavior like this baffled him, and he chose to find an answer not in a psychological condition but in reaction to Puritan religiosity: by the Restoration "every appearance of devotion was looked upon as puritanical, and . . . it has ever since been out of countenance among us" (*S* 458).[13] In this explanation, fulfilling his dual role as censor and popular journalist, he tampered lightly with historical evidence in order to achieve what was for him a moral end. He satisfied national prejudice by rapping dissenters gently on the knuckles. He called the gentry to task without widening the split between them and ecclesiastical authority. And he minimized their conduct as a caprice, irritating and foolish, but in the long run incapable of doing serious damage to a church that had already survived many eccentricities.

For six years, from 1710 to 1716, he wrote about various forms of spiritual imbalance in England. One of these forms, to which he gave much of his attention, was deism. As a fashionable system of belief, its values were debated in coffeehouses and college halls or fulminated against in Anglican churches. Yet the term itself was never precisely defined. Many divines, particularly of High Church bent, used it indiscriminately against all religious beliefs different from theirs. *Deism* thus was applied to a spectrum of opposed attitudes, from those that rejected Old Testament literalism to a Latitudinarianism enunciated, for instance, by Tillotson. Even rationalists like Bentley identified sceptics with deists who, "to avoid the odious name of atheists, would shelter and screen themselves under a new one of deists, which is not quite so obnoxious."[14]

Addison's reactions to deism were ambivalent. In December 1709 he lumped together without any distinction the "deist, atheist, or freethinker," whom figuratively he would rather beat as brutes than tolerate (*T* 111). Eleven months later he softened his severity when he personified deism in *Tatler* 257 as "an half-naked awkward country wench, who with proper ornaments and education would have made an agreeable and beautiful appearance; but for want of those advantages, was such a spectacle as a man would blush to look upon." Her nakedness (which may be taken for the absence of mysteries and rituals of faith) embarrassed him, although he saw in her capacity for reason a latent religious beauty.

For the next few years, at least, he continued to rationalize his moderate position. "The atheist," he concluded in *Spectator* 186, "has not found his post tenable, and is therefore retired into deism, and a disbelief of revealed religion only." By 1716, however, in *The Drummer,* he had reverted to his former intractable opinion. At the outset of the comedy the fatuous Tinsel, whose name suggests not only the false glitter of deism but also its well-known advocate Matthew Tindal, disclaims the label *atheist:* "Oh, my dear, that's an old-fashioned word—I'm a freethinker, child." And so Addison found another name for an old sickness. He had ceased to argue that there was a reputable choice between the infidelities of atheism and deism. Aiming at significant political office for himself, he could no longer afford his earlier forbearance. The freethinking Tinsel symbolizes Addison's need to condemn the ignorance attributed to deism, to deny respectability to thinking that violated orthodox Christianity.

On the whole, his bifocal outlook on deism is understandable only within the context of his age. Like many of his contemporaries, he advocated a formal devotion, which "opens the mind to great conceptions, and fills it with more sublime ideas than any that are to be met with in the most exalted science" (*S* 201). Simultaneously he joined the many who distrusted religiosity, which they linked with the abuse of scriptural authority in the sixteenth and seventeenth centuries: by Catholics when they tied Protestants to the stake, Protestants when they beheaded Catholics, political absolutists when they killed for the divine right of kings, and republicans when they executed their monarch. Addison and other Anglicans, fearful of zeal, must have been refreshed by deistic reliance on reason and the findings of natural science to prove the wisdom and power of God. The deists, moreover, satisfied certain conditions of Addison's inquiry after truth; they dared to reason for themselves, evaluate what they saw, and exercise divinely bestowed curiosity.

He was nevertheless offended by the deist, who dismissed as superfluous the place of revelation in belief. He himself declared that piety demands not only the evidence of reason and demonstration but also the inspiration of faith; and he fortified his aversion to deistic bareness with the authority of liberal Anglicanism. Hence he could disavow, as had Samuel Clarke before him, "modern deists, who contend that there was no want, no need of a revelation; that philosophy and right reason was of itself sufficiently able, to instruct and preserve men in the practice of their duty; and that nothing was to be expected from revelation."[15] No wonder, then, that Addison, who found philosophy a poor substitute for religious belief, personified deism as incomplete, a "half-naked awkward country wench."

But what distressed him most about freethinkers was their patronizing intellectualism. After watching a deist airily relegate the "dry matters" of the Judaeo-Christian tradition to obsolescence, Addison sharply narrowed the margins of his tolerance. The portrait of Tinsel foreshadowed his support in January 1718/19 of Lord Guernsey's motion for a restrictive clause to be added to a bill for strengthening the Protestant interest, "that any person when he comes to take the oath of abjuration, and other oaths, subsequent to his receiving the sacrament, in order to his qualification, shall acknowledge that the Holy Scriptures of the Old and New Testament were given by divine inspiration, and shall acknowledge his firm faith and belief in the ever-blessed Trinity."[16] The amendment, aimed partially at deistic infiltration into high office, was defeated. Addison would not risk majority disapproval to support another amendment subsequently moved by Lord Guernsey.

All the while that he isolated and analyzed sources of religious alienation in England, he had in mind a specific against them, "a strong steady masculine piety" (*S* 201). The phrase now is frustratingly imprecise. But in its own time it had the advantage of deliberate vagueness, which evoked a series of rousing virtues: patriotism, bravery, independence, content, shrewdness, honesty, reasonableness, trustworthiness, fortitude, fidelity, charity, sociability, politeness, obedience, thrift, cleanliness, awe, temperance, and reverence. The phrase is an example of Addison's occasional use of a journalistic generality. Having almost as many positive connotations as there were readers, it was designed to flatter his audience into moral action.

A statement of such vigorous piety synthesized his religious values. He recognized as basic to belief brightness of soul and equability of mind. The gospel was literally good news, which brought to the faithful a happiness expressive of God's plenitude and love. He shared John Scott's confidence that religion was not "intended for a Medusa's head to transform men into monuments of stone"; that contrarily it provided serenity, cheerfulness of temper, vivacity, and courage. He agreed with the Latitudinarian that piety and modest joy were natural correlatives, and Christian pessimism was impossible. "The true spirit of religion," he said, "cheers, as well as composes, the soul; it banishes indeed all levity of behaviour, all vicious and dissolute mirth, but in exchange fills the mind with a perpetual serenity, uninterrupted cheerfulness, and an habitual inclination to please others, as well as to be pleased in itself" (*S* 494).[17]

Addison was no sentimentalist; he knew from experience that life is a series of disappointments to be endured. Scripture also told him that man is a creature of vanity and weakness, wanton desires and corrupt reason, delusive hope and real depravity. He did not repress this knowledge, but he brought it into perspective. He therefore acknowledged that man is a feeble being who through right choice may meliorate his degeneracy and so achieve earthly redemption. Addison's optimism was founded on the orthodox doctrine that man's will lies entirely within personal control and may be used as well for good as for evil.

His faith was a proselytizer's, worldly and strangely outgoing for one who was both shy and cerebral. In his periodicals he emphasized the rewards of piety—perhaps as a lure to his City friends—and translated manna into familiar language. He dangled before his readers the assurance that God bestowed on the devout not only ease of mind but material prosperity. He seems to have mesmerized himself with Tillotson's oft-repeated premise that the "business" of religion is likewise "a mighty advantage to men's estates," for it calls down "God's more especial providence and peculiar blessing which usually attends good men in their undertakings and crowns them with good success."[18] Addison, turning to poetry, celebrated this businesslike piety:

> Thy bounteous hand with worldly bliss
> Has made my cup run o'er,

And in a kind and faithful friend
  Has doubled all my store.

Ten thousand thousand precious gifts
  My daily thanks employ,
Nor is the least a cheerful heart,
  That tastes those gifts with joy.

[*S* 453]

In his religious life he once more managed to attune his materialistic interests to a tireless spiritual dedication. And he did so without hypocrisy or intellectual contortion. He recognized that the faithful must offer themselves "without show or ostentation" to serve God, "the proper object of adoration" (*S* 207). He advanced faith as a source of discipline and humility, which, with the guidance of a rational church, harmonized the relationship between God and individual. In the Addisonian ethic, religious belief never encouraged withdrawal from community obligations; on the contrary, it thrust man into them. Christianity for him was a worldly power that warred against private sin and public vice; it taught industry and the responsibilities of free subjects to princes, and of Christians one to another. It quieted "noise and clamour, slander and calumny, treason and perjury"; contrarily, it exalted "peaceable behaviour, a love of truth, and a submission to superiors" (*F* 52). Addison's definition of a "strong steady masculine piety" merged finally with the social lessons and moderation of Low Church Anglicanism.

He conceived the Good Man or Christian Hero as one "very much strengthened by reason and principle." He was valorous but also cautious; he was bold but also discreet. He could love but also detest all who he thought disrupted the social order: merchants who sold out the community to fatten their purses, Jacobites or absolutists who sacrificed freedom for passive obedience and nonresistance, atheistic bigots and zealots who contested "the religion of their country." Addison's Christian Hero loathed this last group who repaid God's bounty with the meanness of "pride, spleen and cavil" (*S* 381). He despised them as arrogant fools who vainly tried to impose their notions of "random chance" on the divine contrivance of the universe and the stability of their social world.[19]

There is validity in Addison's charge that his age hastened a religious decline already begun during the Restoration. There is validity too in his oversimple belief that much of the religious indifference of his contemporaries was a reaction to the quarrelsome theology of the interregnum and the tension engendered by the Catholic revival during the reign of James II. Certainly early in the eighteenth century devout Anglicans were wary of religious enthusiasm, which they tried to restrain through reason and ecclesiastical discipline. But as much as Addison admired moderation, he understood its deadening effect not only on laymen but on the religious establishment itself. Probably he remembered the New Testament disavowal of those who were "neither cold nor hot." At any rate, he agreed with the lower clergy who tried "to show their respective congregations, the vast difference between that moderation which is a virtue, and that moderation so fashionable and so much recommended, which is nothing but lukewarmness in religion, and indifference in everything, that relates to the service of God." To this extent at least, he thought like a Tory churchman when he admitted that reason can be regulated into common sense, and morality into canniness. What he particularly feared was that moderation, so finely separated from lukewarmness, could be diluted even further into infidelity and ignorance.[20]

During his lifetime the Anglican church was fighting for its spiritual existence. It was cheated of potential saints and martyrs by the expulsion of Nonjurors, like Law, and mild Puritans, like Baxter. It could not claim a single devotional classic; it could not point to many preachers whose oratory merited praise. Its theological ideas were static, derivative, and utilitarian.[21] Many Anglicans were capable of only a ready-made faith, and some could not even achieve that. Despite these signs of spiritual weakness, the church was physically secure and prosperous. Anne was devoted to its well-being. Both parties fought for its approval and were reluctant to hazard a general election without it. Mobs, though written off by either side as ignorant and factional, were loudly Anglican at various times between 1705 and 1716. The church's enemies were few and tired: Catholics were despised by most Englishmen; and dissenters, despite Tory alarums, were falling off in numbers.

Most of these testimonies of church solidarity, however, showed party commitment rather than religious purpose. In 1703, for example, when Parliament rejected the bad-penny bill against occasional conformity, a verbal storm broke out. According to Swift: "It was so universal, that I observed the dogs in the streets much more contumelious and quarrelsome than usual; and the very night before the bill went up, a committee of Whig and Tory cats, had a very warm and loud debate upon the roof of our house. But why should we wonder at that, when the very ladies are split asunder into High Church and Low, and out of zeal for religion, have hardly time to say their prayers?" Addison was as aware as Swift that religious feeling was being overwhelmed by political excitement; the church was being invoked by prelates and politicians alike to screen party maneuvers. Over the years, both as Mr. Spectator and as the true-blue Freeholder, he denounced this self-proliferating confusion. It made for an unruliness, he said, that swept from country parishes through the universities, always to the detriment of pastoral care and sound learning. He had reason to fear party polemics were stunting the intellectual growth of the Anglican community.[22]

At the same time he must have admitted—at least to himself—that the very structure of the church dictated its political involvement. Since the reign of William III, Anglican bishops had played dual roles. They were political leaders as well as religious guides, chosen by the king to support his various programs of Protestant toleration in the three kingdoms. Then, under Anne, the Whig bishops intensified their factional activity to advance causes repellent to the predominantly Tory lower clergy—occasional conformity, comprehension, the impeachment of Sacheverell. These priests subsequently berated many of their bishops as heretics, or Low Churchmen who were, Sacheverell said, "trimming villain[s] under all governments . . . drawn by private gain and animosities, to pursue such methods as really will subvert our constitution, and overturn the foundations of peace and order in church and state." When these High Fliers were silenced by ecclesiastical discipline, the Tory pamphleteers attacked the "Church Whigs" as timeservers worse even than Judas, as "false and perfidious . . . shuffling treacherous Latitudinarians . . . sots and bigots . . . monsters . . . apostates and renegades . . . false traitors . . . crafty, faithless, insidious persons."[23]

In time large numbers of the lower clergy boldly identified themselves with the principles, dogmas, and personalities on which they claimed the Catholic heritage of the church was based. In the split among Anglicans, defiant High Churchmen opposed many of the bishops who argued for "the present Protestant Establishment." The insurgents carried their conservatism into the political issues of indefeasible hereditary right, nonresistance, the legitimacy of the Pretender, and legislative extermination of dissent. By thus flatly opposing the major tenets of the Revolution Settlement, many in the priesthood took issue with both canonical and civil authority. It was against this extralegal position that Whig clergy and laymen fought. None pinpointed the struggle more forthrightly than Steele, especially in 1714, when he insisted "that the clergy have nothing to say to us concerning government, but as other men have it, from the laws themselves."[24]

Addison, who rarely minimized political opposition—in this instance, clerical influence on the people—never confronted the defiant clerics as openly as Steele. Because he habitually respected authority, Addison was reluctant to attack the hierarchy even if they were blatant Tories like Sacheverell or Atterbury. Whatever anger he felt toward priests whose public actions offended him he generally restrained or kept to himself. But during a national crisis, as in the early years of George I's reign, he must have persuaded himself that discretion can be cowardice. In 1715–16 he spoke out against the duplicity of the Church of England party. And he urgently fought what he regarded as an unholy alliance between the Tory leadership and the High Churchmen. He hoped to discredit their image of the Anglican church "lying bleeding of the wounds she has received in the house of her friends.—Her priests sighing, and she in bitterness, because her adversaries are chief, and her enemies at present prosper."[25]

A professional party writer, Addison recognized that this image made for effective propaganda. It was so effective that the people of Durham County, usually unwilling to pay their taxes, agreed to do so "cheerfully" with the appointment of the Tory ministry in 1710. They were willing to break their own contentious precedent because, as one of the gentry reported to Robert Harley, "they now think their church out of danger." For a period of six years, and most emphatically during the Jacobite rebellion, Addison protested against the Tory charge that the Whig bishops were "now associated with the dissenters, in order to undermine, and blow up the present constitution in church and state." He refused to remain simply defensive, however, and condemned the impious tumults stirred up in the name of the church. He castigated the rioters, stressing their unattractive personalities and dubious motivation. He traced the political origin of religious tags used to split England into angry party divisions. He drew a moral lesson from the slogan "The church is in danger," weighing its effects on a people who too easily abandoned intelligence for prejudice.[26]

Mob action of any kind was hateful to him as a breakdown of reason, responsibility, and order. When, as in 1715, he deduced Tory connivance behind public disorder, he reacted with moral outrage. In that year "a tumultuary rabble," somehow joined in the interest of faith, destroyed several meetinghouses, like those at Dudley, West Bromwich, and Oldbury (*F* 28). Often the magistrates' leniency toward the rioters amounted to complicity. Addison did not delude himself into assuming that these mischievous, localized sorties indicated subversion on a grand scale or that they were part of a design to overthrow England's constitutional government. Yet he did connect them with the scheming of the Tories, who by creating an atmosphere of discontent and uneasiness hoped to scramble back into power. Hence he ignored the London rioting led by men who lacked significant class identity and who, according to the *Flying-Post* of 23–26 April 1715, "insulted those that were passing the streets about their lawful occasions, robbed them of their hats, wigs, etc., buffeted them, and threatened farther mischief if they would not huzza 'God bless the Queen and High Church.' " Instead he blamed the violence and looting of 1715–16 on the landed gentry, whom he had long identified with hidebound Toryism. He condemned them and their hangers-on for indifference to the right of property, for hypocritically manipulating the church to conceal their political pique and party ambitions.[27]

From among these rioters he chose two type figures for satirical dissection: the bloated publican who avowed "his zeal for the prosperity of the church . . . by repeated bumpers," and the Tory fox hunter who concurred with him that "there is scarce a Presbyterian in the whole county, except the bishop" (*F* 22). The fox hunter, a flat, undeveloped character, personifies the stupidity often attributed to the squirearchy by the Whigs. Maynwaring, for example, mockingly declared that there were some "honest Tories"—and the fox hunter would be one—"whose fault was folly only. They were so silly as to believe the church was in danger, and so zealous as to give into any thing which they thought would recover it out of it." The inane fox hunter earned the *Freeholder*'s derisive memorial as one of "these rural statesmen." But since he was not malicious, his ending is a happy one; for Addison, having forgotten what he once wrote about the "renegado," allowed him to enjoy a political change of heart. In the fox hunter's last appearance he glowed with the contentment that rightly belonged to "a convert to the present establishment, and a good subject to King George" (*F* 47).[28]

Addison's Whig readers must have chortled comfortably at the fox hunter, dense but likeable, a windy, mindless repeater of Tory harangue. His "High Church innkeeper" was also meant to provoke guffaws; he was "a lusty, jolly fellow, that lives well, at least three yards in the girth, and the best Church of England man upon the road." But Addison seems to have changed his intention in midcaricature, so that the publican ceased to be a mere object of laughable condescension and became disgusting. His body was "swelled . . . to a prodigious size" and his complexion "worked up . . . to a standing crimson." He was a diseased creature whose appearance of bonhomie hid an inner hostility toward those who did not think as he did. He was not at all what he appeared, even as Tory concern for national piety cloaked its desire for supremacy. Like Tory policy he was destructive: to be devout was to raze a few meetinghouses. And like Tory morality he was hypocritical: "He had not time to go to church himself. . . . and had scarce any other notion of religion, but that it consisted in hating Presbyterians" (*F* 22).[29] This bloated sack of flesh synthesized what Addison denounced as Tory ambition during the last four years of Anne's reign and the first two years of George I's.

In 1710, long before he created the two grotesques, he determined to expose the religious cant of the Tories. He spoke for his party in that year of Whig exodus when he complained that the terms *High Church* and *Low Church* were the cry of every hack in the pay of the Harley–St. John ministry. With a plainness that only a political loser could afford, Addison said these epithets "do not so much denote a principle, as they distinguish a party. They are like words of battle, that have nothing to do with their original signification, but are only given out to keep a body of men together, and to let them know friends from enemies" (*T* 220). They had no more Christian validity for him than the Tory slogan "The church is in danger," which he first heard in 1705 upon the return of a Whig majority to the Commons. Thereafter he heard it repeated whenever the Tories strove for a return to power, as in 1710; or whenever they thought their power at stake, as from 1714 to the outbreak of the Jacobite rebellion.

During this long period he never discussed the charge at length or tried to rebut it. Then on 27 April 1716 he described it as "the late cry of the church," as though it were an issue that belonged to the past. His thesis, built on a mixture of exaggeration and forthright analysis, enabled him to examine "how this cry of the church has corrupted the morals of both parties." The argument proper begins:

> The late cry of the church has been an artifice of the same kind with that made use of by the hypocrites of the last age, and has had as fatal an influence upon religion. If a man would but seriously consider how much greater comfort he would receive in the last moments of his life from a reflection that he has made one virtuous man, than that he has made a thousand Tories, we should not see the zeal of so many good men turned off from its proper end, and employed in making such a kind of converts. What satisfaction will it be to an immoral man, at such a time, to think he is a good Whig! or to one that is conscious of sedition, perjury, or rebellion, that he dies with the reputation of a High Churchman! [*F* 37]

The passage is remarkable. Addressed to both Whigs and Tories, it generalizes grandly on the transience of political commitment and on the moral life as the key to salvation. But beneath the flow of bland words it associates the Tories with hypocrisy, with Puritanlike "artifice," reducing "the late cry of the church" to a cheap call for political conversion—which in part it was.[30]

There is nothing impartial about this statement; on the contrary, it suggests an author who had been patiently waiting to vent his hostility. In many ways the spring of 1716 was the perfect time for such an explosion: the rebellion was over, a majority of Englishmen supported the Hanoverian succession and the Whig-dominated Parliament, and the "late cry" was denounced as a political fiction by many who had once followed Sacheverell. The broad appeal of Addison's argument was strengthened by a technique perfected in the *Freeholder*. That is, he adjusted his position to Whig advantage by suppressing certain substantive details. While he made much of the fact that power-hungry men exploited the claim that the church was imperiled, he concealed his awareness that many men of good will believed the claim to be valid. Large numbers of apolitical parish priests were convinced of the threat to the church; nor could anyone suspect the motives of bishops as devout as Ken, Bull, and Beveridge, all of whom had this conviction. When Addison refused integrity to those who voiced the cry or even accepted it, he chose to forget that he had once labeled as "excessively stupid" anyone "who believes that there is no virtue but on his own side, and that there are not men as honest as himself who may differ from him in political principles" (*S* 243).

The essay was directed only in part to a general audience, those to whom the *Freeholder* overtly spoke. Additionally it was meant for the Whig leaders, whom Addison heard in party councils express fear—genuine or not—that "a very considerable schism is formed in the church and every day increases by the joint industry of the Tory and non-juring clergy, whose congregations . . . are grown to be very numerous."[31] The essay thus spoke to men who made Whig policy and were ready to continue the political war under religious banners. It was just this kind of struggle that Addison wished to avoid. Moreover, as a warning to the Whigs prepared to follow Tory precedent, he detailed the harmful effects of the "late cry" on the party that exploited it:

> [It] fills the minds of weak men, who fall into the snare, with groundless fears and apprehensions, unspeakable rage towards their fellow-subjects, wrong ideas of persons whom they are not acquainted with, and uncharitable interpretations of those actions of which they are not competent judges. It instills into their minds the utmost virulence and bitterness, instead of that charity, which is the perfection and ornament of religion, and the most indispensable and necessary means for attaining the end of it. In a word, among these mistaken zealots, it sanctifies cruelty and injustice, riots and treason.

He made clear by broad implication that what had happened to the Tories might well happen to the Whigs if they too used the church for political maneuvering. His analysis is a magnificent piece of journalistic strategy. It sniped at the Tories, his public target. Yet it also pleaded with the two parties to leave the church free from the backbiting of factional disputes.

When he surveyed the state of religion in England, he admitted the loss of conviction that seemed to have befallen a "nation of saints," or at least a devout people (*F* 37). But he consoled himself that this was but a temporary emptiness to be followed in time by a return to active belief and practice. He realized further that the fate of the church was inseparable from politics. Church and state were one; priest, member of Parliament, bishop, and king's minister alike were sworn to support the political and religious establishment. Atterbury wrote of it as "a constitution where the external government of the church is so closely interwoven with that of the state, and so exactly adapted to it, in all its parts, as that it can flourish only when that does; and must, as it always has hitherto done, decline, die, and revive with it. In a word, where the interest of prince, and subject, priest, and people, are perpetually the same; and the only fatal mistake that ever happens in our politics, is, when they are thought to be divided."[32]

Addison did not object to this union, only to its distortion. He found distasteful the enmity with which some of the lower clergy viewed the Revolution Settlement but applauded the bishops' support of it. He deplored as well the hypocrisy of political leaders—more often Tory than Whig, he would say—who used the church for their own aspirations. Politics, in short, colored his attitude toward the Anglican establishment even as it colored almost every other concern of his life. But his relationship with the church was more than political; he looked to it with "filial tenderness and duty." Ultimately he wanted the church to bless a state constructed on principles of Whiggish liberalism; and in return he expected the state to honor the faith and morality of an enlightened church.

CHAPTER NINE

THE NATURE OF BELIEF

AFTER the return of Charles II to England, religious inquiry, whether guided by reason or the *testimony of the spirit,* was centered on what and how man is to believe. Addison favored curiosity that might strengthen faith, but he became uneasy when the search for truth was so obsessive that it could not be separated from a desire to proselyte. Specifically, he feared the missionary ardor of such investigation, whose intensity, accompanied often by self-deception and arrogance, inhibited free debate:

There is nothing in which men more deceive themselves than in what the world calls zeal. There are so many passions which hide themselves under it, and so many mischiefs arising from it, that some have gone so far as to say it would have been for the benefit of mankind if it had never been reckoned in the catalogue of virtues. It is certain where it is once laudable and prudential it is an hundred times criminal and erroneous, nor can it be otherwise if we consider that it operates with equal violence in all religions, however opposite they may be to one another, and in all the subdivisions of each religion in particular.

The introductory paragraph of *Spectator* 185 at first appears to be an open attack on all religious proselyters, an impression amplified because Addison never names institutions, only traits. This impression is dissipated as soon as he identifies proselyting zeal with "pride, interest, or ill nature," with persecution and cruelty, even with "opinions full of contradiction and impossibility"; then there can be no doubt that he is engaged in a flanking attack on dissenters, Catholics, and atheists. But when he speaks about "true and genuine" zeal, he is thinking hospitably of Anglican dedication identified by the church as *enthusiasmus triumphatus.* In *Spectator* 186, as he continues this exposition, Addison's intention is clearer. The second essay, cast in the form of a letter from his "worthy friend the clergyman," advances the premise that Anglican conversion is good; all other, bad.

By introducing the letter of the clergyman, whose ardor urges conviction in "the religion of [his] country," Addison achieves a useful contrapuntal effect. He and the parson, their two voices representing the congregation and the pulpit, are passionate in a single cause. Here—as elsewhere—the *Spectator*'s physical limitations were advantageously used by Addison, for although the compressed format obliged him to break his exposition into two parts, the letter broadens its range. Through the clergyman's presence, Addison vigorously implied that conversion—when of the Church of England variety—was charitable and benevolent. The Anglican missionary, the essayist could assert, brought to the bewildered and doubting the glorious "prospect of a future state" and the serene cheerfulness that sustains those bowed down by "disappointments and misfortunes, pain and sickness, death itself."

By identifying him only as a clergyman and not as an Anglican proselyter, Addison granted him a purity of purpose that he refused other religious enthusiasts. This is special pleading, to be sure; but far from pretending disinterest, he wrote on this occasion as a thoroughgoing Anglican. He was as sure as any man could hope to be that his church had paved a smooth path to salvation. This was an expectation fostered by his having been brought up to distinguish between suspect religiosity—non-Anglican—and the "true and warrantable enthusiasm of devout and holy souls"—Anglican. Under the influence of men as different as More and Sprat, he regarded Church of England zeal as the attribute of those who had been inspirited by a "delicious sense of the divine life." Through their fervor, they braced the establishment and transmitted answers to individuals who might otherwise have sought vainly for God's truth.[1]

On the surface, Addison's defense of Anglican enthusiasm is remarkable because it appears to substitute subjective authority for empirical tests. But this is only a parenthetical interruption of his declared longing for belief grounded in the certainty of knowledge and of his devotion to an individual inquiry after truth. One of the dominant themes of the *Spectator,* indeed, is intellectual liberation, which is summed up in the aphorism "The mind of man naturally hates everything that looks like a restraint upon it" (*S* 412). There is a refrainlike insistence through most of the essays that all unverified conclusions, even those advanced by the church or its ardent disciples, can be put to rational tests. Why else was man divinely endowed with reason if not to pursue knowledge to the full limits allowed by his gift? Addison related the efforts of the Anglican proselyter and the intellectual seeker by defining a common ground for religious and secular inquiry. Man's noblest obligation, he proposed, is to discover truth for the apprehension of the divine being and the wisdom of pleasing him. On many Saturdays Addison detailed in the *Spectator* his own proofs for God's existence, sharing his knowledge with all who desired a well-marked direction to the moral life. Even if he knew that he was being ridiculed as a "parson in a tye wig" or "a priest in his heart," he would not have altered his course. In a practical journalistic way he mediated between the *Ecclesia Anglicana* and the secular world; his aim was to entice dissidents of all persuasions into "the religion of their country" and thus to secure their political as well as moral regeneration.[2]

Whatever lofty hopes Addison had for human endeavor, he never let his attention stray from pragmatic necessity. He continued to be utilitarian in his search for religious truth. As a moral idealist he equated the contemplation of the divine and "the exercise of virtue" (*S* 93). But as a man of the world, conscious of the spiritual needs of his contemporaries, he would not allow the religious experience to remain private. The knowledge derived from it had to be disseminated and translated against a background of worldly affairs, its insights used to further temporal goodness. He would not, for example, urge others to ponder the Incarnation and sufferings of Christ merely as an academic lesson in the articles of faith. Such a study fulfilled its purpose only when it led the believer beyond dogma "to a firm trust and reliance on the mercies of our maker." The example of Christ taught his followers to "love . . . even the most inconsiderable of mankind" and to guard more strictly their "purity" of mind and soul. In Addison's ethic, which had little room for mystic meditation or prolonged retreat, "the history of our blessed Saviour" had a threefold significance: it gave precedent and authority for man's spiritual duty; it cleansed him of concealed vanity and error; it taught him to apply socially the rule of obedience and sacrifice (*S* 186). Addison affirmed that salvation is won in earthly struggle. It is wrested from life not through abstruse speculation on doctrine but through rational charity and tolerance that humbly emulate divine benevolence. He was convinced that morality was and had to be the practical essence of piety.[3]

He subscribed to an Anglican tradition that charted two separate but contiguous roads to religious truth: revelation, the source of faith; and reason, the source of spiritual knowledge. This separation forced him to reject certain Latitudinarians whose scheme of practical morality he otherwise set up as a guide to conduct—Glanvill and Barrow and Stillingfleet, for instance. They insisted that since God's truth was singular, there could be but one approach to it. And they forced this oneness when they categorized "the belief of our reason . . . an exercise of faith and faith . . . an act of reason."[4] Always a realist, Addison drew back from this thesis, for there was nothing in his experience to convince him that faith and knowledge interlock, no matter how much he might have wished they did.

If he had accepted Glanvill's telescoped equation, he would have had to repudiate Locke's assertion that "faith stands by itself, and upon grounds of its own; nor can be removed from them, and placed on those of knowledge. Their grounds are so far from being the same, or having anything common, that when it is brought to certainty, faith is destroyed; 'tis knowledge then, and faith no longer." Addison believed in this distinction, stating tersely that faith is no longer faith when it is "lost in conviction" (*S* 459). The idea is so crisply phrased, so undeveloped, that one suspects he was afraid of it. Undoubtedly, he distrusted the ability of a general audience to understand its subtlety. But more particularly he must have feared the reaction of those fideistic readers who would interpret the separation between faith and knowledge as a prelude to religious subversion and so to social upheaval. Nor would this anxiety have been unfounded. Even Locke, virtually unchallenged in his role as epistemologist, had been scolded by the liberal Stillingfleet for attempting "to start such new methods of certainty" as only "leave men's minds more doubtful than before." Addison, when he remembered this dialogue, was probably hard pressed to find his way out of a dilemma. He did not want to promote scepticism; and according to Stillingfleet, he would do just that if he upheld Locke's argument. Moreover, while he was eager to avoid the recrimination of the world, he was reluctant to earn popular approval at the cost of truth. There could be no happy resolution for him. He therefore stated his own commitment and left it abruptly.[5]

The commitment is made twice in the *Spectator,* where unequivocally he asserted that knowledge provides factual certainty and faith the assurance of transcendent truth. He thus implied that faith occupies a lower plane of proven reliability than does knowledge derived from rational or empirical demonstration. But he also hinted that the two, though separate and different, are complementary. It is easy enough to reconstruct the concern with which Addison decided to defend Locke. But in fact he was needlessly worried, for the distinction between faith and knowledge had become current among theologians by the early eighteenth century, and in the sermons of the period the idea appears frequently, shorn of any implied value judgment. According to Silver-Tongued Bates, for example, "'Tis true, no article of faith is really repugnant to reason; for God is the author of natural as well as of supernatural light, and he cannot contradict himself: they are emanations from him, and though different, yet not destructive of each other."[6]

If Addison disclaimed a doctrine held by a few Latitudinarians, he was nonetheless moved by the charity of the group as a whole. He had seen or read so much of the havoc caused by religious schism that he wished to avoid its horrors, whether of acrimony and cruelty or of "slaughter and bloodshed" (*S* 185). The Latitudinarians taught him to despise religious persecution and the zealotry that prompts it. But they also gave him innumerable lessons in optimism, bolstering his hope that devout belief secures virtue against sin, love against darkness, and prosperity against selfishness. They helped him frame a rule of conduct devoted to the practical benefit of society, a steady reminder that in public life people are moved by inner pressure—of conscience, for example, or of a sense of responsibility to others. Indeed the Latitudinarians counseled him to look beyond society to the individual, who could learn to apply the generous affections and to avoid whatever impairs morality. And finally, the example of their leader Tillotson supported Addison's eagerness to evaluate evidence, balance probabilities, and make rational decisions in spiritual as well as in secular problems.

Like Tillotson especially, he honored the right to doubt and to use scientific method in a search for theological answers. The bishop had insisted that even the most inviolable doctrines "are vehemently to be suspected which decline trial, and are so loth to be brought into the light; which will not endure a fair examination, but magisterially require an implicit faith." Similarly Addison asserted the need to examine all dogma and indeed to reject as inauthentic any "which does not contribute to the confirmation or improvement of morality" (*S* 459). In assuming "all liberty of enquiry and judgment in matters of religion"—the words are Tillotson's—both men aimed not to revise standards of orthodoxy but to prove that Christian verity could triumphantly withstand any test.[7] Addison himself delighted in such intellectual freedom, because it relieved him of the need to believe unquestioningly. He therefore correlated the spirit of his own inquiry after truth with the Latitudinarian's exaltation of liberty of conscience. And he practiced much of this open-mindedness in his daily associations. Morally buoyant, he enjoyed the conversation of men like Whiston, Berkeley, Clarke, and Ambrose Philips; he debated their heterodox opinions with them; and he supported their right to question, even to depart from Anglican doctrine.

The debt he owed to Tillotson and other Latitudinarians must be extended to the Cambridge Platonists, gentle and retiring academics like Whichcote, More, and Culverwel. Although the Latitudinarians were separated from the Cambridge group by a generation or two, there was such amity of purpose between them that anyone borrowing from the one would in a sense be borrowing from the other. Addison was attracted to the private spirituality emphasized by the Cambridge thinkers who opposed the busywork of church politics. He identified his own concentration on virtue with the way in which they subordinated ritualistic observance to moral action. Like them, he saw a common cause between Anglicans and trinitarian dissenters. If he could not convert the latter to the Church of England, he would at least keep them in its benign shadow through tolerant concessions. Finally, he echoed both the words and spirit of the Cambridge group when he urged that religious rationalism, based on a scientific methodology, be liberalized to accommodate and complement revelation.

The interest of both the Latitudinarians and the Cambridge divines in scientific inquiry brought Addison to the physico-theologians, who taught him to look to the immensity and magnificence of nature as the center from which radiated his own proofs for the existence of God. These men, liberated from the old dogmas about eternity, sought their theological answers in mathematics, biology, chemistry, and physics. As scientists, they derived from their discipline, according to Newton, the skill, vision, and tenacity to reach "propositions inferred by general induction from phenomena as accurately or very nearly true." Since these propositions were verifiable to a hitherto unrealizable degree, the natural philosopher assumed that they permitted continuous progress toward discovery of the First Cause. Yearning for a perception of divinity that translated speculation and hope into certainty and fact, Addison became an articulate spokesman for natural philosophy. In both the *Tatler* and the *Spectator* he defended the new science. And yet, although he followed its advances, he rarely wrote about them in specific detail because he wished to avoid the fault that he attributed in *Spectator* 297 to Milton, an ostentatious show of learning. Addison's defense of the new science was assured, but neither original nor precise. His ideas reflected the values of scientists like Sprat, Boyle, Bentley, and Newton, whose Christianity had no visible flaws; and of clerics like More, Glanvill, Bates, and Fleetwood, who in successive generations voiced the church's support of natural philosophy.[8]

His enthusiasm for the new science demanded rejection of scholastic disputation. Attired in his Master's gown at the Encaenia of 7 July 1693, he decried the arrogant inflexibility of the Schoolmen and their ignorance of experimental techniques. Almost brutally—despite the Latin eloquence of his oration—he rejoiced that he lived in an age that saw them and their pseudo science reduced to nothingness and blown away by the progressive winds of natural philosophy. A young orator impressed by the clichés of his time, he celebrated the fact that theaters like the Sheldonian needed no longer ring "with encomia on the Stagyrite, who greater than his own Alexander, had long unopposed, triumphed in our school desks, and had the whole world for his pupils." Not yet prepared to be "with caution bold," he swaggeringly emancipated scholars from the necessity of "a blind veneration to that barbarous peripatetic jingle, to obscure scholastic terms of art, once held as oracles." Now they had but to "consult the dictates of [their] own senses, and by late invented engines force nature herself to discover plainly her most hidden recesses." To supplant the old tyrants he paid homage to Descartes, Boyle, and Newton as Christians who dedicated their wisdom and technical skill, their discoveries and demonstrations, to the glory of God visible everywhere in "this vast machine" of created matter. In all three he was attracted to an intellectual audacity and independence that "scorned to be any longer bounded within the straits and crystalline walls of an Aristotelic world," or to be ensnared in its trifling verbal propositions and syllogisms.[9]

His condemnation of the Schoolmen is of a piece with the intellectual temper of his world. Like the sophisticated scientists whom he admired at this time, he failed to understand that advances made by the new science began in the speculations of the Scholastics. Again, with confidence in Augustan superiority, he could not appreciate the Schoolmen's humanistic view of a universe whose beneficence satisfied the hopes of ordinary men. That he may have had in his last few months second thoughts about the unrestrained statements in the *Oration* is indicated by its absence from his *Collected Works* (1721), but more probably he was unwilling to preserve among mature works a derivative collegiate exercise. Whatever explanation may be advanced for his advising Tickell to omit the *Oration,* the fact remains that as late as 6 September 1714 Addison made no concessions in his war against the Schoolmen. He attacked them for authoritarianism and for verbal cleverness that concealed vapidity. "For my own part," he said in *Spectator* 590, "I look upon [their] propositions as words that have no ideas annexed to them; and think men had better own their ignorance, than advance doctrines, by which they mean nothing, and which indeed are self-contradictory." He accused them, in effect, of false learning that brought them perilously close to religious perversity.

At best, then, he would have left the Schoolmen unread. The new scientists, on the other hand, captured his loyalty, for they combined the appeals of reason and vision, scientific inquiry and religious elevation. The physico-theologians, and particularly Boyle, convinced him that they were devoted to advancing the morally good life. Their experimental philosophy, they said, was never an end in itself but a means of proving God's existence and "divers of [his] chief attributes." Even when an Oxford tutor susceptible to knowledge for its own sake, Addison valued the mathematical probing of the universe as a spiritual exercise. And for the rest of his life he insisted that the ultimate function of science was to consider "the several ends of Providence which are served by . . . and the wonders of divine wisdom which appear in" natural phenomena (*S* 393). He was sure that scientific truth realized itself only when it was harmonized with the theological assumption that God exists and must be adored.[10]

He applauded science as a means of fixing what he called the moral habits of the mind and of disproving random chance as the First Cause. He applauded science when its conclusions brought disbelievers teleological certainty and taught the devout lessons in humility, awe, and duty to God and man. Addison's respect for the Christian endeavor of natural philosophers was unqualified. But he feared that among individuals of "little genius" scientific research might degenerate into preoccupation with "insects, reptiles, animalcules, and . . . trifling rarities." He saw this happen to a whole generation of virtuosi, who forgot their obligation to help mend the world in which they had been placed (*T* 216). Such men as these, in Newton's words, also forgot that "every true step made in [natural] philosophy brings us *not immediately* to the knowledge of the First Cause, yet it brings us near to it, and on that account is to be highly valued." Addison lamented the virtuosi's waste of intelligence and aptitude and effort. But he admitted that in the scheme of things such prodigality was unimportant. What was important was ever-present nature, whose divine essence was accessible even to the unlettered. To one who approached the "beauties of the creation" in simple piety and love, "every field and wood" became consecrated, every "ordinary walk . . . a morning or evening sacrifice" (*S* 393).[11]

He constructed a scheme of piety for himself by reversing the values of the Schoolmen, clarifying the significance of the virtuosi's investigations, and borrowing several of the conclusions promulgated by natural philosophers and rational Anglicans. Several related premises are at the core of his scheme: morality transcends but does not deny ritual; spirituality makes an act subordinate to the doer's intention; virtue is the goal of existence and the essence of happiness; and Christology—in the words of Boyle, whom he admired as much as he did Newton—discerns "the nature of God by the light of reason" and "the knowledge of His will, or positive laws [by] His own revelation." Addison's concept of God was conventional, fashioned by his age. His system of belief was rational and directed toward an operable morality, the good of the social whole. As an individual he could not easily surrender himself to the mysteries of the Christian experience; yet in his devotion he was always an obedient Anglican.[12]

His own doubts were few, for once he was "thoroughly convinced of the truth of any article" and its reasonableness, he would never again "call it into question." Even if he forgot the initial arguments, he managed "to retain the conviction which they once produced." To account for such pious tenacity, he had an analogy: "It is in this manner that the mathematician proceeds upon propositions which he has once demonstrated, and though the demonstration may have slipped out of his memory, he builds upon the truth, because he knows it was demonstrated" (*S* 465). Basic to his moral and doctrinal belief was the postulate of *a* god as the First Cause on whose transcendence and immanence everything else depended, even as corollaries in Euclid followed from first propositions.

From the Restoration through the reign of Anne most Anglicans shaped their inquiry after truth around two premises of rational belief, "that there is a God who rules the world, and that the souls of men are capable of subsisting after death." These were a priori conclusions, not liable to serious question even by many deists, and the Anglican faithful needed only to supply their proofs. The mere act of substantiating such glorious proofs enhanced the beauty of the moral life and so functioned practically. But Addison magnified the process of demonstration as a challenge to human ingenuity and wisdom, an exercise in pious gratitude, "an entertainment . . . adapted to the nature of man," for "curiosity is one of the strongest and most lasting appetites implanted in us, and . . . [religious] admiration is one of our most pleasing passions" (*S* 237).[13]

Occasionally, however, he and his sources found the demonstration difficult and fugitive. To ease its formulation, some, like Tillotson, partitioned the "doctrine of the gospel" into "1. The things to be believed by us," and "2. The duties to be practised." Where Tillotson led the way to divine truth, Addison was not far behind. He too found religion divisible "under two general heads. The first comprehends what we are to believe, the other what we are to practise" (*S* 459). According to his postulate the two heads were separate but linked by human striving to fulfill sacred duty.[14]

The first division, "whatever is revealed to us in the Holy Writings, and which we could not have obtained the knowledge of by the light of nature," he called "faith." Tracing its origin to Anglican dogma, he defined it as the counterpart of national orthodoxy. His attitude toward faith verged on ambiguity if only because of his reticence. Certainly he regarded doctrinal observance as necessary to salvation. His argument with the deists focused on what he judged to be their heinous rejection of faith in worship. But it is not likely that he accepted every one of the Thirty-nine Articles. Even an Anglican as redoubtable as Johnson did not, agreeing only not to preach against them. In much the same spirit Addison rarely commented on particular dogmas. He remained aloof from the trinitarian controversy despite his friendship with Hoadly, Whiston, and Clarke. Still he was no fideist, for he responded to simple piety and appreciated the Lockean reduction of Christianity to a single doctrine: belief in Jesus as the Messiah, the Anointed, whose mission was authenticated by prophecy and miracle.

Yet such a reduction, while precise and uncluttered, was too stringent for him. In his treatise *Of the Christian Religion,* he went beyond Locke to emphasize Christ's divinity and affirmed his belief in Jesus as "God and Saviour," in the "miracles he wrought, and the many attestations of his divine mission, which were to be met with in the history of his life" (*MW,* 2:421). By adding the word *God* to Locke's initial formula and connecting that word with the idea of the liberator, whether called "Messiah" or "Saviour," he was able to achieve, according to Latitudinarian standards, an orthodox union of the metaphysical and historical, the supernatural and natural. His avowal of faith was obviously restrained, but it was for him even more than for Locke "a settled and sure principle of assent and assurance," which permitted "no manner of room for doubt or hesitation."[15]

Morality, the second of the "two general heads" under which he considered religion, included rational belief in the existence of God, the immortality of the human soul, and "all those duties" made mandatory "by reason or natural religion." Morality had the consent of "all the civilized nations of the world." And its dicta, governed by the law of nature, went beyond creed or church. Unlimited by time or place and illuminated "by the light of nature," morality differed from faith in that it was capable of demonstration and had the certainty of fact (*S* 459).[16] When Addison made his separation between natural and revealed religion, he accepted a current Anglican premise. He did, however, sharpen the distinction by substituting a new terminology for tired vogue words.

His division was not absolute, but neither did it imply equality; on the contrary, he posited morality as the primary condition of the religious experience. Authority for this choice reposed in the theological writing of Locke and the sermons of Tillotson. But the support he desired most he found in Scripture—from Isaiah and Amos to Romans and Revelations—where he learned (through the interpretation of the Cambridge divines) that "God hath rejected his own institutions; when they have been made final, put in competition with morals, or made compensation for morals." Ritual and dogma, in short, must never be allowed to obscure moral duty. Similarly he had deduced from the rebukes of Jesus to the scribes and Pharisees that ceremony must be subordinated to justice, honesty, and mercy; that the essence of devotion is locked in the soul of man. He followed his sources—from Holy Writ to Locke and the rational Anglicans—to a like conclusion: "A good intention joined to a good action, gives it its proper force and efficacy; joined to an evil action, extenuates its malignity, and in some cases may take it wholly away; and joined to an indifferent action, turns it to a virtue, and makes it meritorious, as far as human actions can be so" (*S* 213).[17] That final clause hovers like a mild reproach. Even the best of men, he appears to sigh, cannot quite come to terms with their ideals. But imperfection is modified by the desire to strive upward, and the effort invites admiration.

While he granted precedence to morality, he stressed that the inherent beauty of revelation gave impetus to human goodness by enlarging on "amiable ideas of the Supreme Being" and, conversely, on "the blackness and deformity of vice." Implicitly he acknowledged that the controversy within the church over the relative merits of natural and revealed religion was near to preciosity. Whatever position was taken, there was consensus that reason no less than revelation obliged men to do what was right. Addison himself clearly gave pre-eminence to morality but admitted that it could not be divorced from faith. Separate but related by God's unity, "faith and morality naturally produce each other" (*S* 465). The pilgrim could not travel one road, hence, without entering on the other; and both led him finally to eternal judgment.[18]

When Addison argued in print that morality was more essential than faith to salvation, he set forth the essence of his own religious belief. But almost any journalistic observation that he made had to serve a public as well as a private intention. His purpose was to pique the curiosity of freethinkers, whom in spectatorial days he had often wanted to conciliate and attract into the Church of England. *Spectator* 459, for example, so stressed the function of morality in divine worship that no deist could presumably take exception to prescribed forms. Addison even risked near heresy to emphasize that "no article of faith can be true" if it undermines morality. Appealing to the ethical core of deistic belief, he declared "that the greatest friend of morality, or natural religion, cannot possibly apprehend any danger from embracing Christianity, as it is preserved pure and uncorrupt in the doctrines of our national church." With such statements he hoped to reassure the deists that revelation in Anglican belief was compatible with their rational morality.

Earlier, in *Spectator* 186, he admitted to accepting "the great received articles of the Christian religion . . . so clearly proved from the authority of that divine revelation in which they are delivered, that it is impossible for those who have ears to hear and eyes to see, not to be convinced of them." As a concession to the deists, however, he was careful to insist that not *all* articles needed to be believed, only those that were "great." And as a further concession, he allowed for the faint possibility of error even in those. Nevertheless, he could "find no ill consequences in adhering" to them; for, right or wrong, they furthered the great ethical goal of Christianity, and that was what really counted. The Incarnation and suffering of Christ he thus found to be productive of "such habits of virtue in the mind of man, that, . . . supposing it were possible for us to be mistaken in them, the infidel himself must at least allow that no other system of religion could so effectually contribute to the heightening of morality."

Remarks like these clarify several truths about Addison: first, that, if pressed, he might hedge on the authenticity of certain dogmas, even those fundamental to orthodoxy; second, that he was an enthusiastic defender of Christian morality; and third, that for all his sophistication he was occasionally naïve in his dismissal of religious complexities. Because of his confidence that even an "erroneous" article of faith was a persuasive argument for Anglican loyalty, he underestimated the determined scepticism of his "infidels." Eager to abide by the ethical truths of Christianity, he assumed that all reasonable men agreed that doctrinal details should be subordinated to pious intention and performance. Obviously Addison could not understand why anyone, even a deist, should sacrifice the integrity of the moral whole to quibbles over lesser problems in revelatory truth.

For the last eight years of his life his religious ideas remained constant. If at the end he was proud of dying as a Christian, it was as a Christian who proclaimed the triumph of virtue rather than the efficacy of faith. Indeed, he was so revolted by the moral failure of those he branded as persistent, voluntary sinners that he flatly struck their names from the rolls of those to be saved.[19] For Addison, then, the quintessence of Christianity was not ritualistic performance, elaborate ecclesiastical government, or resplendent cathedrals. He measured its true worth again and again by its redemptive message to men faced with moral choice, by its advocacy of public engagement, and by its promise of peace both here and in the world to come.

CHAPTER TEN

THE PROOF FOR DIVINITY

IN 1682, with the aid of a metaphor inspired by his own Pyrrhonism, Dryden had asserted his belief that "they who would prove religion by reason do but weaken the cause which they endeavour to support: 'tis to take away the pillars of our faith, and to prop it only with a twig." Like other fideists, he fretted that rational piety encouraged arrogant rejection of the revealed word of God for the half-truths of man. But this was a minority concern in England and his therefore a minority voice. By the last decade of the seventeenth century most Anglicans held the existence of God to be the most obvious proposition that reason discovers, its proof equivalent to mathematical certainty. According to the dominant Latitudinarian argument, "It is every man's duty, who hath ability and capacity for it, to understand the grounds of his religion," to try its doctrines and to establish its truths in the invincibility of fact.[1]

Addison himself, for personal and altruistic reasons, was eager to set forth in the *Spectator* various demonstrations for divinity. By defining the basis of his own belief, he intended a lesson in religious understanding, to show the need for obedience to ecclesiastical authority and submission to supernal will. Along the way he would clarify his thinking and that of others about mortal preparation for eternal judgment. He would allow himself—and his audience vicariously—to engage in disputation that had an exciting immediacy. For during his generation God was once more fashionable, and one could talk about him without being accused of Puritan tendencies. But most significantly, Addison's effort to affirm the presence and attributes of divinity was pragmatic. He strove to resolve certain doubts that inhibited piety, to moderate religious antagonism, and to correct error. Since he wrote and thought as an Anglican, he meant to strengthen national orthodoxy. Through precept and statement, characterization and anecdote, allegory and drawing-room comedy, he found contexts for the Latitudinarian figure "Religion, placed in a soul of exquisite knowledge and abilities, as in a castle, finds not only habitation, but defence."[2]

The religious rationalists—scientists or liberal clerics or Whig journalists—began their proof for divine existence in the structure of the physical universe and in the multitudinous living forms that bore witness to His wisdom and creativity. So sure were they of finding in nature the evidence they sought that they rhapsodized both their own proof and God's benevolent power in a series of rhetorical questions: "What more likely to make this vast world, to stretch forth the heavens and lay the foundations of the earth, and to form these and all things of nothing, than infinite power? what more likely to communicate being, and so many degrees of happiness to so many several sorts of creatures than infinite goodness?" Addison could readily answer Tillotson's questions because he too sought his answers in nature. The essayist, even more comprehensively than the clergyman, used the term *nature* for man's entire environment—everything from the atoms to the planets, from the minutest forms of animal being to the angelic host. Accordingly each element, from the least animate to the most vital, was both ordered by and suffused with God's spirit. "Every particle of matter," Addison found, "is actuated by this Almighty Being which passes through it." And for man as well, "the Divinity is with him, and in him, and everywhere about him" (*S* 571). All of the essays written to demonstrate the Godhead were intellectualized. But each expressed a controlled joy in the omnipotent skill responsible for the natural world. Here was creativity without blemish, intricate in design, diverse in detail, sublime in wholeness. Here in nature to proclaim His glory was harmony, beautiful and predictable.[3]

Profoundly moved, Addison envisaged the immeasurable creation "as the temple of God, which he has built with his own hands, and which is filled with his presence" (*S* 565). But not content to react emotionally, he wanted also to understand and to explain why cosmic vastness evoked such admiration and finally provided evidence of a divine being. His answer was humbly speculative; it "may be," he said in *Spectator* 413, because

> the Supreme Author of our being has so formed the soul of man, that nothing but himself can be its last, adequate, and proper happiness. Because, therefore, a great part of our happiness must arise from the con-

> templation of his being, that he might give our souls a just relish of such a contemplation, he has made them naturally delight in the apprehension of what is great or unlimited. Our admiration, which is a very pleasing motion of the mind, immediately rises at the consideration of any object that takes up a great deal of room in the fancy, and, by consequence, will improve into the highest pitch of astonishment and devotion when we contemplate his nature, that is neither circumscribed by time nor place, nor to be comprehended by the largest capacity of a created being.

On this hypothesis he predicated the sublimity of an unbounded nature that inspired him and every other rational being to believe in the creative presence of God. As from a mystic impulse, his intelligence then led inexorably to the idea that the universe was the product of infinite power, prompted by infinite goodness, and located within infinite space.

Ever the popular journalist while serving as both teacher and proselyter, he faced the need to make religious abstractions intelligible to a lay audience. He conceded that the vastness of the universe, a difficult notion to assimilate, had to be related to a more familiar and manageable object. He remembered Thomas Burnet's sublimated awe before the expanse of the ocean and the height of the mountains. Like his "sacred" teacher, Addison was caught up in the joy of reverence when he wrote poetically of "the hoary Alpine hills" and "the Tyrrhene seas." More important, he responded to Burnet's suggestion that he correlate the sea, its "foaming billows" like so many "floating mountains," with the immensity of God's cosmos. At the same time he subscribed to a generally accepted inference from the *Essay concerning Human Understanding:* the greater the object, the loftier the intellectual reaction. As he surveyed the ocean, "the biggest object that he can see in motion," he added to the thought of the Cartesian Burnet and the empirical Locke measures of Longinian idealism and his own aesthetics. He therefore found it "impossible . . . to survey this world of fluid matter, without thinking on the hand that first poured it out, and made a proper channel for its reception. . . . The imagination prompts the understanding, and by the greatness of the sensible object, produces in it the idea of a being who is neither circumscribed by time nor space" (*S* 489).[4]

Along with other rationalists Addison moved from the size of the universe as evidence of supernal being to the argument from design. The latter is actually an argument from order in which the orderly whole of the universe implies an architect of absolute will and intelligence. This proof originated with Augustine's effort to Christianize the Platonic emphasis on universal harmony. Then Aquinas rephrased it in the postulate that there is a knowing "somewhat" by which our natural objects are arranged in relation to an end, and that this "somewhat" must be called God. From these scholastic beginnings, the proof was expanded by the principles of hierarchy (with its corollary of plenitude) and union. In the seventeenth century it was given mechanical precision by the Cartesians. Malebranche, for example, reasoning mathematically, equated cosmic order with "the essential and necessary will of God, according to which, and by which he wills whatever he wills, for God loves order, he wills nothing but order, his will always follows order."[5]

Addison was heir to all these contributions filling out the argument from design. He tried to soften the Cartesian interpretation, which attracted him, with his own sense of beauty and the Anglican concept of benevolence—God's boundless and loving creativity. He never quite turned his back on the geometric exactitude that Descartes or Malebranche imposed on the supernal plan. But he was sufficiently liberated to see the harmony of the universe in terms of a divine loveliness throughout the entire hierarchical scheme of being. He viewed the universe as the dramatic sanctification of order, set in motion by God's transcendence and unified by His immanence. He praised this divine harmony as the creation not of mechanism or blind chance, but of an intelligent and benign agent.[6]

Addison spent little time on the argument from design as an abstraction, although he made categorically clear his belief that the universe was a "curious and well-contrived" frame with "the same concatenation and subserviency, the same necessity and usefulness, the same beauty and harmony in all and every of its parts . . ." (*S* 543). He desired not to justify the argument but to use it for moral instruction. Indeed he would have it work as a theodicy that moved the mind to a purpose larger than itself and so allayed egocentric discontent or even grief. When he disallowed the possibility of error in the argument, he attested in *Spectator* 237 to the order of the universe, that is, to "the beautiful connections between incidents" that are separated by time and space. Yet he was too exact an empiricist, too earnest a realist, to deny "the promiscuous distribution of good and evil to the virtuous and the wicked in this world." Like a teacher who achieves rapport with a class by an occasional confession of ignorance, he was "puzzled, and at a loss what to pronounce upon so mysterious a dispensation." He could only suspend judgment, hopeful that God's order would in time justify what at the suspended moment appeared to be irrational and unjust: "Thus those parts in the moral world which have not an absolute, may yet have a relative beauty, in respect of some other parts concealed from us, but open to His eye before whom *Past, Present,* and *To come,* are set together in one point of view; and those events, the permission of which seems now to accuse His goodness, may in the consummation of things, both magnify His goodness and exalt His wisdom."

He asked, in short, that his readers remember their imperfect intelligence and inability to evaluate matters of which they knew "neither the antecedents nor the consequents, the beginning nor the end." They were to trust that God, who possessed all knowledge, was the author of all good. The argument from design was important to him as a demonstration of divinity, but it was no less significant as an example of religious need and obligation.[7]

Addison's major proof for divine existence was based on natural data. It had the advantage of current acceptance and empirical certainty that other demonstrations lacked. To enhance for his audience the familiarity of his argument, he turned to post-Restoration thinkers whose Christianity was respectable and well known, liberal and reasonable. He borrowed—as he often did—from such Latitudinarians as Tillotson, Barrow, and Bates; from natural philosophers like Boyle, Ray, Burnet, and Newton; from various Boyle lecturers, Bentley, Clarke, Derham; and of course from Locke.

At intervals, from 23 August to 25 October 1712, he took up in the *Spectator* the subsidiary theorems related to the teleological argument. He spoke fleetingly of the structure of the planets and earth, which "proclaim" themselves as "the works of such a being as we define God to be" (*S* 465). But he distrusted his ability to deal with evidence of this kind. Abstract mathematical conclusions drawn from celestial bodies and other lifeless phenomena—those unverified by the senses—worried him. Like Boyle he could never be sure that such conclusions were a "clear and cogent argument" to establish "the wisdom and design of the world." Moreover, he was humanist enough to believe that the inanimate universe bore only peripherally on man's moral condition. "Dead matter," he said by way of dismissal, was but a background for animal activity, particularly for human industry. It was thus "subservient to beings . . . conscious of their existence"; there was "no more of the one than what was necessary for the existence of the other." His central concern was "the world of life. . . . all those animals with which every part of the universe is furnished. The material world is only the shell of the universe: the world of life are its inhabitants" (*S* 519).[8]

As tangible evidence for his demonstration of a supernal being, he concentrated on the number of animal species—on their variety apparent in hierarchical arrangement and on their physiological and instinctive properties adjusted not only to survival but to constructive function. Whether through the senses, the perceptive imagination, or the understanding, he beheld "the world of life" with reverence. "The whole chasm in nature," he said, "from a plant to a man, is filled up with diverse kinds of creatures, rising one over another, by such a gentle and easy ascent, that the little transitions and deviations from one species to another, are almost insensible." Although the language is simple and colorless, its restrained awe promotes belief. Here on the scale of being were multitudes, various in form and function but all unified and made mutually dependent by "the exuberant and overflowing goodness of the Supreme Being, whose mercy extends to all his works" (*S* 519).[9]

This metaphor of continuum has as its corollary the assumption made earlier in *Spectator* 289 that only "an intelligent supervisor" could have planned for the perpetuation of each species by maintaining a "nice proportion" between male and female, birth and death. "Chance," he was sure, "could never hold the balance with so steady a hand." Indeed, it is possible to determine with reasonable assurance how the idea came to him and what use he made of it. From John Ray he learned of the "one thing necessary to the conservation of the species of animals; that is, the keeping up constantly in the world a due numerical proportion between the sexes of male and female, doth necessarily infer a superintending Providence." The speculations of another natural philosopher, William Derham, enabled Addison to move upward from the example of simple animal life to that of man himself and to relate the concept of balance to the notion of a ratio between birth and death. According to Derham, "There is a certain rate and proportion in the propagation of mankind: Such a number marry, so many are born, such a number die; in proportion to the number of persons in every nation, county or parish. And as to births . . . [there] is the proportion of males and females, not in a wide proportion, not an uncertain, accidental number at all adventures, but nearly equal."[10]

With these ideas fixed in his mind, Addison transported his readers to a London coffeehouse where Mr. Spectator asked the proprietor for last week's "bill of mortality," an account of christenings and deaths issued every Wednesday by the London Company of Parish Clerks. As the silent figure perused the bill, his first reaction was characteristically moral. He meditated on the time when he could "escape out of this world of sorrows, into that condition of existence" that offered a prospect of happiness beyond human conception. The essay's readers were now empathically relaxed in intimate smoke-filled surroundings and ennobled by comfortable thoughts of eternity. But Mr. Spectator was not yet finished with his interpretation of the bill of mortality, which he used also as an argument for divinity: "How can we, without supposing ourselves under the constant care of a Supreme Being, give any possible account for that nice proportion which we find in every great city, between the deaths and births of its inhabitants, and between the number of males, and that of females, who are brought into the world?" The bill, he said, was not only a symbol establishing God's existence but a guarantee of divine solicitude. It was a statistical promise that the human world (after all, the concern of his readers) would be neither "overcharged with multitudes" nor allowed to wither into a desert.

The approach and details of Addison's physico-theological quest for God are almost clichés of English religious thought after the Restoration. Indeed, one might write of his quest what Johnson was to say of Pope's *Essay on Man:* "Surely a man of no very comprehensive search may venture to say that he has heard all this before."[11] But Addison's intention was not to introduce untried religious ideas in a journal designed for a large and general public. What gives his proof vitality—and hence an impression of newness—is the inventiveness and dignity with which it carries his conviction: it derives energy from optimistic precepts and illustrations, and joy from a consciousness of God's vast and ordered universe. What gives it permanence is its ingenious, consistent use of religious knowledge to guide the individual and stabilize his world. And all this it does without any sacrifice of fluency and civility.

His proof gave him ammunition for repudiating the atheists, who, in their defense of chance, dismissed the idea of supernal design in the universe and its subsequent reflection in social order. It permitted him to lash out in anger or more often to laugh at the folly of men who refused to recognize "as an incontested principle" that only "a thinking and all-wise Being" could effect and maintain nature's "uniformity and consistence" (*S* 543). He ridiculed the atheists and their suppositions in both the *Tatler* and the *Spectator*. He later dramatized certain of his attitudes in *The Drummer,* where to establish Tinsel's inanity in the first scene he allowed the grotesque to boast: "Oh, I shall then have time to read you such lectures of motions, atoms, and nature—that you shall learn to think as freely as the best of us, and be convinced in less than a month, that all about us is chancework." This was a comic recapitulation of Boyle's statement that "the physical arguments of atheists [are] very few"; and it was also Addison's mocking judgment of their intellectual flabbiness.[12]

The physico-theological proof, additionally, furnished Addison with arguments for the devout. He could thus deny that mechanistic force in the universe predicated a depersonalized First Mover, that it enhanced the cause of materialism or altered the concept of a benevolent and merciful God. He could use his proofs to presuppose, as had Leibnitz before him, that in natural phenomena everything happened mechanically but at the same time metaphysically; that mechanical operations had divine origin. Moreover, Latitudinarian literature, particularly the religio-scientific works of Boyle, inspired Addison in many of the *Spectator*'s Saturday essays to embrace the idea of a God whose love effected the ordered plenitude of the universe.

But he would not be trapped into reproducing Boyle's self-defeating image of the Creator as a craftsman whose unlimited ingenuity could build a "house," a "ship," a "watch," a "fowling piece," or a "windmill." Addison recognized the need to cast aside any suggestion that God was merely a master of the slide rule and a power impersonally involved with his own creation. When, as in *Spectators* 121 and 543, he spoke of God as the "all-wise contriver," his thoughts of the deity were supramundane, divorced from neoclassic denotations of the inventor or schemer. Rather he intended the descriptive phrase to connote a grand, infinite designer, who allowed his measureless control of mechanical principles to function only as an instrument of bounty. The God of the *Spectator* expressed an infinite love for all his handiwork and a "goodness . . . of so communicative a nature, that it seems to delight in the conferring of existence upon every degree of perceptive being" (*S* 519).[13]

For all the practicality of the physico-theological proof and its empirically derived data, Addison occasionally pushed against its restrictions. In one instance he argued for the existence of an ascending order of creatures superior to man. He did so even against Locke's warning that such speculation, without a basis in clear, distinct ideas, was idle hypothesis. And from time to time he felt the incongruity of sorting out tangible, sensory material for proof of an immaterial being.[14] Throughout the *Spectator* he scattered demonstrations for the existence of God that, while relying on the light of reason, differed in approach and technique from the physico-theological argument. One of these was a psychological proof deeply embedded in human consciousness and spiritual need; a second was based on the philosophical concept of eternity; and a third was derived from ideas on the immortality of the soul. It is almost as if, by vanquishing disbelief among his readers, Addison wished to compensate for his failure to take religious orders.

His psychological proof for the being of God has a double focus. According to it, God exists because man is incapable of living as a moral agent without Him and because man experiences divinity within himself. The psychological was the most personal of Addison's demonstrations. It allowed him a high degree of intimacy with an audience that shared his weakness and, like him, required the support of God's loving kindness. It allowed him to portray man as a being whose grimness tempered spectatorial optimism, which could otherwise have become cloying. His portrait showed a creature beaten down by fear, envy, and ignorance, "a very helpless and a very wretched being," beset by calamities and dangers "which he could not foresee, nor have prevented, had he foreseen them" (*S* 441). The purpose of his short and joyless life eludes man, who sees existence as little more than an occupancy that lasts only long enough for him to beget progeny. For all his power to hope, he is frightened by the suspicion that death alone is conclusive. As Addison filled in more and more of the details of the portrait and identified himself with it, he commented almost entreatingly, "that were there any doubt of a Providence, yet it certainly would be very desirable there should be such a Being of infinite wisdom and goodness, on whose direction we might rely in the conduct of human life" (*S* 293). For a short moment he reveals himself as a petitioner who, without his usual calm and self-reliance, seeks desperately for strength from God.[15]

This psychological brief, published on 5 February 1712, was far from an irrefutable demonstration. It was an intimation based on yearning for God's certainty, because man could not survive either his flawed nature or his external trials without supernal intercession. Although it reflected an egoistic attitude toward divine power, this proof was also a humble one that had been fostered by religious thinkers pre-eminent since the Restoration. Like Tillotson, Bates, and Clarke, Addison acknowledged that his optimistic vision of the universe was sometimes darkened by the specter of man's agony.[16]

While Latitudinarian dicta encouraged his psychological proof for divine existence, he was nevertheless anxious about its subjectivity. Subsequently, he tried to test it empirically. A good man, he said in *Spectator* 571, experienced the essence of God in his virtuous thoughts, the comforts and refreshments that his soul enjoyed, and all the "ravishing joys and inward satisfactions" that carried him toward truth. Here, as in his other religious essays in the *Spectator,* he imbues an orthodox concept with a multiple function and couches its statement in prose familiar in tone and deceptively simple. Thus he called into play the doctrine of divine immanence without naming it and used the doctrine first to support his psychological proof for God's existence and then to teach the moral lesson that always followed from each of his demonstrations. Emboldened by the precedent of Seneca and Scripture, the truth of nature and revelation, he reminded his readers: "There is a Holy Spirit residing in us, who watches and observes both good and evil men, and will treat us after the same manner that we treat Him."

He concluded his psychological argument for divinity on Friday, 23 July 1714. His next effort to affirm the divine presence centered on a demonstration recognized in his day as "a metaphysical abstracted proof of a deity." Because it was based on the philosophical notion of eternity and surrounded by abstruse speculation, he regarded its subject matter as proper for intellectual pondering rather than for pious meditation. He presented its details therefore with scholarly detachment, an objectivity that is not often found in his religious papers. The argument itself, he knew, had long been debated "by men famous for their penetration and force of understanding," but he apparently chose Locke as the immediate source for his own troubled hypothesis. According to the philosopher, man knows "by an intuitive certainty, that bare *nothing can no more produce any real being, than it can be equal to two right angles.* If, therefore, we know there is some real being, and that nonentity cannot produce any real being, it is an evident demonstration, that *from eternity there has been something;* since what was not from eternity had a beginning; and what had a beginning must be produced by something else." In his essay Addison elaborated on Locke's elliptic, cragged description while codifying its distinct but related premises: that obviously no being is self-created, for otherwise it must have acted before it was, a patent contradiction; that consequently something must have been "from all eternity"; that no created being, according to empirical notions of time and duration, could have existed from all eternity; and that "this eternal Being must therefore be the great author of nature, the Ancient of Days, who, being at an infinite distance in his perfections from all finite and created beings, exists in a quite different manner from them, and in a manner of which they can have no idea" (*S* 590).[17]

This, Addison's only attempt to use a metaphysical argument, appears in one of his last *Spectator* essays. As a proof, it was recondite without providing certainty; yet its frequent appearance in works other than his own made it one that he thought proper for a comprehensive periodical. Journalistic duty in this instance is not to be confused with private conviction, and the essayist made his reservations apparent, aware that he was in good company. From Boyle he had learned that such a proof was inferior, dependent on "so irrelative" a quality as to be founded on "mere speculation." Tillotson had warned him that it was a subject of disputation much favored by the Schoolmen and hence suspect. From his personal need for God's assurance, Addison sensed that such a demonstration began in arrogance and led to intellectual quibbling. As if he felt that its erudition stood between himself and the Divine, his final words on the argument from eternity came not from the "natural dictates of reason" spelled out by his philosophical sources but from scriptural authority. The piety of his conclusion in no way mitigated an uneasiness obvious throughout *Spectator* 590. Nor did it make more germane the "one useful inference" that he elicited from the argument: the need to be grateful for "the good will, which prompted our Creator to adapt existence to beings, in whom it is not necessary." This moral message he had used so many times before and for so many different purposes that at this late point in the *Spectator* it seems only perfunctory.[18]

His demonstrations of divinity were in varying degrees exercises in stern intellectuality and piety, in wisdom and virtue. For the most part these were derivative proofs recast from the thinking of others. Only the related argument, focused on the immortality of the soul, has a ring of originality, and then but in certain details. He proposed to convince his readers that the immortality of the soul was beyond question and that the certainty of this truth was in itself proof of the greater one, that God exists. Such was the assumption he hoped to develop from the simple premise earlier enunciated by Tillotson: "He that goes about to prove the soul's immortality, supposeth the existence of a Deity, that there is a God." Addison felt certain that were he able to establish the deathlessness of the human spirit, he could then presume the being of God. The task was a difficult one that demanded long consideration. He therefore approached the problem as early as 7 July 1711 and as late as 29 September 1714; during those three years he dealt with it in casual statements and entire essays.[19]

He argued for the soul's immortality by building on an old and often contradictory tradition. His borrowings extended from Socrates and Plato to the early Church Fathers and Augustine; from Aristotle to Aquinas; from the physico-theologians such as Boyle and Bentley to Latitudinarian bishops and chaplains like Clarke, who had been accused of heterodoxy. Influenced by some more than by others, he cast aside any premise contrary to rational Christian belief. For example, he was attracted to the Platonic vision of immortality with its ideal of virtuous service, but he did not accept its corollaries of the soul's pre-existence or the doctrine of opposites. If in the course of his demonstration he minimized details gathered from classical philosophy, he also tried to keep his argument free of fideistic pressure. Hence, he held himself aloof from the controversy over bodily resurrection associated with the orthodox interpretation of immortality. And because he seldom alluded to the Sacrifice and the Redemption of Christ, which made glorious the hope of eternal life for man, his talk about immortality comes close to being but bare philosophy. Seemingly comfortable only in the moderate piety of a Tillotson or Bates, he summarized the Latitudinarian postulates for the immortality of the soul:

> *First,* From the nature of the soul itself, and particularly its immateriality; which though not absolutely necessary to the eternity of its duration, has . . . been evinced to almost a demonstration.
>
> *Secondly,* From its passions and sentiments, as particularly from its love of existence, its horrour of annihilation, and its hopes of immortality, with that secret satisfaction which it finds in the practice of virtue, and that uneasiness which follows in it upon the commission of vice.
>
> *Thirdly,* From the nature of the Supreme Being, whose justice, goodness, wisdom, and veracity are all concerned in this great point. [*S* 111][20]

He stated his précis flatly, perhaps because he was restrained by the metaphysical nature of a subject that he tried to handle experientially, or because he was oppressed by the weight of authoritative opinion, most of which he had to ignore. But more likely the pedestrian prose of his summary resulted from haste. He skimmed over what was commonly known in order to argue for his own vision of the immortal life, which he did not "remember to have seen opened and improved by others who have written on this subject." In romanticized language he contemplated the immortality of the soul from its "perpetual progress . . . to its perfection, without a possibility of ever arriving at it." But he was in fact not quite the innovator he claimed to be in *Spectator* 111. Perhaps he responded subconsciously to the biblical intimation of progressive change for souls in the life hereafter: "But we all, with open face beholding as in a glass the glory of the Lord, are changed into the same image from glory to glory, even as by the Spirit of the Lord." Perhaps he remembered and extended the medieval and patristic image of man's pilgrimage from this life to the next, an image given Protestant sanction in such works as Donne's *Of the Progress of the Soul* and Bunyan's *Pilgrim's Progress.* Immediately relevant for Addison, however, was Henry More's argument, which brushes a traditional orthodoxy with a new concept:

> For considering how small degrees of purification the souls of almost all men get in this life, even theirs who pass vulgarly for honest and good

men, it will plainly follow that very few arrive to the aethereal vehicle immediately upon quitting their terrestrial body, that being a privilege that has appurtained to none but very noble and heroical spirits indeed, of which history records but very few. But that there may be degrees of purity and excellency in the aerial bodies, is a thing that is not to be denied, so that a just Nemesis will find out every one after death.[21]

The concept of progression hinted by More was atypical of Protestantism, which held to a belief in the static perfection of the heavenly life. Not only did reformational eschatology embrace Christ's view of alternative and absolute destinies (heaven and hell), but it wished to avoid association with the Catholic doctrine of purgatory. But where More implied the "privilege" of happy alteration, Addison asserted that the human potential for growth—moral, emotional, and intellectual—terminated neither in this life nor the next. With rhapsodic intensity he wrote: "To look upon the soul as going on from strength to strength, to consider that she is to shine forever with new accessions of glory, and brighten to all eternity: that she will be still adding virtue to virtue, and knowledge to knowledge, carries in it something wonderfully agreeable to that ambition which is natural to the mind of man. Nay, it must be a prospect pleasing to God himself, to see his creation for ever beautifying in his eyes, and drawing nearer to him, by greater degrees of resemblance" (*S* 111).

Although the immortality of the soul was a subject important enough for his last contribution to the *Spectator,* he did not discuss further the concept of man's endless perfectibility. Rather *Spectator* 600 described in sensuous biblical imagery the rapture of the soul when it is released from the body and for the first time is able to fulfill all its faculties of understanding, will, memory, imagination, "the senses both outward and inward." As Addison warmed to his vision of hope, he conjured up the heavenly life as a state that promised not perfection but perfect happiness for the whole man. Indeed, his ultimate proof for spiritual immortality depended simply on the belief that God "has thus naturally qualified the soul for it, and made it a being capable of receiving so much bliss." This condition alone, he suggested, established the eternality of the human spirit, which, as Richard Bentley had written earlier, "doth necessarily evince the existence of a supreme and spiritual being."[22]

It must have become apparent to Addison that what began casually—the introduction of religious subjects into the *Spectator*—had caught on. These discussions compelled interest as long as they were comfortably sandwiched between essays dealing with less ponderous and more secular matters. Gradually he must have conceived a plan to present with unobtrusive regularity chapters for a layman's manual of piety, detailing and demonstrating the bases of rational Anglicanism. He knew from his reading in many such manuals that his would be incomplete if it did not treat the divine attributes. For the sake of wholeness he therefore devoted one essay to an analysis of how man framed his ideas of divinity and another, about two years later, to a moral disquisition on omniscience and omnipresence.

He was reluctant to tackle the problem of the divine attributes, lest he become like Simonides, who, "the more he contemplated the nature of the Deity, found that he waded but the more out of his depth; and that he lost himself in the thought, instead of finding an end of it" (*S* 531). He himself probably felt little need to catalogue God's perfections, for he was convinced by Barrow's supposition that when one professes belief in Him, all His excellencies are acknowledged. And what mattered to Addison was belief, sturdy and unfaltering. Moreover, he was rarely anthropomorphic in his thinking. Because he regarded God's nature as perfect and infinite, he judged it close to presumption for man to deduce from his own motives and characteristics those of the Godhead. He believed in a God whose order he could never fully fathom but in whose "overflowing" goodness and wisdom he trusted (*S* 519).[23]

He therefore isolated for discussion only two of the divine attributes. His choice must have been dictated by duty to the social good; that is, he intended to reassure those who were troubled by the notion of a universe functioning with machinelike precision and made up of a plurality of inhabited worlds scattered through bewildering reaches of space. If thinkers as bold as Pascal and Newton could become frightened by the eternal silence of endless matter, then what must be the anxiety of ordinary men everywhere? Addison therefore wrote to restore the security of those who thought themselves "overlooked amidst the immensity of nature, and lost among that infinite variety of creatures, which in all probability swarm through all these immeasurable regions of matter." He countered their pessimism with the vision of a God who "passes through, actuates and supports the whole frame of nature" and who in His omnipresence is united to "every motion that arises in the whole material world" (*S* 565). Drawing his evidence from natural philosophy and Holy Writ, he reminded his readers that God was not separated from them but was in His omniscience privy to all their thoughts. Just as he made each demonstration for the existence of God serve an ethical purpose, so in his study of the divine attributes he clarified man's need to obey a protective being who transcends time and space.[24]

Addison's loyalty to the "religion of his country" was without question. He respected the ecclesiastical structure; he admired the devotional services of the church and the expression of humble goodness in the Book of Common Prayer. Unlike many of his time he customarily treated Anglican clergymen—whether High or Low, Tory or Whig—with deference. Whenever the church was under attack, he rose quickly to defend the institution, its ritualistic observances, and its dogmas. But throughout the *Spectator* in his own inquiry after truth, he stressed not parochialism but the principles on which all Protestants, and indeed all Christians, could agree. The tenets that he proclaimed were a willing submission to the authority of Scripture, a belief in the Trinity and Christ the Redeemer, confidence in the immortality of the soul, and a discriminating practice of charity. His call to worship was always moral and for the most part rational. It was given both direction and dimension by the Lockean premise that "our proper employment lies in those enquiries, and in that sort of knowledge which is most suited to our natural capacities, and carries in it our greatest interest, i.e., the condition of our eternal estate." Ethics—the studied pursuit of the good life—was for Locke and Addison "the proper science and business of mankind in general."[25] Addison's religious statement sometimes suggests the sobriety of mathematical proof and even the cogency of an exercise in civil liberty. But this restraint is counterbalanced by his adamant refusal to separate private spirituality from a concern for the social whole or to indulge in empty ritualism at the expense of his own soul.

AFTERWORD

ARMORED GENIUS

THE products of a clubbable, gregarious age, many Augustan authors attract almost as much attention to their personalities as to their writings. Addison, for whom the printed page is the only allowable intimacy between himself and his readers, appears as a public man—political pamphleteer, dramatist, versifier, and essayist. The essential human being is so obscured that it is not possible strongly to like or dislike him. Mr. Spectator is much closer to us than Mr. Addison. When we turn to his letters for an expression of personality, we are disappointed, for his correspondence, devoted largely to official business, is not often lightened by the easy candor of friendship.

He was taciturn among strangers or rivals, and yet his contemporaries testify that among acquaintances he was a companionable man. Lady Mary Wortley Montagu thought him "the best company in the world." For several years he enjoyed amiable exchanges with Pope, according to whom he "was perfect good company with intimates" and a "charming" conversationalist. Swift, a lifelong friend despite bitter political differences, would have concurred. Such conviviality as Addison exhibited, however, was not often released before the wine bottles were unstopped. Until the glasses were filled several times, he held his thoughts in prolonged silence, even in the congenial setting of a tavern.[1]

The intimates of his late evening hours were not necessarily bound to him by ties of affection, mutual esteem, or trust. Indeed, lasting associations require a reciprocity in which he was reluctant to engage. This may help to explain why he was seemingly more comfortable with mediocre dependents than among men of strong will and talent. He was "mute," for example, when he was with men such as Halifax and Stanhope, whom he acknowledged to be his superiors. He could not help being overshadowed by the genius and volatile personalities of Swift and Pope. But he dominated a circle of lesser men. Exacting deference from those he befriended, he could patronize or abuse them. He let young men like Thomas Burnet or Ambrose Philips play cupbearer to his Jove; he rewarded them with journalistic assignments and, in the case of Philips, even with lodgings in his own house. He had tolerant contempt for the poetry of Eustace Budgell; yet he was willing to correct his cousin's epilogue to *The Distressed Mother* and to reward him with political employment. The unequal association ended in 1717, when the younger man dared to quarrel—against his patron's wishes—with Lord Bolton.[2] And in that same year the friendship between Steele and the now powerful secretary of state began to crack so that by 1719 the split was irreparable.

Behind Addison's correct exterior lurked a formidable capacity for pique and animus. His vindictiveness, however, often yielded to the demands of utility. After Tickell, for example, defected from his "senate" in 1713, Addison gave no sign of nursing a grudge: journalistic ability, such as Tickell's, forwarded Whig aims, and he was prepared to welcome the prodigal son when he returned. Although he elicited little affection from his coterie, some genuinely appreciated his literary or organizational talents. Others, however, fawned on him as a source of political doles. And still others subjected him to hostility that ranged from loathing to backstairs gossip. They questioned his virility and made broad jokes about his pallid marriage.[3] Although the privacy he cherished was invaded by slanderous rumors, he concealed whatever he knew or felt about this malice.

His austere façade seldom betrays a human failing. It is unimportant that in 1713, when he wrote a propagandistic paean to port, he also permitted numerous advertisements for French wines to appear in the *Guardian*. And—along with many other respectable men, among them Sir Robert Walpole—he had claret and burgundy smuggled through Dublin to stock his Whig cellar. It is clear that as did other teachers of morality about whom Imlac spoke, Addison discoursed like an angel and lived like a man. He wore several masks, whether deliberately or compulsively; and who the real man is we can rarely be sure.

Although few men of his time were privileged to penetrate the "stiff sort of silence," as Pope called his dignified restraint, or to enjoy his conversational wit, Addison perpetuated himself in his writings. He tried to clothe the feeling individual in armor, but in Johnson's judgment, he was destined "to pass through futurity protected only by his genius."[4] And his genius is not inconsiderable. In his periodicals, especially in his social exegeses, he defines himself as a human being; in them he glows with rational complaisance, a virtue that he aimed for in his own life and recommended as the great palliative for his world. "Complaisance," he wrote in *Guardian* 162,

> renders a superior amiable, an equal agreeable, and an inferior acceptable. It smooths distinction, sweetens conversation, and makes everyone in the company pleased with himself. It produces good-nature and mutual benevolence, encourages the timorous, soothes the turbulent, humanizes the fierce, and distinguishes a society of civilized persons from a confusion of savages. In a word, complaisance is a virtue that blends all orders of men together in a friendly intercourse of words and actions, and is suited to that equality in human nature, which everyone ought to consider, so far as is consistent with the order and economy of the world.

The statement is idealistic. Setting a premium upon civilized coexistence, it urges the give-and-take of tolerance and fair play. At the same time, Addison puts his readers on guard against illusory appearance. The ideal human condition, he intimated, should not be confused with man's state as it is. The civilization he soberly viewed was shadowed by unhappiness, anguish, loneliness, and poverty. He did not minimize these miseries, but tried to make them supportable without upsetting the order and economy of the world. Throughout his periodicals he quietly celebrated the status quo. He was the intelligent observer looking with approval at the rise of Sir Andrew while preaching to the gentry the need for social commitment and to the poor the virtue of obedient toil. Along with the merchant he plainly revered the establishment and its props—the Bank of England, the Exchange, public credit, the Acts of Uniformity, Toleration, and Settlement—indeed, whatever in his opinion contributed to a "just and regular economy."

Yet he never closed his eyes to the dangers inherent in the behavior of his City friends. As this group extended its influence over England, he saw his country's vitality weakened by greed and venality, its good will by competitive ruthlessness. He watched British patriotism reduced to insularity, and economic daring bloodied by wars and slavery. He witnessed the decline of religious fortitude, as Anglican loyalties were diverted to faction and faith was made lukewarm by pious truisms. But while he deplored this gathering degeneration, his usual reaction was no more than restrained perturbation. His expressions of anger startle, if only because they are so unexpected as to seem intrusive, alien to the dispassion of their creator. Although he pre-empted the right to be a censor, the conscience of a comfortable generation, he regarded his country's stability as too precious to be endangered by radical criticism. He had no serious quarrel with his environment; he was confident that useful meaning would be extracted even from defects in the social fabric, which would somehow serve the irrefutable order and economy of the world that he enjoyed.

As one who generally spoke for and conformed to majority opinion, he propagandized any value or law or juridical decision in support of "nations, professions, and communities," those very groups detested by Swift. With man in the mass as his principal subject, Addison noted intellectual pretension and moral pettiness but subordinated them to evidence of positive worth. Just as his attitude toward society is general rather than particular, so is it genial rather than captious. In his eyes the human species, though far from perfect, is more good than bad, more regenerate than lost; it is redeemable rather than hopelessly corrupt. Only after he had accounted for the well-being of the whole did he turn his attention to "John, Peter, Thomas, and so forth."[5] In terms of the democratic ideal, as we interpret it, he can hope for little sympathetic understanding. But he must be examined by the prevailing standards of his culture, no matter how distant they may seem from ours. He is important today, not because his ethos is the same as ours, but because he illuminates a vital age out of which our ethos has gradually evolved.

And he is important to us as a man of letters whose prose style and intellectual attitudes are perfectly reconciled. His moderation is voiced in language that suggests the ease of conversation and usually avoids passion and metaphorical richness. His is, as Johnson said, "the model of the middle style; on grave subjects not formal, on light occasions not groveling; pure without scrupulosity, and exact without apparent elaboration; always equable, and always easy, without glowing words or pointed sentences. Addison never deviates from his track to snatch a grace; he seeks no ambitious ornaments, and tries no hazardous innovations. His page is always luminous, but never blazes in unexpected splendour."[6] His style, in short, is that of a man secure in the middle station against both the pull of cold rationality and rampant imagination, who persuaded with tact and taught with humility.

In finely crafted essays, moreover, he captured the spirit of his times as no one else was able to do. As a social thinker he exhibits both the weakness and the enlightenment of Augustan England. Although lacking intellectual originality, he had a genius for embracing and communicating contemporary social issues, both large and small. His literary concern with the fops and their ladies was no less than his concern with England's mercantile wars and Protestant succession. He had a sure instinct for singling out ideas that were much in men's minds and for explaining them in a style that was at once plain and relaxed. His readers identified themselves with the point of view of his essays even as he identified himself with the thinking of the public which, paradoxically, he helped formulate.

Satire figures in his essays, but it is so modified by complaisance that it rarely bites and almost always supports his balanced estimate of mankind. At times, indeed, the satire becomes so painless as to be indistinguishable from pleasant comedy. The class types that he drew are the outgrowth of his usually unembittered and mildly amused social experience. Some—like the Tory fox hunter, the High Church publican, and Second-Sighted Sawney—want credibility. Others, however, especially Sir Roger, Sir Andrew, and Will Wimble, are characters memorable for their individuality. Simultaneously, each represents a large segment of mankind and behaves in a manner indigenous to his world, if not always to ours.

As evocations of a serene and informed imagination, they inhabit a fascinating, variable gallery. We cannot help sensing through them the presence of Addison, but it is Addison the observer and artist, the barely visible author. The private man—husband, brother, friend—is not even hinted at; he seems to move in altogether another orbit. We may regret a division of personality, but it is precisely this split that made his literary achievement possible. By withholding his private life, he turns attention almost exclusively to the printed page, the outlet for his creative energy.

It would be rash to attribute to him the poetic fire or soaring passion of a Stephen Dedalus, but he has a similar need for aesthetic distance and for effacing himself. Without achieving the absolute detachment of Joyce's hero, the essayist is triumphantly remote, having nearly refined himself out of our awareness. His characters and their ideas are therefore appealingly direct. We can imagine ourselves in a dialogue with the keen-eyed Spectator, or the Freeholder loyal to George I, or even the Old Whig devoted to the shibboleth of mixed government. On first acquaintance we are inclined to be suspicious of Addisonian plasticity. But we soon learn that just because he is pliable, he can fulfill his special talent. For the man who becomes smoothly enfolded in majority opinion also effaces himself to good purpose. By doing so, he loses himself in the crowd and leaves the monument of his work to tower in the open.

Like any public servant, Addison early reconciled himself to certain compromises that were an inevitable part of social obligation as well as of personal success. Infrequently his compromises were forced by a desire to play to power; more often they were dictated by loyalty to a beleaguered patron or ministry or party. But whatever induced them, they fell—usually but not always—into that gray area where moral principles are not at issue. Tempering his compromises with a humane interest in his fellow Englishman, he geared them to the cause of moral utility. He worked, for instance, to fulfill Whig ambitions but not at the cost of orderly government. Or if his sense of justice was party-directed, it did not dilute his belief in British freedom and the civil rights of the individual. As a Christian, he made devotion integral to his daily existence and rejected the nominal faith of many contemporaries. His piety sometimes smacked of patriotism, but it was nonetheless genuine. He made no secret of his respect for public and private wealth. But while he indulged his taste for property and restrained luxury, he remembered his indebtedness to the community and the state. Finally, his praise of good breeding was inseparable from his conviction that civility is the antidote to instinctual self-interest and the basis of an amiable and benevolent society.

He was at home in his world, recording and sometimes even rising above the identifying marks of the age. He observed this world with concern, his meliorating attention more on folly than vice. As a spectator who had the insights of a historian and the conscience of a moral philosopher, he exposed the trivial and fleeting, the silly and mean. He did not believe that his was the best of all possible worlds, but he hoped to effect a moral reawakening that would refresh the human spirit through good will and gladden the heart through profit.

APPENDIX

SHORT TITLES

NOTES

BIBLIOGRAPHY

INDEX

APPENDIX

THE 1714 EDITION OF

THE TRIAL OF COUNT TARIFF

THE polemic intention of *The Trial of Count Tariff* is emphasized in the 1714 edition.[1] Making only minor changes in the new edition, Addison, for example, allows 17 June to stand erroneously for the day on which the treaty was defeated. But in the 1714 edition there is a postscript dated 28 July, from London, which reads:

Sir,
Liberty is so invaluable a Jewel, and so much the Birth-right of every Englishman, as well as the Glory of the present Reign, that 'tis not doubted you'll so far approve of the inclos'd, as to incert it, it being the Copy of an Epilogue in Praise of Liberty, pronounc'd with wonderful Applause at a late Dramatick Performance of several young Gentlemen, who for their own Diversion Acted the Play call'd Julius Caesar.

> Wonder no more Great *Julius Caesar* fell,
> No *Brutus* strove *Rome's* Bondage to expell;
> Mankind's obliged Invasion to suppress,
> His noblest boast of Freedom to confess.
> How vile's the Wretch by Slav'ry made Tame,
> Who dares not glory in the Patriot's Name,
> Nor in his Country's Cause, just Liberty proclaim!
> 'Tis pity they who Liberty despise,
> Shou'd want a Tyrant for their Exercise:
> 'Tis pity but they shou'd be all oppress'd,
> Who covet Chains, and made themselves the Just.
> As they who scorn the Light, should never see;
> So they who wou'd be Slaves shou'd ne'er be free.
> The best of Subjects still to Law appeal;
> But if oppress'd in Virtue's Cause, Rebel;
> Will Force to Force, and Right to Wrong oppose,
> And Nature's Laws engage with Nature's Foes:
> Such to the Parent Monarch Reverence pay,

His just Commands most willingly obey,
But scorn those Scepters which the Tyrants sway.
Mountains of murther'd Heroes bury'd lye,
Beneath the Column of our Liberty.
You Britain's, who this Liberty enjoy.
Oh! keep it safe, do not your selves destroy:
Our Fathers kept the spotless Virgin chaste,
The Monument of their Immortal Actions past:
Our Fathers Blood this Promise does require:
That we shou'd hand it down again entire:
Posterity wou'd curse us in our Graves,
That we left free ourselves, shou'd leave 'em Slaves.
LIBERTY is Life, and every Passive Slave,
Moves only in the Narrow Circle of his Grave:
'Tis Natures brightest, choicest Gift to Men,
Born in their Blood, and run thro' ev'rey Vein;
And all but Mad men will the Gift Maintain.

Shakespeare's *Julius Caesar* probably was performed at Oxford or Cambridge, many of whose "young gentlemen" and fellows were politically active, especially in the election of 1714. And the epilogue, a bad imitation of the sober liberalism of *Cato,* was probably written by a Whig attached to one of the universities or having close university ties. If an Oxonian, he might have been Henry Carey, Thomas Tickell, Edward Young, or Digby Cotes; if a Cantabrigian, Laurence Eusden.[2] Of these possibilities, Eusden seems the likeliest, for he courted Addison and Steele for at least three years, during which he contributed letters that Steele incorporated in *Spectators* 54 (2 May 1711), 78 (30 May 1711), and 87 (9 June 1711). *Spectator* 618 (Philips, Tickell; 10 November 1714) mentions "an epistolary poem, just published by Mr. Eusden on the king's accession to the throne: wherein [are] many . . . noble and beautiful strokes of poetry." Eusden contributed another letter to *Guardian* 124 (3 August 1713), and a translation from Claudian to *Guardians* 127 (6 August 1713) and 164 (18 September 1713). He wrote commendatory verses for the seventh edition of *Cato* as well (see the advertisement in *Guardian* 92 of 26 June 1713). And in 1714 he wrote and had published *A Letter to Mr. Addison, on the King's Accession to the Throne.* Because of his loyalty to the Whigs and to Addison, he was made poet laureate on 24 December 1718, largely—it is to be suspected—through the intercession of Addison himself.

Regardless of the authorship of the postscript, *The Trial of Count Tariff* continued to serve as a party pamphlet. It was reissued in 1714 in order to meet certain political contingencies. By July 1714 the friction between Harley and St. John "visibly prognosticated an approaching change in the ministry" and the queen, as was generally known, had not long to live.[3] In this critical year the Whigs looked forward to the general election for added numbers in Parliament and for control of the ministry. They began their campaign considerably before the election, contending that the Tory ministry, ignorant of commercial affairs, had betrayed the interests of England. The Whigs were aided by the parliamentary debate on the Tory-written Anglo-Spanish commercial treaty of 1713. The debate, which began on 30 June 1714, brought forth much scandalous information on the treaty and on Arthur Moore's criminal manipulation of it.[4] When Addison reissued *The Trial of Count Tariff* in the midsummer of 1714, he allowed his readers to know that he had prophesied the disastrous consequences of the Assiento, also the handiwork of Arthur Moore. At the same time he drew attention to the inadequacies of the Spanish trade by reviewing those of the French trade, for which the same Tory ministry was responsible. Finally, the postscript to this new issue emphasized the 1714 Whig election cry "The Succession in Danger" and the party's love of liberty, limited monarchy, constitutional law, and natural rights. Each of these shibboleths was silently contrasted with the alleged Tory doctrines of nonresistance, passive obedience, and hereditary right.

Practically, *The Trial of Count Tariff* performed in 1714 as much of an election service to the Whig cause as it did in 1713. Apparently Addison was only too willing, as were most Whigs, to turn Tory handling of trade agreements into a *cause célèbre,* into "a DOCTOR SACHEVERELL."

SHORT TITLES

[Except for individual sermons in collected works, the date of first publication appears in brackets if an edition other than the first is listed.]

WORKS BY ADDISON

F	*Freeholder* [1715–16], in *Works,* vols. 4, 5
G	*Guardian* [1713], in *Works,* vol. 4
Letters	Walter Graham, ed., *The Letters of Joseph Addison* (Oxford, 1941)
MW	A. C. Guthkelch, ed., *The Miscellaneous Works of Joseph Addison,* 2 vols. (London, 1914)
OW	*Old Whig* [1719], in *Works,* vol. 5
Remarks	*Remarks on Several Parts of Italy, etc.* [1705], in *MW,* vol. 2
S	Donald F. Bond, ed., *Spectator* [1711–12, 1714], 5 vols. (Oxford, 1965)
T	*Tatler* [1709–11], in *Works,* vol. 2
Trial	*The Late Trial and Conviction of Count Tariff* [1713], in *MW,* vol. 2
War	*The Present State of the War, and the Necessity of an Augmentation, Considered* [1708], in *MW,* vol. 2
WE	*Whig Examiner* [1710], in *Works,* vol. 4
Works	Henry G. Bohn, ed., *The Works of Joseph Addison,* with notes by Richard Hurd, D.D., 6 vols. (London, 1877–78)

OTHER WORKS

Barbon, *Discourse*	Nicholas Barbon, *A Discourse of Trade* [1690], in *A Reprint of Economic Tracts,* ed. Jacob H. Hollander (Baltimore, 1905)

Barrow, *Works*	Isaac Barrow, *The Works of the Late Learned Isaac Barrow . . .*, 3 vols. (London, 1700)
Bates, *Works*	William Bates, *The Works of the Late Reverend and Learned W. Bates* (London, 1700)
Bentley, *Confutation*	Richard Bentley, *A Confutation of Atheism* [1692], in Letsome and Nicholl, *Defence*, vol. 1
Berkeley, *Works*	A. A. Luce and T. E. Jessop, eds., *The Works of George Berkeley, Bishop of Cloyne*, 9 vols. (London, 1948–57)
Boyer, *History*	Abel Boyer, *The History of the Life and Reign of Queen Anne* (London, 1722)
Boyer, *State*	Abel Boyer, *The Political State of Great Britain*, 38 vols. (London, 1711–29); vol. 5 (1713), vol. 6 (1713), vol. 8 (1714)
Burnet, *History*	Gilbert Burnet, *The History of His Own Time* [1724–34], 2d ed., 6 vols. (Oxford, 1833)
Child, *New Discourse*	Josiah Child, *A New Discourse of Trade* [1693], (London, 1740)
Defoe, *Crusoe*	Daniel Defoe, *The Life and Strange Surprising Adventures of Robinson Crusoe, of York, Mariner; The Farther Adventures of Robinson Crusoe;* and *Serious Reflections during the Life and Surprising Adventures of Robinson Crusoe, with His Vision of the Angelic World* [1719–20], ed. George A. Aitken, 3 vols. (London, 1895)
Dryden, *Poems*	James Kinsley, ed., *The Poems of John Dryden*, 4 vols. (Oxford, 1958)
HMC, *Portland*	Historical Manuscripts Commission, *The Manuscripts of His Grace the Duke of Portland*, 10 vols. (1891–1931); vol. 4 (London, 1897), vol. 5 (London, 1899)
Hooker, *Polity*	Richard Hooker, *Of the Laws of Ecclesiastical Polity* [1594], *Eight Books* (London, 1662)
HR	*The Historical Register*, 23 vols. (London, 1717–[39]); vol. 1 (1717), vol. 2 (1717), vol. 4 (1719). Also 2 vols. (London, 1724)

Letsome and Nicholl, *Defence*	Sampson Letsome and John Nicholl, eds., *A Defence of Natural and Revealed Religion: Being a Collection of the Sermons Preached at the Lecture Founded by the Honourable Robert Boyle,* 3 vols. (London, 1739). Bracketed inserts refer to dates of delivery.
Locke, *Second Treatise*	John Locke, *Second Treatise of Government* [1690], in *Two Treatises of Government,* ed. Thomas I. Cook (New York, 1947)
PH	*Cobbett's Parliamentary History of England* ..., 36 vols. (London, 1806–20); vol. 6 (1810), vol. 7 (1811)
South, *Sermons*	Robert South, *Thirty-Six Sermons and Discourses on Several Subjects and Occasions,* 5th ed., 2 vols. (London, 1728)
Steele, *Englishman*	Richard Steele, *Englishman* [1713–14, 1715], ed. Rae Blanchard (Oxford, 1955)
Steele, *Tracts*	Richard Steele, *Tracts and Pamphlets,* ed. Rae Blanchard (Baltimore, 1944)
Swift, *Correspondence*	Harold Williams, ed., *The Correspondence of Jonathan Swift,* 5 vols. (Oxford, 1963–65)
Temple, *Works*	William Temple, *The Works of Sir William Temple* ..., 4 vols. (London, 1770)
Tillotson, *Works*	John Tillotson, *The Works of the Most Reverend Dr. John Tillotson* ..., 5th ed., 3 vols. (London, 1735)

NOTES

INTRODUCTION. THE MIDDLE PATH

1. Samuel Johnson, *The History of Rasselas, Prince of Abyssinia* [1759], chap. 1.
2. See *T* 192.
3. Aristotle *Politics* (ed. Richard McKeon; New York, 1941) 1. 2. 1253a31–32, 2.
4. Alexander Pope, *An Essay on Man* [1733, 1734], bk. 3, l. 114. See *T* 117.
5. Pope, *Windsor-Forest* [1713], ll. 13–16.

1. THE SQUIRE AND THE MERCHANT

1. Daniel Defoe, *Crusoe,* 1:107, 246–47; and *The Family Instructor* [1715], 8th ed. (London, 1720), 1:208–9; Rev. Richard Steele, *The Religious Tradesman* [1684], (Charlestown, Mass., 1804), pp. 4–6.
2. For similar approval of the middle class, see Defoe, *Crusoe,* 1:2–4; and *The Complete English Tradesman,* 2 vols. (London, 1726–27), pt. 1, 2:106–7; Richard Steele, *The Conscious Lovers* [1722], (London, 1723), act 1, sc. 1. Addison's choice of the biblical quotation and his interpretation of it have been a commonplace of Protestant thinking since the time of Elizabeth. See Richard Hooker, *Polity,* 5. 76. 5; Rev. Richard Steele, *The Husbandman's Calling* [1672], (Boston, 1713), pp. 36–38; William Bates, *Spiritual Perfection,* in *Works,* p. 632.
3. Edward Chamberlayne, *Angliae Notitia; or, The Present State of England* (London, 1669), p. 444. Cf. Defoe, *Tradesman,* pt. 1, 2:34.
4. John Aikin, *Monthly Magazine* 9 (Feb. 1800): 2–3.
5. Defoe, *Tradesman,* 1:368–69. The characteristics and behavior of Sir Roger as seen during Mr. Spectator's visit to the squire's country house are developed by Addison in *S* 131 also. Sir Roger's death, as well as his earlier fear of Sir Andrew's republicanism and of his participation in the Pope's Procession, are also the invention of Addison. Steele's contribution to the portrait of the squire is primarily the detail of the old man's love for the perverse widow. The squire's hunting prowess is described in *S* 115. For Addison's sentimental regard for Sir Roger, see *Addisoniana,* 2 vols. (London, 1803), 1:70–71, 71–72. For further speculation regarding Addison's desire to kill off Sir Roger, see *S* 517, n. 2.
6. Nicholas Barbon, *Discourse,* p. 9; Defoe, *Tradesman,* pt. 1, 2:79–80. Cf.

Defoe, *A General History of Trade* (London, [Aug.], 1713), pp. 47–46 [misnumbered].

7. See also Great Britain, *Calendar of State Papers, Domestic Series, 1651–52* (London, 1877), p. 263; William Petyt, *Britannia Languens* (London, 1680), sec. 8; Charles King, ed., *British Merchant; or, Commerce Preserved* [1713–14], 3 vols. (London, 1721), 1:1; Roger Coke, *Treatise I* (London, 1671), pp. 84–85; Josiah Child, *New Discourse*, pp. xl–xli; Anon., *An Elegy on the Death of Trade* [1698], in *The Harleian Miscellany*, 12 vols. (London, 1808–11), 10:351–59. See similar charges by Latitudinarians: Edward Tenison, *The Excellency and Usefulness of a Public Spirit. A Sermon . . .* (London, 1711), pp. 7–8; John Scott, *The Christian Life* (London, 1681), p. 177.

8. Cf. *S* 26; William Temple, *Observations upon the United Provinces of the Netherlands* [1673], in *Works*, 1:154.

9. Defoe, *Tradesman*, pt. 1, 2:56. See also Aristotle *Nicomachean Ethics* (ed. Richard McKeon; New York, 1941) 1144b–1145a. The defense of prudence by middle-class apostles may be found in the following: William Ames, "Of Prudence," in *Conscience* (London, 1639), bk. 3, chap. 9; Rev. Richard Steele, *Religious Tradesman*, pp. 51–52; Defoe, *Crusoe*, 1:4; and *Family Instructor*, 1:66 et passim. Addison's ambivalent views on prudence may be found in *S* 225 also.

10. Cf. *S* 34, *S* 243, *S* 483. The association of hypocrisy with the middle class (tarred with the brush of Puritanism) is discussed also by Defoe, *The Poor Man's Plea* [1698], in *A True Collection of the Writings of the Author of "The True Born Englishman"* (London, 1703), pp. 288–89 et passim; and *Crusoe*, 3:71; and by John Barrington, *The Interest of England Considered, in Respect to Protestants Dissenting from the Established Church with Some Thoughts about Occasional Conformity* (London, 1703), p. 2. Addison discussed the causes of such hypocrisy and its characteristics in *S* 458 and *S* 494 also.

11. Cf. *S* 458. The association of irreverence with the gentry is common in middle-class thought. See, for example, Defoe, *Poor Man's Plea*, in *True Collection*, p. 294, and chap. 8 of this volume.

12. Defoe, *Tradesman*, 1:371; and *A Plan of the English Commerce* (London, 1728), pp. 12–13; see also *Review*, 6 Mar. 1705. For a similar statement by Addison, see *G* 137. It is just this kind of fluidity that is condemned by Chamberlayne, *Angliae Notitia*, pp. 434–36. Defoe's attack on the *Spectator* is in the *Review* of 14 Aug. 1711.

13. See primarily Jonathan Swift's *Conduct of the Allies* [1711], in *Political Tracts, 1711–13*, ed. Herbert Davis (Princeton, 1951), for the shrewd exploitation of the different interests between "moneyed" and "landed" estates.

14. George Berkeley, *Maxims concerning Patriotism* [1750], in *Works,* vol. 6, nos. 3, 33; Chamberlayne, *Angliae Notitia,* pp. 434–36. Defoe discusses the falsity of this attitude in *Tradesman,* pt. 1, 2:31.

15. See George Lillo, *The London Merchant* (London, 1731), act 1, sc. 1, for a realistic presentation of Elizabethan middle-class confidence and pride.

16. *S* 108, *S* 119. Cf. Defoe, *Plan,* pp. 6–7, 80–81.

17. See *G* 158 and *S* 317; see also Scott, *Christian Life,* pp. 345–46.

2. The Social Virtues

1. Jean Calvin, *Institutes of the Christian Religion* [trans. T. N., 1561], ed. John T. McNeill, trans. Ford Lewis Battles, 2 vols. (Philadelphia, 1960), 3. 10. 6. Cf. *S* 115. See also William Ames, "Of Liberality and Pity," in *Conscience* (London, 1639), bk. 5, chap. 49; Richard Baxter, *A Christian Directory* (London, 1673), p. 133 et passim; John Scott, *The Christian Life* (London, 1681), pp. 353–54; John Locke, *Second Treatise,* 5:34; Daniel Defoe, *Crusoe,* 1:2, 3:191; Rev. Richard Steele, *The Religious Tradesman* [1684], (Charlestown, Mass., 1804), pp. 12–13, 14–15, 82–85; Anon. [at times attrib. R. Allestree], *The Whole Duty of Man* [1658], (London, 1714), passim; William Horsely, *The Universal Merchant* (London, 1753), p. xv.

2. Rev. Richard Steele, *Religious Tradesman,* p. 16; Defoe, *Review,* 18 Jan. 1706; George Berkeley, *The Querist* [1735–37, 1750], in *Works,* vol. 6, no. 3. Addison's tags are from *T* 97, *S* 73, and *S* 10.

3. Locke, *Some Thoughts concerning Education* (London, 1693), secs. 38, 54, 56.

4. For his dissection of a beau's head and a coquette's heart, see *S* 275; on Aurelia and Fulvia, *S* 15. See also *S* 323, *T* 110, *T* 116, *G* 106. Cf. Baxter, *Christian Directory,* p. 452 et passim; Anon., *Whole Duty,* p. 159; Rev. Richard Steele, *Religious Tradesman,* p. 16; Isaac Barrow, *Of Industry in General,* in *Works,* 3:199.

5. Addison found the allegory of Prodicus in Xenophon *Memorabilia* (trans. E. C. Marchant; London and New York, 1923) 2. 1. 21–33. For the unhappy immortality that lies in wait for the idle, see *S* 317.

6. See *S* 115, *T* 103. Few of his contemporaries stress to the same extent this aspect of labor. A notable exception is Barrow, *Of Industry,* in *Works,* 3:194–95.

7. Addison's view of the penitential nature of labor was shunned by many of his contemporaries, who believed that labor virtually assures redemption. See, e.g., Francis Gastrell, *The Religious Education of Poor Children Recommended* (London, 1707), pp. 13–14.

8. Cf. Baxter, *Christian Directory,* p. 133; Gilbert Burnet, *History,* 6:212; Berkeley, *Querist,* in *Works,* vol. 6, no. 201; Rev. Richard Steele, *The Husbandman's Calling* [1672], (Boston, 1713), pp. 6–7; and *Religious Tradesman,* pp. 14–15; William Law, *A Serious Call to a Devout and Holy Life* [1729 (Dec. 1728)], (London, 1955), pp. 15, 48; Barrow, *Of Industry,* in *Works,* 3:198; John Tillotson, *Of Diligence in Our General and Particular Calling,* in *Works,* 3:365.

9. Addison joined with Scott to justify "larger portions of recreation" for those of wealth and station than for those "of meaner circumstances, who having not yet made a competent provision for their families, are obliged in justice to a more constant industry, lest they fall under St. Paul's censure of being worse than infidels" (*Christian Life,* p. 360). Addison admired Scott's work; see *S* 447.

10. Daniel Defoe, *The Complete English Tradesman,* 2 vols. (London, 1726–27), 1:118–19; see also p. 47, and cf. Rev. Richard Steele, *Religious Tradesman,* pp. 54–93; George Lillo, *The London Merchant* (London, 1731), act 2, sc. 1. For his condemnation of idleness in the gentry, see *S* 123; cf. Burnet, *History,* 6:212.

11. Calvin, *Institutes,* 3. 7. 5; 3. 8. 39 and 45; Quintilian *Institutio oratoria,* 4 vols. (trans. H. E. Butler; London and Cambridge, Mass., 1936) 5. 11. 24. Cf. Baxter, *Christian Directory,* p. 448; Barrow, *Of Industry,* in *Works,* 3:181 ff. For Addison's ants, see also *G* 156.

12. Rev. Richard Steele, *Religious Tradesman,* p. 61. See also *S* 55; cf. Francis Bacon, "Of Expense," in *Essays or Counsels Civil or Moral* [1625], in *Works,* ed. James Spedding, R. L. Ellis, and D. D. Heath (London, 1861), vol. 6; George MacKenzie, *The Moral History of Frugality* [1711], in *Essays upon Several Moral Subjects* (London, 1713), p. 293.

13. For typical Stoic attacks on physical self-indulgence—drunkenness, for example—see Seneca, Epistle 83, in *Works* (trans. Thomas Lodge; London, 1620); and *Epictetus His Morals, with Simplicius His Comment,* trans. George Stanhope (London, 1694), p. 329. For a partial list of Addison's attacks upon such immoderation, see *T* 148, *T* 162, *T* 240, *G* 120, *S* 195.

14. Calvin, *Institutes,* 3. 10. 4.

15. See *S* 294 and *S* 346 (Steele); see also *G* 166. Cf. Baxter, *Christian Directory,* pp. 128, 631–32, and bk. 4, pp. 143, 146–47; Tillotson, *The Children of This World Wiser Than the Children of Light,* in *Works,* 2:482; Robert South, *A Sermon on Proverbs i. 32, the Prosperity of Fools Shall Destroy Them,* in *Sermons,* 2:23; John Ray, *Three Physico-Theological Discourses* [1692], 2d ed. (London, 1693), pp. 390–91; John Wilkins, *Of the Principles and Duties of Natural Religion* [1675], 7th ed. (London, 1715), pp. 292–93.

16. MacKenzie, *Moral History,* in *Essays,* p. 307; Nicholas Barbon, *Discourse,* p. 27.

17. Berkeley, *An Essay toward Preventing the Ruin of Great Britain* [1721], in *Works,* 6:74. In the *Englishman* (vol. 1, no. 4) Richard Steele sets himself up as censor in the tradition of Mr. Spectator. Steele recognized the clamor for sumptuary legislation but rejected such legal restraints. The two leading exponents of such legislation in Addison's day were Berkeley, *Essay,* in *Works,* 6:75–76; and *Querist,* in *Works,* vol. 6, no. 57; Defoe, *An Essay on Ways and Means for the Advancement of Trade* (London, 1726), passim. But Defoe was not always certain about the efficacy of sumptuary laws: see *Some Objections Humbly Offered . . . Relating to the Present Intended Relief of Prisoners* (London, 1729), p. 21; *Mercurius Politicus* (London, 1716–20), p. 67.

18. Cf. MacKenzie, *Moral History,* in *Essays,* p. 317; Thomas Mun, *England's Treasure by Foreign Trade* [1664], (New York, 1895), pp. 81–82; Defoe, *Tradesman,* pt. 2, 2:103–5, 105–8; and *A General History of Trade* (London, [July], 1713), p. 27. For Addison's exasperation with the importation of French "fopperies," see *S* 45.

19. Jean Jacques Rousseau, *A Discourse on the Origin of Inequality* [1754], in *The Social Contract and Other Discourses,* trans. G. D. H. Cole (New York and London, 1950), p. 270.

20. See *T* 123. Addison's conviction is supported—at least in theory—by the following: Defoe, *Crusoe,* 2:54, 112; Rev. Richard Steele, *Religious Tradesman,* p. 129; G. Fox[?], *An Epistle by Way of Caution, to Shopkeepers, Merchants and Factors* (London, 1710), passim. Yet Defoe often took a flexible view of commercial honesty; see *Tradesman,* 1:275; pt. 1, 2:47–48; *Mercator* (1713–14), no. 27.

21. *S* 177; Calvin, *Institutes,* 3. 7. 6. See also Law, *Serious Call,* pp. 82–83; see also *S* 232, by either John Hughes or Henry Martyn, for a stiffening even of Addison's attitude.

22. Addison discusses this in *S* 549 also. Cf. Anon., *Whole Duty,* pp. 353–54; Defoe, *Crusoe,* 3:18; and *Giving Alms No Charity* [1704], in *A Second Volume of the Writings of the Author of "The True Born Englishman"* (London, 1705), pp. 430–31.

23. Samuel Johnson, *Review of Soame Jenyns' "Free Enquiry into the Nature and Origin of Evil"* [1757], in *Works,* 11 vols. (Oxford, 1825), 6:57. The charity-school movement was started by the Latitudinarians, Patrick and Tenison. For Addison's indebtedness to the Latitudinarian temper, see chap. 9 of this volume. His evaluation of the charity-school movement had Anglican support. See Tillotson, *The Example of Jesus in Doing Good,* in *Works,* 1:152; White Kennett, *The Charity of Schools for Poor Children Recommended* (London, 1706), pp. 4, 5, 8, 11–12; and *Glory to*

God and Gratitude to Benefactors (London, 1709), p. 15; Gastrell, *Religious Education,* pp. 6, 17, et passim; Ofspring Blackall, *The Rules and Measures of Alms-Giving, and the Manifold Advantages of Charity-Schools* (London, 1708), pp. 24–25, 27 ff.; John Jackson, *The Blessedness of Communicating to Charity-Schools* (London, 1710), passim; George Smalridge, *The Royal Benefactress; or, The Great Charity of Educating Poor Children* (London, 1710), passim; William Dawes, *The Excellency of the Charity of Charity-Schools* (London, 1713), passim. For middle-class support of Addison's position, see Anon., *An Account of Charity-Schools Lately Erected in Great Britain and Ireland* (London, 1710), p. 1; *S* 294 (Steele); Defoe, *Charity Still a Christian Virtue* (London, 1719), passim. For an attack on what is seen as the hypocrisy of the charity-school movement, see Bernard Mandeville, *On Charity and Charity-Schools* (London, 1723), passim.

24. William Petty, *A Treatise of Taxes and Contributions* [1662], in *Economic Writings,* ed. Charles Henry Hull, 2 vols. (Cambridge, 1899), 1:29; Edward Chamberlayne, *England's Wants* (London, 1667), p. 7; Berkeley, *Querist,* in *Works,* vol. 6, no. 372.

25. See also Anon., *Whole Duty,* p. 150; Calvin, *Institutes,* 3. 10. 6; Ames, "Of Contentment," in *Conscience,* bk. 5, chap. 57; Defoe, *Crusoe,* 1:150, 174, 185–86; William Bates, *The Great Duty of Resignation,* in *Works,* p. 282; Steele, *Lover* [1715], no. 26, in *Periodical Journalism, 1714–16,* ed. Rae Blanchard (Oxford, 1959).

26. See also *S* 289. For classical use of this image, see the summary in Tillotson, *Good Men Strangers and Sojourners upon Earth,* in *Works,* 2:91. (See particularly Seneca *Dialogues* 6. 21. 1, and *Epistulae morales* 120. 14; *Epictetus,* pp. 127, 371–72.) Epictetus was a popular eighteenth-century model for contentment; e.g., Wilkins, *Principles,* pp. 209 ff.

27. The idea of a large population as the key to prosperity is expressed by the following: S. W., *The Golden Fleece* (London, 1656), pp. 79–80 [misnumbered]; Petty, *Treatise,* in *Writings,* 1:34, 108, 117; Mun, *England's Treasure,* p. 31; William Temple, *Of Popular Discontents,* in *Works,* 3:60; John Graunt, *Natural and Political Observations upon the Bills of Mortality* [1662], in Petty, *Writings,* 2:377–78; John Houghton, *England's Great Happiness* (London, 1677), pp. 9–10; Josiah Child, *New Discourse,* p. xi; Horsely, *Merchant,* p. xv.

28. For Addison's view of the father's role, see also *G* 165; cf. Defoe, *The Family Instructor* [1715], 8th ed. (London, 1720); 1:232; Bates, *Spiritual Perfection,* in *Works,* pp. 662–63. For Addison's view of woman's domestic role, see *S* 73, *S* 81, *S* 295. For his view of children's duties, see, e.g., *S* 181, *S* 189. See also Ames, "Of the Mutual Obligation between Parents and Children," in *Conscience,* bk. 5, chap. 22; Anon., *Whole Duty,* pp. 275–82;

Bates, *Spiritual Perfection,* in *Works,* pp. 662–63; Steele, *The Conscious Lovers* [1722], (London, 1723), act 1, sc. 2, and act 3, sc. 1; Lillo, *Merchant,* act 1, sc. 1; Defoe, *Family Instructor,* 1:79, 88; and *Crusoe,* 1:7, 43; and *Review,* supp. 4 (Dec. 1704), supp. 5 (Jan. 1705).

29. Locke, *Second Treatise,* 6:58; and *Some Thoughts concerning Education,* secs. 41–42. For Addison's involvement with Defoe, see *Review,* 12 Oct. 1711. William Fleetwood (*The Relative Duties of Parents and Children, Husbands and Wives, Masters and Servants, Considered in Sixteen Sermons* [London, 1705], pp. 53–54) raises the same question dramatized by Addison and answers it as irresolutely.

30. Cf. Child, *New Discourse,* p. 163.

31. Defoe, *Tradesman,* pt. 1, 2:154, 156. See Rev. Richard Steele, *Religious Tradesman,* pp. 228–29.

32. Cf., e.g., *Tradesman,* pt. 1, 2:163–64, "For there is something so absurd in the life of imprudent expence that a man bred in business can never fall into it, unless he has first forfeited all his former capacities, and is no more able to make any judgment of things."

3. The Mercantilist Principle

1. John Locke, *A Second Letter concerning Toleration* (London, 1690), p. 2. The idea that trade leads to war and that war stimulates trade is stated in *The Continuation of the Life of Edward, Earl of Clarendon,* 3 vols. (Oxford, 1759), 2:376 ff.; and Charles D'Avenant, *That Foreign Trade is Beneficial to England,* in *Political and Commercial Works,* 5 vols. (London, 1771), 1:348. It is implied throughout the *British Merchant; or, Commerce Preserved* [1713–14], ed. Charles King, 3 vols. (London, 1721), a strong influence on Addison's economic thinking.

2. *S* 2 (Steele). For similar statements, see Nicholas Barbon, *Discourse,* pp. 5, 23; Dudley North, *Discourses upon Trade* [1691], p. 37, in *A Reprint of Economic Tracts,* ed. Jacob H. Hollander (Baltimore, 1907); Locke, *Some Considerations of the Consequences of the Lowering of Interest, and Raising the Value of Money* [1691], in *Works,* 3 vols. (London, 1714), 2:8, and *Second Treatise,* 5:42; Daniel Defoe, *A General History of Trade* (London, [July], 1713), pp. 29–30; Anon., *Delenda Carthago; or, The True Interest of England . . . ,* in *A Collection of Scarce and Valuable Papers* (London, 1712), p. 235. For Addison's tributes to Marlborough and Shovell, see *The Campaign* (*MW,* 1:163) and *S* 26; for his announcement of the latter's death, see his letters to Charles Montagu, 28 Oct. 1707, and to Christian Cole, 21 Oct. 1707, *Letters,* pp. 79–80, 81.

3. Defoe, *Review,* 19 Apr. 1705, and *A Plan of the English Commerce* (London, 1728), pp. 52–53. See also Josiah Child, *New Discourse,* p. 209;

William Petyt, *Britannia Languens* (London, 1680), p. 238; D'Avenant, *An Essay upon Ways and Means* [1695], in *Works*, 1:16; and *That Foreign Trade Is Beneficial*, in *Works*, 1:348.

4. Cf. Alexander Pope, *Essay on Man*, bk. 1, ll. 107–8.

5. In, for example, the anonymous Whig pamphlet, *A Letter to the Honourable A——r M——re, Com——ner of Trade and Plantation* (London, 1714), p. 24. Whig hatred of Moore was evident as early as 1711 in a broadside by Arthur Maynwaring, *An Excellent New Song, Called Credit Restored* . . . (London).

6. *British Merchant* 3:256–58. This journal did not appear until almost two months after the defeat of the commercial treaties. According to the advertisement in *G* 128, its first number appeared on 7 August 1713. Several months in the planning stage, it organized the attack, both before and during publication, upon the commercial treaties of Utrecht and the Assiento.

7. Aristotle *Politics* (ed. Richard McKeon; New York, 1941) 4. 11. 1295a25–29, 1295b35–36. See *F* 1; *S* 119; *S* 287; *Remarks*, pp. 220–21. Cf. Aristotle *Politics* 5. 11. 1313a19–34.

8. See Algernon Sidney, *Discourses concerning Government* (London, 1698), pp. 200–206 [chap. 2, sec. 25].

9. *Remarks*, pp. 220–21; Sidney, *Discourses*, pp. 200–206 [chap. 2, sec. 25]. Cf. James Harrington, *Oceana*, ed. John Toland (London, 1700), p. 105.

10. *War*, p. 262. Cf. William Temple, *Observations upon the United Provinces of the Netherlands* [1673], in *Works*, 1:195–96; George MacKenzie, *The Moral History of Frugality* [1711], in *Essays upon Several Moral Subjects* (London, 1713), pp. 347–48.

11. *T* 161; Harrington, *Oceana*, p. 105. Cf. Aristotle *Politics* 4. 4. 1292a25–30; White Kennett, *The Happiness of This Church and Nation Briefly Intimated* . . . (London, 1705), p. 13; Charles Mordaunt, *Remarks on a Pamphlet Entitled, The Thoughts of a Member of the Lower House, etc.* (London, 1719), p. 19; Jonathan Swift, *Contests and Dissensions in Athens and Rome* [1701], in *A Tale of a Tub with Other Early Works, 1696–1707*, ed. Herbert Davis (Oxford, 1965), p. 227.

12. William Petty, *Political Arithmetic* [1690], in *Economic Writings*, ed. Charles Henry Hull, 2 vols. (Cambridge, 1899), 1:272; *War*, p. 248. Cf. the anonymous *A Compendious History of the Taxes of France and of the Oppressive Methods of Raising Them* [1694], in *The Harleian Miscellany*, 12 vols. (London, 1808–11), 10:200–221; Defoe, *Giving Alms No Charity* [1704], in *A Second Volume of the Writings of the Author of "The True Born Englishman"* (London, 1705), p. 422.

13. *F* 10 (cf. Locke, *Second Treatise*, 7:90, 91). See also *T* 161; *F* 18; John Cary, *An Essay towards the Settlement of a National Credit* (Lon-

don, 1696), passim; Anon., *The Grand Concernments of England Ensured* (London, 1659), pp. 15–17; Defoe, *The Chimera* (London, 1720), p. 5; Matthew Tindal[?], *An Essay concerning Obedience to the Supreme Powers, and the Duty of Subjects in All Revolutions* [1694], in *A Collection of State Tracts,* 3 vols. (London, 1705–7), 2 (1705):435. The economic arguments of Addison, which underlie his attack on absolute monarchy, are everywhere dependent on Locke; see *Second Treatise,* 18:202–10.

14. Swift, *The History of the Four Last Years of the Queen* [1758], ed. Herbert Davis with an introduction by Harold Williams (Princeton, 1951), pp. 69–70; and *The Conduct of the Allies* [1711], in *Political Tracts, 1711–13,* ed. Herbert Davis (Princeton, 1951), pp. 53–54. For the continuing attack upon the Bank of England, see William Paterson[?], *A Brief Account of the Intended Bank of England* (London, 1694); Anon., *Reasons Offered against the Continuance of the Bank in a Letter to a Member of Parliament* (London, 1707); John Broughton[?], *The Vindication and Advancement of Our National Constitution and Credit* (London, 1710); Anon., *An Essay towards the History of the Last Ministry and Parliament* (London, 1710), pp. 58–72; Defoe[?; also attributed to Simon Clement], *Faults on Both Sides* (London, 1710).

15. It is interesting that Defoe and Swift both visualize credit as a lady; see Defoe's *Review,* 21 Dec. 1710, and Swift's *Examiner* 37. The intellectual concept of Addison's allegory may be found in a letter to Joseph Keally, 5 Aug. 1710, *Letters,* pp. 228–29.

16. Addison consistently declared the political neutrality of the *Spectator;* see, for example, *S* 16, *S* 262, *S* 556. For Addison on allegory, see *S* 512.

17. Defoe[?], *Faults,* p. 44; Anon., *The Age of Wonders* [1710], in *Political Ballads of the Seventeenth and Eighteenth Centuries,* 2 vols. (London, 1860), 2:68–73; cf. Thomas Smith to Harley, 28 Jan. 1711/12, in HMC, *Portland,* 5:140.

18. Gilbert Burnet, *History,* 5:21. See *T* 161 and cf. Kennett, *Happiness,* p. 7.

19. Barbon, *Discourse,* p. 19.

20. Defoe, *Plan,* p. 141.

21. Anon., *A Letter to a Country Gentleman: Setting Forth the Causes of the Decay and Ruin of Trade* [1698], in *Harleian Miscellany,* 10:363. Cf. Roger Coke's similar personification, in *Treatise II* (London, 1671), "Preface to the Reader." A description of the source of England's power may be found in Defoe, *Plan,* p. 52.

22. *F* 42. For the merchant as benefactor, see also the anonymous pamphlet *Advice to Whigs and Tories* (London, 1714), p. 29; Defoe, *Plan,* p. 54; and *Review,* 20 Jan. 1708.

23. North, *Discourses,* p. 16, in *A Reprint;* D'Avenant, *An Essay on the East India Trade* [1696], in *Works,* 1:98–99, 104. Cf. Petty, *Political Arithmetic,* in *Writings,* 1:258.

24. Abel Boyer, *State,* 6:169. Cf. Burnet, *History,* 6:161–64. The two articles proposed to repeal all tariff prohibitions respecting Great Britain and France not in force prior to 18 September 1664, to levy no higher duties on French than on other foreign goods brought into England, and to restore the French tariff of 1664 for English exports to France, except for "manufactures of wool, sugar, salted fish and the product of whales," which were to be the subject of a special agreement; pending this agreement they were to come under the "duties appointed by the tariff of the 7th of December 1699."

25. It was advertised in *Guardian* 94 (29 June) for publication on the following day.

26. Defoe, *Memoirs of Count Tariff* (London, 1713), p. 46; the equation of the Sacheverell incident and the commercial treaties of Utrecht was an example of Defoe's justifiable Tory cynicism. Addison's contempt for Defoe and *Mercator,* Defoe's journal of economics, is suggested by the name of one of the *Trial*'s three villains, Mercator. Defoe's connection with the journal was a notorious secret. It was described as "a paper which is now certainly known to be written by Daniel Foe, a fellow who has prostituted his pen in the vilest manner to all parties" and who "notwithstanding his fair pretences, is a snake in the grass" (Robert Walpole[?], *A Letter to a West-Country Clothier and Freeholder* [London, 1713], pp. 5–6). Cf. Boyer, *History,* pp. 633–34; Anon., *A Letter from a Tory Freeholder to His Representative in Parliament, upon Her Majesty's Most Gracious Speech to Both Houses on the Subject of Peace, June 6, 1712* (London, 1712), p. 15. For Whig use of the *Trial* in 1714, see Appendix.

27. There were at least twenty-nine petitions; see *House of Commons Journals* 17 (for 1711–14):347–408.

28. He probably wore a cravat made of Turkish raw silk but manufactured in England. Such an article aided the British economy, according to the *British Merchant* 1:2, 24–25; Theodore Janssen, *General Maxims in Trade, Particularly Applied to the Commerce between Great Britain and France* (London, 1713), p. 6. For biblical quotation see John 5:3, 4.

29. *PH,* 6:1212. Cf. *F* 22; *British Merchant* 1:23–24, 203–4; and 2:12–13 et passim.

30. For representative discussions of this concept, see *F* 41; *F* 42; Thomas Mun, *A Discourse of Trade from England into the East-Indies* [1621], (New York, 1930), pp. 1–2; and *England's Treasure by Foreign Trade* [1664], (New York, 1895), pp. 7–8; Edward Misselden, *The Circle of Commerce* (London, 1623), pp. 116–17; Temple, *Observations,* in *Works,*

1:194–95; George Berkeley, *The Querist* [1735–37, 1750], in *Works,* vol. 6, no. 161; William Wood, *A Survey of Trade* [1718], 2d ed. (London, 1719), p. 85.

31. *F* 41. Cf. *HR,* 2 (1724):287–88.

32. Coke, *Treatise II,* "Preface"; Barbon, *Discourse,* p. 31; John Tillotson, *The Wisdom of God in the Creation of the World,* in *Works,* 2:554; Defoe, *General History* (Aug.), pp. 7–8; Kennett, *Happiness,* p. 8.

33. *Remarks,* pp. 216–17. Cf. Defoe, *Plan,* pp. 17–18, 99; Barbon, *Discourse,* p. 22.

34. Cf. Barbon, *Discourse,* p. 21; Kennett, *Happiness,* p. 8; Defoe, *General History* (July), pp. 3–4; Richard Steele, "The Dedication to Sir John Fellows," in *A Nation a Family* [1720], in *Tracts,* p. 577.

35. Cf. Barbon, *Discourse,* pp. 22–23; Anon., *An Address to the Good People of Great Britain Occasioned by the Report from the Committee of Secrecy* (Dublin, 1716), pp. 5–6; Defoe, *The Complete English Tradesman,* 2 vols. (London, 1726–27), 1:381–82; Steele, *Englishman,* vol. 2, no. 17.

4. The War of Economic Right

1. William Temple, *Observations upon the United Provinces of the Netherlands* [1673], in *Works,* 1:203. See *War,* p. 242; cf. John Locke, *Some Considerations of the Consequences of the Lowering of Interest, and Raising the Value of Money* [1691], in *Works,* 3 vols. (London, 1714), 2:7; William Petyt, *Britannia Languens* (London, 1680), p. 140; Philopatris [pseud.], *A Treatise Wherein Is Demonstrated That the East India Trade Is the Most National of All Foreign Trades* (London, 1681), p. 7 (this pamphlet is sometimes attributed to Josiah Child); David Hume, *Essays, Moral, Political, and Literary,* ed. T. H. Green and T. H. Grose, 2 vols. (London, 1907), 1:345. Addison takes pleasure in pointing to the Netherlands' increasing poverty as a result of her involvement in the War of the Spanish Succession; see, for example, *War,* p. 262.

2. Daniel Defoe, *Armageddon* (London, 1711), pp. 4–5; and *Crusoe,* 3:233–34.

3. See also William Cecil Burghley, *Notes by Burghley on Trade, Fishing, and Shipping* [1581], in *Tudor Economic Documents,* ed. R. H. Tawney and E. Power, 3 vols. (London, 1924), 2:124–25; Arthur Young, *Reflections on the Present State of Affairs* (London, 1759), p. 21. In the seventeenth century Holland vied with France as England's most dangerous economic rival. The House of Commons resolved in 1664 that the Dutch "damages, affronts, and injuries" were "the greatest obstruction of our foreign trade" (*House of Commons Journals* 8 (1660–67):548; Anon., *Delenda Carthago; or, The True Interest of England, in Relation to*

France and Holland, in *A Collection of Scarce and Valuable Papers* [London, 1712], p. 236). By the following century, however, Holland was no longer a threat.

4. Johnson, *An Essay on the Origin and Importance of Small Tracts and Fugitive Pieces* [1744], in *Works,* 11 vols. (Oxford, 1825), 5:192.

5. According to Defoe, wool is "the greatest and best of our trading produce, the soul and life of our whole commerce, and the fund of all our prosperity and success in that commerce" (*A Plan of the English Commerce* [London, 1728], p. 155; *Review,* 25 Apr. 1713). See also Nicholas Barbon, *Discourse,* p. 10; Child, *New Discourse,* p. 155.

6. *War* was published early in 1708. Typical of the popular demand in 1707–8 for a continuation of the war are the following: John Mackqueen, *A Divine and Moral Essay on Courage, Its Rise and Progress* (London, 1707), p. 61; John Glanvill, *A Poem Occasioned by the Successes of the Present War* (London, 1707), p. 10; Henry Brookes, *Daphnis* (London, 1707), passim; Gilbert Burnet, *A Thanksgiving Sermon Preached before the Queen, and the Two Houses of Parliament, at St. Paul's* (London, 1707), pp. 23–24; Nicholas Rowe, *A Poem upon the Late Glorious Successes of Her Majesty's Arms* (London, 1707), passim; John Gaynam, *Marlborough Still Conquers* (London, 1708), p. 15; Charles Gildon[?], *Libertas Triumphans* (London, 1708), passim. See also the advertisement for *A Philippic Oration* on the last pages of Richard Blackmore's *The Kit-Cats. A Poem* (London, 1708, 1709).

7. *House of Lords Journals* 18 (for 1705–9):398–99. Cf. *PH,* 6:608, 601–10.

8. For his statement on the need for troop increases, see also *War,* p. 247; on mercenaries, pp. 255–56. For an anticipatory statement of Addison's view, see Anon., *The Claims of the People of England Essayed* [1701], in *A Collection of State Tracts, Published during the Reign of King William III* (London, 1707).

9. For Marlborough's similar recommendation, see *PH,* 6:607–8.

10. Samuel Clarke, *A Thanksgiving Sermon before the Honorable House of Commons* (London, 1709), p. 15; Jonathan Swift to Robert Hunter, 12 Jan. 1708/9, *Correspondence,* 1:121. The people were much agitated by the deliberately stalled peace talks, both at The Hague and in 1710 at Gertruydenberg. For the severity of the Whig peace conditions, see the biased report of Swift, *The Conduct of the Allies* [1711], in *Political Tracts, 1711–13,* ed. Herbert Davis (Princeton, 1951), p. 50.

11. The *Examiner* continued to serve as a Tory propaganda vehicle until 26 July 1714, one day before Harley's dismissal. From 1710 to 1712 the Tories particularly exploited the idea of Whigs as warmongers: Swift's letter to Archbishop King, 9 Sept. 1710, *Correspondence,* 1:174; Henry St.

John, *A Letter to the Examiner* (London, 1710), pp. 6–7, 9–10; and Swift, *The Conduct of the Allies,* pp. 41, 42–43, et passim; see also Defoe: *An Essay at a Plain Exposition of the Difficult Phrase A Good Peace* (London, 1711), p. 7; *Reasons Why a Party among Us, and Also among the Confederates, Are Obstinately Bent against a Treaty of Peace with the French at This Time* (London, 1711), pp. 7–8; *Reasons Why This Nation Ought to Put a Speedy End to This Expensive War* [1711], 2d ed. (London, 1711), passim; [?], *The Conduct of Parties in England . . .* (London, 1712), pp. 41–42.

12. Defoe, *An Essay at a Plain Exposition . . .*, p. 6. For Maynwaring's influence on the *Whig Examiner,* see John Oldmixon, *The Life and Posthumous Works of Arthur Maynwaring* (London, 1715), p. 158. There is, however, no evidence that Maynwaring wrote the *Whig Examiner.*

13. *Examiner* 5. Abusive references to the *Tatler* in the *Examiner* and other Tory writing placed responsibility on Richard Steele. As he complained to William Congreve in his dedication (1721) to *The Drummer:* "Many of the writings now published as [Addison's], I have been very patiently traduced and calumniated for. . . ." (Addison's *Works,* 6:310).

14. There is no originality in Addison's *Whig Examiner* arguments. They may be found in many Whig pamphlets during 1709 and 1710. See, for example, White Kennett, *Glory to God and Gratitude to Benefactors* (London, 1709), passim; Anon., *The Duke of Marlborough's Letter, in Answer to the French King's Proposals of Peace* (London, 1709), passim; Clarke, *A Thanksgiving Sermon,* pp. 2–3, 22; Benjamin Hoadly, *The Election Dialogue,* in *A Collection of Several Papers Printed in the Year 1710* (London, 1718), pp. 121–22; Anon., *Considerations on Peace and War* (London, 1710), pp. 40–43, 47.

15. John Gay, *The Present State of Wit* (London, 1711), pp. 8–9.

16. *Examiner* 3.

17. Oldmixon, *Maynwaring,* p. 169.

18. Historical Manuscripts Commission, *The Appendix to the Seventh Report* (London, 1879), 7:239; Abel Boyer, *History,* p. 641; and *State,* 6:21.

19. Cf. letters to Ambrose Philips, 23 Dec. 1710, and to Joshua Dawson, 21 Sept. 1710, *Letters,* pp. 249, 238.

20. For the Whig interpretation of the *Examiner*'s purpose, see *Mr. Steele's Apology for Himself and His Writings* [Oct. 1714], in *Tracts,* p. 300. For the Tory view of the *Examiner*'s function, see Swift, *Examiner* 37, and *Memoirs Relating to That Change Which Happened in the Queen's Ministry in the Year 1710. Written in 1714* [1765], in *Political Tracts, 1713–19,* ed. Herbert Davis and Irvin Ehrenpreis (Princeton, 1953), pp. 123–25.

21. See also *WE* 1.

22. Swift, *The History of the Four Last Years of the Queen* [1758], ed. Herbert Davis, with an introduction by Harold Williams (Princeton, 1951), pp. 5–7. This was exactly the procedure followed; see, for example, such Whig pamphlets as George Ridpath, *Some Thoughts concerning the Peace* (London, 1713); Anon., *Advice to Whigs and Tories* (London, 1714); Anon., *A Letter to the Examiner, Suggesting Proper Heads, for Vindicating His Masters* (London, 1714). This particular Whig strategy was known to the Tory high command as early as 1711; see Charles Lawton to Harley, 30 Sept. 1711, in HMC, *Portland,* 5:94.

23. Cf. George I's address to both houses of Parliament on 21 Mar. 1714/15, in *HR,* 1 (1724):111–12. The king's statement is of course a reflection of the concerted attitude of the Whig leaders.

24. *Addisoniana,* 2 vols. (London, 1803), 1:74.

25. See *Trial,* p. 269, for other material in the paragraph. For Whig knowledge of Tory dealings with the French, see Burnet, *History,* 6:69–70, 72. Much was revealed when Matthew Prior was discovered at Dover as he returned from a secret session with the French in July 1711 (Swift, *History,* p. 46). That the Tories deliberately concealed the documents, "except two or three," relating to these negotiations was revealed by Walpole and his Committee of Secrecy; see Anon., *A Report from the Committee of Secrecy . . . Relating to the Late Negotiations of Peace and Commerce, etc. Reported on the Ninth of June, 1715 by the Right Honourable Robert Walpole* (London, 1715), pp. 5–6 et passim. See also Anon., *An Address to the Good People of Great Britain, Occasioned by the Report from the Committee of Secrecy* (Dublin, 1716).

5. Whiggism

1. James Sutherland, "The Last Years of Joseph Addison," in *Background for Queen Anne,* pp. 127–28.

2. Mary Manley, *The Secret Memoirs . . . of Several Persons of Quality . . . from the New Atalantis* [1709], 7th ed. (London, 1736), pp. 218–19. Mrs. Manley was in no position to be critical of Addison's political involvement. In several letters (19 July 1711 to 20 Aug. 1714) to the earl of Oxford, she revealed her desire to become a Tory writer; see HMC, *Portland,* 5:55, 95–96, 453, 458, 491. Ultimately she became one. For Addison's slurring remarks on Mrs. Manley, see *T* 229, *T* 243, *S* 37, *G* 107.

3. Horace, Satire 3, bk. 1, in *Satires, Epistles, and Ars Poetica* (trans. H. Rushton Fairclough; Cambridge, Mass., and London, 1947); Seneca, Epistle 120, in *Works* (trans. Thomas Lodge; London, 1620); *Epictetus His Morals with Simplicius His Comment,* trans. George Stanhope (London, 1694), pp. 139–40; Cicero *Tusculan Disputations,* trans. J. E. King (London

and New York, 1927), pp. 359–61; Jean de La Bruyère, "Of Man," in *Characters* [1699], 3d ed. (London, 1702), p. 212.

4. Bishop Berkeley reports the example of Addison's Whig loyalty. Using it as evidence, he finds Addison "more earnest in the Whig cause than Mr. Steele" (Historical Manuscripts Commission, *The Appendix to the Seventh Report* [London, 1879], 7:238). For Steele's relations with Harley, see his letter to the latter, 9 Oct. 1710, *The Correspondence of Richard Steele,* ed. Rae Blanchard (Oxford, 1941), p. 43, n. 1.

5. Addison to Jacob Tonson, May 1703, *Letters,* pp. 39–40.

6. Midleton's letter to Thomas Brodrick, 14 Dec. 1719, in William Coxe, *The Memoirs of the Life and Administration of Sir Robert Walpole,* 3 vols. (London, 1798), 2:173. That Bolton was probably the "great man" may be deduced from a memorandum written by Midleton sometime between 1725 and 1729 (Coxe, *Memoirs,* 2:178–80). It is ironical that when the recommendation was made, Addison was already dead.

7. Jonathan Swift, *The Journal to Stella* [1766–68], ed. Harold Williams, 2 vols. (Oxford, 1948), 12 Oct. 1710. For an example of Addison's failure to estimate public opinion accurately, see his letter to Sunderland, 20 May 1710, *Letters,* p. 218.

8. Joseph Spence, *Observations, Anecdotes, and Characters of Books and Men,* ed. James M. Osborn, 2 vols. (Oxford, 1966), 2:626. For the apocryphal story, see *Biographie universelle, ancienne et moderne* (Paris, 1843), 1:164.

9. For Addison's part in Steele's trial, see *Addisoniana,* 2 vols. (London, 1803), 2:216–18.

10. For his letter to the earl of Stair, June 1717, see the *Annals and Correspondence of the Viscount and the First and Second Earls of Stair,* ed. John Murray Graham, 2 vols. (London, 1875), 2:20–22.

11. See *WE* 5, in which—as a formality—he obliquely censures Sacheverell. Addison's election to Parliament as member for Lostwithiel having been set aside before the trial, he was not obligated to take a parliamentary stand.

12. For Addison's abiding sense of indebtedness to Ormonde, see also his letters to Joseph Keally, 29 Dec. 1710, and Joshua Dawson, 28 June 1711, *Letters,* pp. 251, 263.

13. Algernon Sidney, *Discourses concerning Government* (London, 1698), pp. 70–71 (chap. 2, sec. 3); cf. Cicero *Paradoxa Stoicorum* ("Paradox 1"), in *De oratore,* tr. Harris Rackham, 2 vols. (Cambridge, Mass., and London, 1942), 2:261–63. He wrote the Lords Justices of Ireland, 23 Apr. 1717, that the appointment was "a troublesome post" (*Letters,* p. 357).

14. See his letter to Henry Davenant, 22 Apr. 1717, *Letters,* pp. 356–57. Cf. *S* 469, *F* 39. For a snide and unsubstantiated reason for Addison's as-

sumption of the secretaryship, see HMC, *Egmont Diary,* vol. 1, 1730–33 (London, 1920), p. 105.

15. Letter from Stanhope to Robert Walpole, sent from Hanover on 15 Dec. 1716, in Coxe, *Memoirs,* 2:140; correspondence from George Tilson to Lord Polwarth, HMC, *Report on the Manuscripts of Lord Polwarth* (London, 1911), 1:407, 458, 462.

16. Spence, *Observations,* 1:78; "A Libel on D—— D—— and a Certain Great Lord" [1730], in *The Poems of Jonathan Swift,* ed. Harold Williams, 3 vols. (Oxford, 1937), 2:479–86.

17. Gay to Addison, Dec. 1713, *The Letters of John Gay,* ed. C. F. Burgess (Oxford, 1966), p. 6; Burnet to George Duckett, 1 June 1716, *The Letters of Thomas Burnet to George Duckett, 1712–1722,* ed. D. Nichol Smith (Oxford, 1914), p. 99. Burnet's spite is so patent that it reflects on him rather than on Addison or Pope. What is believable in his statement, however, is that in 1716 the two men went through the motions of cordial association. See also Jervas to Pope, 20 Aug. 1714, *The Correspondence of Alexander Pope,* ed. George Sherburn, 5 vols. (Oxford, 1956), 1:244.

18. Pope's portrait of Addison surrounded by a "little senate" of mediocrities and "by flatterers besieged" is, we believe, witty nastiness that buries its seed of truth in sarcastic exaggeration ("An Epistle from Mr. Pope to Dr. Arbuthnot" [1734], ll. 207–9).

19. Charles Mordaunt, *Remarks on a Pamphlet Entitled, The Thoughts of a Member of the Lower House, etc.* (London, 1719), pp. 4–5.

20. John Trenchard wrote *Some Reflections on a Pamphlet, Called, The Old Whig* (London, 20 Mar.); Eustace Budgell probably wrote the *Moderator* (5 Apr.). John Asgill on 3 April published *The Complicated Question Divided* (London), and Mordaunt's *Remarks* was published on 8 April, as was probably Richard West's *An Enquiry into the Manner of Creating Peers* (London).

21. Gay to Maurice Johnson, Jr., 23 Apr. 1713, *Letters,* pp. 2–3. Addison's relationship with the three Tories concerning the production of *Cato* is cited by John Loftis, *The Politics of Drama in Augustan England,* pp. 59–60. Today we know still other facts that disprove the accusation of his hostile contemporaries. We know, for example, that he had asked St. John and Harley to read the play prior to its casting, that two weeks before opening night (14 April) he dined with the secretary of state and Swift, and that he even invited the author of *The Conduct of the Allies* to attend a rehearsal.

22. *PH,* 6:1223; see also Abel Boyer, *State,* 5:442.

23. For the constant negotiation that went on between Halifax and Harley, see the former's letters addressed to the treasurer between 30 Aug. 1711 and 28 Oct. 1714, in HMC, *Portland,* 5:79, 108, 113–14, 115–16, 120,

125, 131–32, 133–34, 134, 149, 166, 251–52, 254, 268–69, 270–71, 271, 275, 292, 292–93, 346–47, 358, 437, 438, 451, 500. Addison's letter to John Hughes is quoted in part in *Addisoniana,* 1:59.

24. Anne to Marlborough, 3 July 1708, 22 July 1708, HMC, *The Marlborough Papers,* in *Eighth Report* (London, 1881), p. 42; Pope to Caryll, 1 May 1714, *Correspondence,* 1:220–21.

25. For the attack on party "distinction," see Daniel Defoe[?], *The Conduct of Parties in England . . .* (London, 1712), p. 6. The popularity of the idea can be established by Defoe's repetition of it in *An Appeal to Honour and Justice* [London, 1715], in *Later Stuart Tracts,* ed. George A. Aitken (London, 1903), p. 103. Even late seventeenth-century political commentators attributed the rise of parties to William's reign: Anon., *The State of Parties, and of the Public, As Influenced by Those Parties in This Conjunction Offered to Englishmen. Printed about the Year 1692,* in *A Collection of State Tracts,* 3 vols. [London, 1705–7], 2 (1705):211–12.

26. Spence, *Observations,* 1:60.

27. This idea is voiced by men as different in values and personalities as Defoe and Berkeley. Cf. Defoe, *A Hymn to Peace* (London, 1706), p. 16; Berkeley, *The Querist* [1735–37, 1750], in *Works,* vol. 6, no. 309.

28. William Temple, *Of Popular Discontents,* in *Works,* 3:45. See also *S* 126; John Scott, *The Christian Life* (London, 1681), pp. 201–3; Defoe, *The Secret History of the White Staff, . . . ,* pt. 2 (London, 1714), p. 65.

29. *HR,* 1 (1717):112; the earl of Wintoun was not tried with the others.

30. Steele, *A Letter to a Member, etc. concerning the Condemned Lords* [Mar. 1716], in *Tracts,* p. 415.

31. Francis Atterbury, *An Argument to Prove the Affections of the People of England to Be the Best Security of Government* (London, 1716), passim.

32. Stanhope to the commanding officer of His Majesty's forces in Liverpool: Whitehall, 29 Feb. 1715/16, in Great Britain, Public Record Office, *State Papers Domestic* 35, vol. 5, no. 13. Addison makes two bland references to the escape of Nithsdale, in *F* 26 and *F* 34.

33. In pointing out these inadequacies, Addison is acknowledging some truth in Tory propaganda that had voiced these charges for years. See Swift, *Examiners* 25 and 35; and *A Short Character of His Excellency Thomas Earl of Wharton, Lord Lieutenant of Ireland* [1711], in *Examiner and Other Pieces Written in 1710–11,* ed. Herbert Davis (Oxford, 1957); Anon., *Accrostic,* in *Tory Pills to Purge Whig Melancholy,* 2d ed. (London, 1715), p. 61.

34. Swift to Pope, 10 Jan. 1720/21, *Correspondence,* 2:373; cf. *G* 118; see also *S* 439. Addison's hatred for this undercover race may be traced to his unwilling association with them in his days as undersecretary to

both Hedges and Sunderland. Secret service activities were among the duties assigned to the secretary of state's office.

35. For a conventional representation of the jackal-lion tradition, see John Dryden's *Annus Mirabilis* [1667], st. 82, ll. 325–28, in *Poems,* vol. 1; for its repudiation, see the statement by Oliver Goldsmith, in *Collected Works,* ed. Arthur Friedman, 5 vols. (Oxford, 1966), 5:240. Concerning Walsingham's spy system, Conyers Read remarked: "It is hard to find out much . . . and in consequence writers are often apt to erect, upon the basis of a few known facts, an elaborate structure formed for the most part out of their imaginations" (*Mr. Secretary Walsingham and the Policy of Queen Elizabeth,* 3 vols. [Cambridge, Mass., 1925], 2:318).

36. Ps. 10:9. A further precedent for the leonine metaphor might have come from *Paradise Lost,* 11. 182–90; see *S* 363.

37. Addison's displeasure with personal attack is consistently revealed by Thomas Burnet in his *Letters to George Duckett,* passim.

38. For other attacks on party writers, see *S* 124, *S* 125, *S* 507, *F* 35, *F* 40.

39. If in *F* 35 he invites governmental control of the press, he had rejected the idea in the *Spectator*. In *S* 451 he objected to the legislative measure "to oblige every person that writes a book, or a paper, to swear himself the author of it, and enter down in a public register his name and place of abode."

40. Addison discusses justice in *S* 125 and *S* 243, constancy in *S* 162. But see *S* 125 for his more cynical caution against the superpatriot.

6. The Structure of Government

1. Cicero *De re publica,* trans. Clinton Walker Keyes (London and New York, 1928), p. 211. Although this work was not extant in Addison's day, significant passages had been preserved in various medieval sources and later reproduced in all standard seventeenth- and eighteenth-century editions of Cicero's works. See also Thomas Aquinas, *Summa theologica,* pt. 2 (first part), 24; Richard Hooker, *Polity,* bk. 1, passim. (John Locke himself cites "judicious Hooker" throughout his *Treatises of Government.* In Addison's time Bishop Benjamin Hoadly used Hooker's *Ecclesiastical Polity* as the basis for his *Original and Institution of Civil Government* [London, 1710], as did John Willes for his *Present Constitution, and the Protestant Succession Vindicated* [London, 1714].) See also Hugo Grotius, *Of the Rights of War and Peace* [Eng. trans., 1654], 3 vols. (London, 1715), 1:45–48; Samuel Pufendorf, *Of the Law of Nature and Nations* [Eng. trans., 1703], 3d ed. (London, 1717), bk. 2, chap. 3 (especially p. 117);

Richard Cumberland, *A Brief Disquisition of the Law of Nature* (London, 1692), passim; Nathanael Culverwel, *Of the Light of Nature, a Discourse* [1652], (Edinburgh, 1857), pp. 57–80.

2. Grotius, *Rights,* 1:45; see also Culverwel, *Light,* p. 57. For Addison's view of the "ornament of our nature," see *S* 39.

3. For Addison on justice, see also *S* 125, *S* 169, *S* 243, *F* 31.

4. See Cicero *De officiis,* trans. Walter Miller (London and New York, 1913), pp. 29–31. But Addison was himself guilty of this when he refused to vote on Ormonde's fate.

5. Locke, *Second Treatise,* 2:6, 3:21. For Anglican assumption of this interpretation, see William Bates, *The Harmony of the Divine Attributes,* in *Works,* p. 96; Henry Downes, *The Necessity and Usefulness of Laws and the Excellency of Our Own* (Oxford, 1708), p. 4.

6. For a similar definition made by the Whig Lord Mayor of London and by George I to the Lords of the Council on 23 September 1714, see *HR,* 1 (1724):49–50, 53.

7. White Kennett, *A Thanksgiving Sermon for the Blessing of God, in Suppressing the Late Unnatural Rebellion* (London, 1716), p. 19. See also *F* 1 and Daniel Defoe, *Review,* 21 May 1709. On 25 August 1710 Addison wrote Lord Wharton that these slogans were the rhetoric of "fashionable doctrine" (*Letters,* p. 234).

8. Cicero *De re publica,* p. 65; Locke, *Second Treatise,* 4:22. See also Hooker, *Polity,* 1. 8. 10; Eutactus Philodemius [pseud.], *The Original and End of Civil Power* [London, 1649], in *Pamphlets on Religion and Democracy, Sixteenth to Nineteenth Centuries* (San Francisco, 1940), p. 191; William Temple, *An Essay upon the Original and Nature of Government* [1672], in *Works,* 1:30, 51, 52; Algernon Sidney, *Discourses concerning Government* (London, 1698), pp. 24–25, 247–49 (chap. 1, sec. 11; chap. 2, sec. 32). Cf. John Asgill, *The Complicated Question Divided* (London, 1719), p. 15.

9. For Addison's analysis of the law and its relation to the Pretender, see also *F* 16.

10. Aristotle *Politics* (ed. Richard McKeon; New York, 1941) 3. 4. 1277a27, 26.

11. See *OW* 1 and Locke, *Second Treatise,* 8:99; 10:132.

12. J. L. Delolme in his analysis of the "Anglo-Norman constitution" ably refuted this maxim; see his *Constitution of England* (Dublin, 1775), p. 5. Addison also wrote of mixed government in *S* 287 and could have drawn additional sanction for his view from the following: *The History of Polybius the Megalopolitain,* trans. Sir H. S. [1693], 2d ed., 3 vols. (London, 1698), 3:14–15; Cicero *De re publica,* p. 151.

13. Francis Atterbury, *Sermons and Discourses on Several Subjects and Occasions,* 2 vols. (London, 1723), 1:263 ff.; Richard Steele, *Englishman,* vol. 1, no. 28; Sidney, *Discourses,* pp. 130–33 (chap. 2, sec. 16).

14. Steele, *A Letter to Sir M[iles] W[arton] concerning Occasional Peers* [1713], in *Tracts,* p. 76. For the legal statement of the peerage bill, see Great Britain, Public Record Office, *State Papers Domestic* 35, vol. 19, no. 77; *HR,* 4 (1719):130–31; John Oldmixon, *The History of England during the Reigns of King William and Queen Mary, Queen Anne, King George I . . .* (London, 1735), pp. 675–77.

15. Addison's definition of tyranny is based on that of Locke, *Second Treatise,* 18:199, 15:172; the Neo-Stoic Pierre Charron, *Of Wisdom,* trans. George Stanhope [1697], 2d ed. (London, 1707), bk. 3, p. 135; and Sidney, *Discourses,* pp. 12–14, 45–48 (chap. 1, sec. 5; chap. 1, sec. 18).

16. For Bishop Berkeley's remark, see Historical Manuscripts Commission, *The Appendix to the Seventh Report* (London, 1879), 7:238. Cf. *F* 10. For Whig statement, see Anon., *A Collection of Original Letters and Authentic Papers, Relating to the Rebellion, 1715* (Edinburgh, 1730), pp. 43–44.

17. Abel Boyer, *State,* 5:459; *HR,* 1 (1724):45–47, 67–68, 70.

18. For successive announcements of rebellious activity, see *HR,* 1 (1724):334–36; *House of Commons Journals* 18 (for 1714–18):232–346. Cf. Townshend to Horace Walpole, 15/26 Jan. 1715/16, in William Coxe, *The Memoirs of the Life and Administration of Sir Robert Walpole,* 3 vols. (London, 1798), 2:50. Addison's attacks on Jacobitism (e.g., *F* 10) are supported and even anticipated by the following: Benjamin Hoadly, *The Happiness of the Present Establishment . . .* (London, 1708), p. 4; Defoe, *A Letter from Captain Tom to the Mob, Now Raised for Dr. Sacheverel* (London, 1710); Samuel Bradford, *The Reasonableness of Standing Fast in English and in Christian Liberty* (London, 1713); John Barrington, *A Dissuasive from Jacobitism* [1713], 2d ed. (London, 1713); Kennett, *A Thanksgiving-Sermon;* Edmund Gibson, *The Deliverances and Murmurings, of the Israelites, and These Nations, Compared* (London, 1716). See also the following anonymous pamphlets: *The Substance of a Late Conference between the French King, the Pretender, and One of Their Best Friends* (London, 1710); *A Letter to the Patriot, Relating to the Pretender, and the Growth of Popery in the City of York, and Other Parts of Great Britain* (London, 1714); *A Discourse Showing the Reasons Why Protestant Subjects Cannot Enjoy Their Laws, Religion, Liberty and Property under a Popish Prince in a Dialogue between a Romanist and an Englishman* (London, 1714); *Popery and Slavery Reviving . . .* (London, 1714); *British Advice to the Freeholders of Great Britain* (London, 1715), p. 23.

19. Addison to Lord Manchester, 9 Apr. 1708, *Letters,* p. 107.

20. Stephen Poyntz to Secretary Stanhope, 21 Aug./1 Sept. 1716, in Coxe, *Memoirs,* 2:75–76.

21. Addison earlier—in *Trial*—described the Tory propaganda war against the Whigs as one of "misrepresentation," "calumnies," "aspersions," "false and fraudulent" statements, which sought to "traduce" honest reputations. For Lord Somers, see *F* 39.

22. Poyntz to Stanhope, 17/28 Aug. 1716, in Coxe, *Memoirs,* 2:73. For Addison's praise of the Prince of Wales, see *F* 46.

23. In the *Daily Courant* for 2, 6, and 20 Jan. 1715/16 the first three numbers of the *Freeholder* were advertised as available free to any interested reader, an indication that the cost of publication was borne by the party whose views it upheld.

24. For the details of the first suspension, see *HCJ,* 18:233 ff.; *HR,* 1 (1724):336; for those of the second, see *PH,* 7:275–76; *HCJ,* 18:334 ff.

25. For Stanhope's position, see *PH,* 7:275–76. See Cicero *De legibus,* trans. Clinton W. Keyes (London and New York, 1928), p. 467; and *Philippics,* trans. Walter C. A. Ker (London and New York, 1926), p. 291; Locke, *Second Treatise,* 14:160. Cf. Grotius, *Rights,* 1:20–21; Charron, *Of Wisdom,* bk. 3, p. 70.

26. Just four months later, in a calmer period, Addison criticized such deference as pseudo culture and false analogy.

27. *Weekly Journal,* 25 Feb. 1715/16.

28. The objection is William Shippen's, made on the floor of the Commons during the debate on the renewal of suspension (*PH,* 7:275–76); Swift to Pope, 10 Jan. 1720/21, *Correspondence,* 2:373.

29. Gibbon, *The Memoirs of the Life of Edward Gibbon* [1796], ed. G. Birkbeck Hill (London, 1900), p. 19.

30. Gibbon, *Memoirs,* p. 19. For Walpole as author of the preamble to the Septennial Act, see J. H. Plumb, *The Origins of Political Stability: England, 1675–1725,* pp. 173–74.

31. Cicero *The Second Speech against Lucius Sergius Catiline,* in *The Speeches,* trans. Louis F. Lord (Cambridge, Mass., and London, 1937), p. 65.

32. For Addison's portraits of the fox hunter and his publican, see *F* 22, *F* 44, *F* 47; of Sawney, *F* 27. For his attacks on Tory stateswomen, see *F* 4, *F* 8, *F* 11, *F* 15, *F* 23, *F* 32. For the satirical "History of the Pretender's Fourteen Years Reign Digested into Annals," see *F* 36.

7. Civil Liberties and Natural Rights

1. William Blackstone, *Commentaries on the Laws of England,* 4 vols. (London, 1765–69), 1:251.

2. Cf. Blackstone, *Commentaries,* 1:125.

3. Cf. Cicero *De legibus,* trans. Clinton W. Keyes (London and New York, 1928), p. 329; and *De officiis,* trans. Walter Miller (London and New York, 1913), p. 109; Samuel Pufendorf, *Of the Law of Nature and Nations* [Eng. trans., 1703], 3d ed. (London, 1717), bk. 3, chap. 2; John Locke, *Second Treatise,* 2:4–5 (it is with relevance to this particular idea that Locke cites the "judicious Hooker" and the first book of *Ecclesiastical Polity*); William Molyneux, *The Case of Ireland's Being Bound by Acts of Parliament* [1698], p. 150 (as cited by Josiah Tucker, *Notions of Mr. Locke, and His Followers* [Gloucester, 1778], p. 29); Gilbert Burnet, *An Enquiry into the Measures of Submission to the Supreme Authority* (London, 1688), p. 1.

4. Cf. *T* 161; Richard Steele, *The Crisis* [1714], in *Tracts,* p. 137; Daniel Defoe, *An Answer to a Question That Nobody Thinks of, viz., But What If the Queen Should Die?* (London, 1713), p. 18; and *Review,* 13 June 1706, 28 Jan. 1706/7.

5. See, for example, John Dennis[?], *The Danger of Priestcraft to Religion and Government* (London, 1702), p. 4.

6. For Steele's enunciation of the same maxim, see his speech on the peerage bill (8 Dec. 1719) before the Commons in *PH,* 7:609–16.

7. For Whig statements on the right of property as a civil liberty, see Steele, *Englishman,* vol. 1, no. 3; Defoe, *The Original Power of the Collective Body of the People of England Examined and Asserted* (London, 1702), p. 2; and *An Answer to a Question,* pp. 34–35; Ambrose Philips, *An Epistle to the Right Honourable Charles Lord Halifax, One of the Lords Justices Appointed by His Majesty* (London, 1714), pp. 1–2; Henry Downes, *The Necessity and Usefulness of Laws, and the Excellency of Our Own* (Oxford, 1708), p. 20 et passim; Burnet, *An Enquiry,* p. 4. Cf. Addison's defense of the right of rebellion and Locke, *Second Treatise,* 19:232; Cicero *De officiis,* pp. 191, 299; Pierre Charron, *Of Wisdom,* trans. George Stanhope [1697], 2d ed. (London, 1707), bk. 3, pp. 68–69, 135–36, 275; Algernon Sidney, *Discourses concerning Government* (London, 1698), pp. 14–17, 345–48 (chap. 1, sec. 6; chap. 3, sec. 20).

8. Charles Leslie, *The Right of Monarchy Asserted* (London, 1713), pp. 18, 20; this statement is representative of High Church Tory attitudes from the beginning of the century. For Tory contempt of Sacheverell, see Abigail Harley to Edward Harley, 2 Mar. 1709/10, in HMC, *Portland,* 4:533.

9. For Whig interpretation of the principles of the Revolution in terms of Sacheverell, see Arthur Maynwaring, *Four Letters to a Friend in North Britain,* letter 1, 15 June 1710 (London, 1710), p. 3. See also Burnet, *History,* 5:434 ff.; William Fleetwood, *The Thirteenth Chapter to the Ro-*

mans, Vindicated from the Abusive Senses Put upon It (London, 1710); Benjamin Hoadly, *The Jacobite's Hopes Revived by Our Late Tumults and Addresses* (London, 1710), passim; Anon., *The Substance of a Late Conference between the French King, the Pretender, and One of Their Best Friends* (London, 1710), passim.

10. Addison's attack on Sacheverell is a recapitulation of a statement made by Stanhope during the impeachment (Abel Boyer, *History,* p. 415). For Addison's initial approval of Whig silence relative to Sacheverell, see his letter to Sunderland, 20 May 1710, *Letters,* p. 218.

11. This was a segment of the official Whig line in 1715–16; see, for example, William Burscough, *The Revolution Recommended to Our Memories* [1715], 2d ed. (London, 1722), pp. 31–32. Addison gloatingly pointed out evidence of this change in public opinion—from reactionary Toryism to moderate Whiggism—to Charles Delafaye, 7 June 1715, *Letters,* p. 336; see also Historical Manuscripts Commission, *Appendix to Eighth Report* (London, 1881), pt. 1, 8:49.

12. Defoe[?], *Faults on Both Sides* (London, 1710), pp. 47–48. During the Sacheverell trial the moderate Tory attitude was best expressed by George Hooper, bishop of Bath and Wells; see Boyer, *History,* p. 433. While theoretically accepting the doctrine of passive obedience and nonresistance, Jonathan Swift (*Examiner* 34) justified rebellion under a limited monarchy in cases of extreme necessity.

13. Defoe[?], *Faults,* p. 7. See also White Kennett, *A Compassionate Enquiry into the Causes of the Civil War in a Sermon Preached . . . on the Day of Fast for the Martyrdom of King Charles the First* [1704], (London, 1708), p. 2.

14. Addison's position is identical with Steele's in the *Englishman,* vol. 1, no. 56; and with Defoe's in *Original Power,* pp. 5–6; *Review,* 17 July 1707, 10 Mar. 1707/8, 31 Dec. 1709, 18 Feb. 1709/10, 25 Feb. 1709/10, 29 Aug. 1710; and *A Secret History of One Year* (London, 1714), p. 3. The same position is echoed by the Whig bishops: see, for example, Hoadly, *Some Considerations Humbly Offered to the Right Reverend the Lord Bishop of Exeter* [1709], in *Several Tracts Formerly Published: Now Collected into One Volume* (London, 1715), pp. 333 ff.; Burnet, *An Enquiry,* passim. The pamphlet literature on this subject, both pro and con, is enormous. See, for example, the following: Eutactus Philodemius [pseud.], *The Original and End of Civil Power* [1649], in *Pamphlets on Religion and Democracy, Sixteenth to Nineteenth Centuries* (San Francisco, 1940), pp. 198–99, 211; Anon., *An Argument for Self-Defence* [1687?], in *A Collection of Scarce and Valuable Tracts . . . Selected from . . . Libraries; Particularly That of the Late Lord Somers* [*Somers Tracts*], ed. Walter Scott, 2d ed., 13 vols. (London, 1809–15), 10:277–82;

George Hickes, *The Doctrine of Passive Obedience and Jure Divino Disproved* [1689], in *The Harleian Miscellany,* 12 vols. (London, 1808–11), 7:295–98; Peter Allix[?], *An Examination of the Scruples of Those Who Refuse to Take the Oath of Allegiance* (London, 1689), p. 11; Hubert Languet, *Vindiciae contra Tyrannos,* trans. William Walker [1648], (London, 1689), passim; Matthew Tindal[?], *An Essay concerning Obedience to the Supreme Powers, and the Duty of Subjects in All Revolutions* [1694], in *A Collection of State Tracts,* 3 vols. (London, 1705–7), 2 (1705):434 et passim; Thomas Bradbury, *The Lawfulness of Resisting Tyrants* [1714], 4th ed. (London, 1714), passim; John Withers, *The History of Resistance, as Practiced by the Church of England* [1710], in *Somers Tracts,* 12:264; and *The Perjury and Folly of the Late Rebellion Displayed* (London, 1716), pp. 13–14, 18–19.

15. See particularly his description of Nassau in *A Poem to His Majesty* (*MW,* 1:42, ll. 55–59), and that of Somers in *F* 39. For Addison's allegorical presentation of the havoc caused by rebellion, see *F* 27. His concept of restraint was personal, but it also reflected the spirit of Locke (*Second Treatise,* 18:203, 204) and that of contemporaries like Steele (*Englishman,* vol. 2, no. 22).

16. Burnet, *History,* 5:108; Locke, *A Letter concerning Toleration* (London, 1689), passim; William Sherlock, *A Practical Discourse of Religious Assemblies* [1681], 3d ed. (London, 1700), p. 142; Anon., *The Case of Toleration Recognized* (London, 1702), p. 7.

17. Boyer, *History,* p. 103; Burnet, *History,* 5:70–71.

18. The moderate's attitude toward Sacheverell's charge against Godolphin is synthesized by William Wake, bishop of Lincoln, *Speech in the House of Lords, March the Seventeenth at the Opening of the Second Article of the Impeachment against Dr. Sacheverell* (London, 1710), p. 1.

19. Cicero *De natura deorum,* tr. H. Rackham (London and New York, 1933), p. 7; *The History of Polybius the Megalopolitain,* trans. Sir H. S. [1693], 2d ed., 3 vols. (London, 1698), 3:73–74; Charron, *Of Wisdom,* bk. 3, pp. 15, 270–71. For contemporary attitudes toward religion's role in the political arena, see Charles D'Avenant, *An Essay upon the Probable Methods of Making a People Gainers in the Balance of Trade* [1699], in *Political and Commercial Works,* 5 vols. (London, 1771), 2:321; Robert South, *Ecclesiastical Policy the Best Policy: or, Religion the Best Reason of State,* in *Sermons,* 1:46; John Tillotson, *The Advantages of Religion to Societies,* in *Works,* 1:36. The view of religion as a rein upon the human tendency toward political anarchy is further stated by Richard Bentley, *Confutation,* p. 10; John Wilkins, *Of the Principles and Duties of Natural Religion* [1675], 7th ed. (London, 1715), pp. 258 ff.; Edward Stil-

lingfleet, *Origines Sacrae* [1662], 5th ed. (London, 1680), p. 357; Lilly Butler, *Religion No Matter of Shame* [1709], in Letsome and Nicholl, *Defence,* 2:438–39. The view that the piety of a populace gives a state political stability and wealth is also expressed by [George Savile], *The Character of a Trimmer* [1688], 3d ed. (London, 1689), p. 12; Dennis [?], *Danger of Priestcraft,* p. 6; Bradbury, *Eikōn Basilikē* (London, 1715), passim; George Berkeley, *An Essay toward Preventing the Ruin of Great Britain* [1721], in *Works,* 6:79; Steele, *Englishman,* vol. 1., no. 57; Burnet, *History,* 6:211–12; Samuel Clarke, *A Sermon Preached before the Queen at St. James's Chapel* (London, 1710), p. 13.

20. For Addisonian opinions stated in this paragraph, see *T* 257, *S* 185, *F* 39, *F* 54. The salutary relationship between toleration and trade was spelled out as early as 1682 in an anonymous broadside published in London, *Some Sober and Weighty Reasons against Prosecuting Protestant Dissenters.* See also Locke, *A Second Letter concerning Toleration* (London, 1690), p. 2; Josiah Child, *New Discourse,* p. 6; William Temple, *Observations upon the United Provinces of the Netherlands* [1673], in *Works,* 1:77, 180–88; John DeWitt, *The True Interest and Political Maxims of the Republic of Holland and West-Friesland* (London, 1702), pt. 1, pp. 61 ff.; William Petty, *Political Arithmetic* [1690], in *Economic Writings,* ed. Charles Henry Hull, 2 vols. (Cambridge, 1899), 1:263; Steele, *A Letter to a Member of Parliament concerning the Bill for Preventing the Growth of Schism* [1714], in *Tracts,* pp. 251–52.

21. See the letters of Halifax to Harley, 2 and 6 Dec. 1711, in HMC, *Portland,* 5:120, 125; Boyer, *History,* pp. 38 ff., 103, 161–62, 529.

22. *S* 269 is a gently satirical exposure of many of Sir Roger's beliefs, all equally fatuous, but in the long run harmless.

23. Cf. *F* 37; Hoadly, *The Present Delusion of Many Protestants, Considered* (London, 1715), pp. 21–22; A. A. Sykes, *The Safety of the Church under the Present Ministry Considered* (London, 1715), passim; Samuel Bradford, *The Christian Religion the Occasion, Not the Cause of Division* (London, 1716), p. 22.

24. *House of Commons Journals* 18 (1714–18):71, 117; John Oldmixon, *The History of England during the Reigns of King William and Queen Mary, Queen Anne, King George I . . .* (London, 1735), p. 671.

25. See, for example, the following Whig pamphlets, which urged greater freedom for dissenters: Anon., *Reasons Humbly Offered to the Conformists, Why They Should Hold Occasional Communion with Protestant Dissenters* (London, 1702); Anon., *Reflections upon a Late Scandalous and Malicious Pamphlet Entitled, The Shortest Way with Dissenters* (London, 1703); Defoe, *Review,* 22 Nov. 1705, 17 July 1707, 28

Dec. 1710; Anon., *A General View of Our Present Discontents* (London, 1710); Anon., *Britain's Alarm to All True Protestants* (London, 1714); John Barrington, *A Letter from a Layman in Communion with the Church of England, Tho' Dissenting from Her in Some Points* (London, 1714); Thomas Brett, *True Moderation* (London, 1714); Anon., *A Collection of White and Black Lists; or, A View of Those Gentlemen Who Have Given Their Votes in Parliament for and against the Protestant Religion, and Succession, and the Trade and Liberties of Their Country* (London, 1715); Anon., *Reasons for Repealing the Occasional and Schism Acts* (London, 1715); Sykes, *An Answer to the Nonjurors' Charge of Schism upon the Church of England* (London, 1716); Bradford, *Christian Religion;* John Sowter, *The Way to Be Wise and Wealthy; or, The Excellency of Industry and Frugality* (London, 1716); Edmund Calamy, *The Repeal of the Act against Occasional Conformity, Considered,* 2d ed. (London, 1717); Charles Owen, *Plain Reasons* [1715], 3d ed. (London, 1717); Matthew Henry, *A Brief Enquiry into the True Nature of Schism* [1690], (London, 1717); Anon., *Reasons for Enabling Protestant Dissenters to Bear Public Office* (London, 1717); Defoe, *Faction in Power* (London, 1717); Withers, *A Vindication of the Dissenters from the Charge of Rebellion and Being the Authors of Our Civil Wars* (London, 1719). These representative titles fall into a pattern. From 1702 to 1710 the Whigs fought mainly to preserve for the dissenters those liberties permitted them by the Act of Toleration, although the party writers all suggested the hope of enlarged toleration for dissent. In 1711 when the Whigs betrayed the interests of the dissenters, the Whig press was largely silent on the subject. From 1714, the Whigs engaged in an all-out campaign to secure the repeal of the Occasional Conformity and Schism acts.

26. The political origin of Locke's anti-Catholicism is apparent throughout his *Letter concerning Toleration.* Cf. Steele, *An Account of the State of the Roman Catholic Religion throughout the World* [May 1715], in *Tracts,* pp. 349–55.

27. See *F* 12, *F* 54, and, for his description of gypsies, *S* 130.

28. See *F* 5, *F* 36, *F* 49.

8. Church and Party

1. *F* 6. For Richard Steele's similar position, see his *Englishman,* vol. 1, no. 12, and everywhere in *The Christian Hero* [1701], ed. Rae Blanchard (Oxford, 1932). This is a typically Latitudinarian definition of the good man; see John Tillotson's sermons, particularly *Of the Work Assigned to Every Man and the Season for Doing It,* in *Works,* vol. 2.

2. For John Milton on religious diversity, see his antiprelatical pam-

phlets, particularly *The Reason of Church Government Urged Against Prelaty* (London, 1642).

3. John Scott, *The Christian Life* (London, 1681), p. 457. Cf. Joseph Glanvill, *A Blow at Modern Sadducism . . . with Reflections on Drollery and Atheism* [1668], 4th ed. (London, 1688), p. 182.

4. Jonathan Swift, *A Tale of a Tub with Other Early Works, 1696–1707,* ed. Herbert Davis (Oxford, 1965), p. 85; Edward Gibbon, *The History of the Decline and Fall of the Roman Empire* [1776–88], ed. J. B. Bury, 9th ed., 7 vols. (London, 1925), 2:2. That Addison avoided all manner of offensiveness is shown by the note Bishop Hurd appended to *T* 257. He pointed to the essay's "ridicule . . . so guarded and chaste . . . that no part of it is seen to fall on religion itself.—It is to be lamented, that another of our wits, I mean, in the famous *Tale of a Tub,* was either not so discreet, or not so happy."

5. S[imon] P[atrick], *A Brief Account of the New Sect of Latitudinarians* (London, 1662), p. 7. Cf. Benjamin Hoadly, *Four Sermons concerning Impartial Enquiry into Religion* [Jan. 1712/13], in *Several Tracts Formerly Published* (London, 1715), p. 457. See Swift, *Tale of a Tub,* secs. 2, 4.

6. Tillotson, *A Sermon Preached at White-Hall before His Late Majesty* (London, 1686), p. 5; *The Hazard of Being Saved in the Church of Rome,* in *Works,* 1:94; *The Protestant Religion Vindicated from the Charge of Singularity and Novelty,* in *Works,* 1:251; *The Rule of Faith,* in *Works,* 1:527–614; *Sin and Danger of Adding to the Doctrine of the Gospel,* in *Works,* 2:200–206; *Of Miracles Wrought in Confirmation of Christianity,* in *Works,* 3:482. Cf. Edward Stillingfleet, *Scripture and Tradition Compared* (London, 1688), passim; Henry More, *A Brief Discourse of the True Grounds of the Certainty of Faith in Points of Religion,* in *Theological Works* (London, 1708), pp. 765–70; John Williams, *The Divine Authority of the Scriptures* [1694–95], in Letsome and Nicholl, *Defence,* 1:217.

7. For Latitudinarian attacks on Catholic infallibility, see Hoadly, *Four Sermons,* p. 457; Stillingfleet, *A Second Discourse in Vindication of the Protestant Grounds of Faith* (London, 1673), chap. 1; Tillotson, *On the Fifth of November, 1687,* in *Works,* 1:158–66; John Locke, *A Second Letter concerning Toleration* (London, 1690), p. 3.

8. Locke, *Some Thoughts concerning Education* (London, 1693), sec. 66. Cf. *F* 27, *S* 399.

9. Stillingfleet, *Origines Sacrae* [1662], 5th ed. (London, 1680), p. 357; John Dryden, *The Medal* [1682], in *Poems,* vol. 1, l. 166. For definitions of melancholy, see Samuel Johnson's *Dictionary of the English Language* (London, 1755), s.v. "Melancholy"; Robert Burton, *The Anatomy of Mel-*

ancholy, What It Is [1621], ed. Floyd Dell and Paul Jordan-Smith (London and New York, 1930), pt. 3, sec. 4. For Anglican attitudes toward dissent, see, e.g., More, *Enthusiasmus Triumphatus* [1656], (London, 1712), passim; Glanvill, *Philosophia Pia* (London, 1671), pp. 223–24; and *Usefulness of Real Philosophy to Religion,* in *Essays on Several Important Subjects in Philosophy and Religion* (London, 1676), pp. 17–18; George Rust, *A Discourse of the Use of Reason in Matters of Religion* (London, 1683), pp. 32–33; Swift, *Tale of a Tub,* passim.

10. Cf. Tillotson, *Sermon XX. Preached at the First General Meeting of the Gentlemen, and Others, in and near London, Born within the County of York,* in *Works,* 1:174.

11. Swift, *Tale of a Tub,* secs. 6, 9. See also *S* 201.

12. Gilbert Burnet, *History,* 6:208–9. See also William Fleetwood, *A Sermon Preached before the Queen at St. Paul's, August the Nineteenth, 1708* (London, 1708), p. 14.

13. Cf. *F* 37; Isaac Barrow, *Provide Things Honest in the Sight of All Men,* in *Works,* 3:303, 326. For Addison's discussion of the causes of such behavior, see also *S* 458, *S* 494. Thomas Sprat (*The History of the Royal Society of London, for the Improving of Natural Knowledge* [London, 1667], pp. 367–76 [misnumbered]) was one of the first to discuss this cause. By Addison's day it had become a cliché of the establishment. See, for example, Anon., *The Representation of the Present State of Religion, with Regard to the Late Excessive Growth of Infidelity, Heresy, and Profaneness: Drawn Up by the Upper House of Convocation, of the Province of Canterbury, and Transmitted to the Lower House for Their Approbation* [1711], in *The Harleian Miscellany,* 12 vols. (London, 1808–11), 11:163–69.

14. Richard Bentley, *Confutation,* p. 2. For other rational statements, see also Stillingfleet, Preface to *A Letter to a Deist* (London, 1677); John Dennis[?], *The Danger of Priestcraft to Religion and Government* (London, 1702), p. 7. Cf. *T* 111, *S* 186. For violent hostility to deism, see Dryden, Preface to *Religio Laici, or A Layman's Faith* [1682], in *Poems,* vol. 1.

15. Samuel Clarke, *A Discourse concerning the Unchangeable Obligations of Natural Religion, and the Truth and Certainty of the Christian Revelation* [1705], in Letsome and Nicholl, *Defence,* 2:136. See also Robert South, *A Discourse concerning the General Resurrection,* in *Sermons,* 2:75.

16. *Addisoniana,* 2 vols. (London, 1803), 2:70–71. See also *PH,* 7:586.

17. Scott, *Christian Life,* pp. 365–66, 371–72. See also *S* 381; *S* 387; South, *Her Ways Are Ways of Pleasantness,* in *Sermons,* 1:1; Barrow, *The Pleasantness of Religion,* in *Works,* 1:1–11; Tillotson, *Of Sincerity towards God and Man,* in *Works,* 2:5.

18. Tillotson, *The Advantages of Religion to Particular Persons,* in

Works, 1:43; and *Of Diligence in Our General and Particular Calling,* in *Works*, 3:364 et passim.

19. Addison points out the evils of atheism—its pride, its subversive character, its zeal—in *T* 111, *T* 257, *S* 3, *S* 166, *S* 185, *S* 381. Addison's analysis of atheism is supported by the religious temper of the period. For the attack on the atheist's pride, see Josiah Woodward, *Causes of the Modern Infidelity* [1710], in Letsome and Nicholl, *Defence*, 2:545. For the attack on atheists as disrupters of peace and organized society, see John Wilkins, *Of the Principles and Duties of Natural Religion* [1675], 7th ed. (London, 1715), pp. 255–56, 260; Bentley, *Confutation*, pp. 10, 11; Stillingfleet, *Origines Sacrae*, p. 358; South, *For the Wisdom of This World, Is Foolishness with God*, in *Sermons*, 1:122; Lilly Butler, *Religion No Matter of Shame* [1709], in Letsome and Nicholl, *Defence*, 2:440. For the attack on atheistical zeal, see Wilkins, *Principles*, pp. 353–54.

20. John Oldmixon, *The Life and Posthumous Works of Arthur Maynwaring* (London, 1715), p. 29; see also *T* 220.

21. Fleetwood, *Sermon at St. Paul's*, p. 14; Burnet, *Of the Propagation of the Gospel in Foreign Parts* [1704], in *An Account of the Society for Propagating the Gospel in Foreign Parts* (London, 1704), pp. 18–19; Swift, *An Argument to Prove That the Abolishing of Christianity in England May, As Things Now Stand, Be Attended with Some Inconveniences . . .* [1708], in *Bickerstaff Papers and Pamphlets on the Church*, ed. Herbert Davis (Oxford, 1957), passim.

22. Swift to William Tisdall, 16 Dec. 1703, *Correspondence*, 1:38–39. See also *S* 112 and the portraits of the Tory fox hunter and his innkeeper in the *Freeholder*.

23. See, e.g., Henry Sacheverell, *The Character of a Low Churchman* (London, 1702), p. 27 [misnumbered]; and *Political Union* (London, 1710), passim; Charles Leslie, *The New Association of Those Called Moderate Churchmen . . .* [1702], 3d ed. (London, 1702), p. 1. Typical of Tory attacks on the Whig bishops is Joseph Trapp's *Character and Principles of the Present Set of Whigs* (London, 1711), p. 31; see also HMC, *Portland*, 5:435. For a Whig analysis of this attack, see particularly Richard West, *The True Character of a Churchman* (London, 1702), passim; Daniel Defoe, *King William's Affection to the Church of England Examined* [1703], 4th ed. (London, 1703), p. 23.

24. Hoadly makes clear the religious split between the upper and lower clergy; see his *Serious Advice to the Good People of England*, in *A Collection of Several Papers Printed in the Year 1710* (London, 1718), p. 22. For Steele's statement, see *The Romish Ecclesiastical History of Late Years* [1714], in *Tracts*, p. 227. Cf. George I's "Directions to the Clergy on Dec.

11, 1714," in *HR,* 1 (1724):77–78; for the political stand of High Church clerics, see the anonymous *Tory Pills to Purge Whig Melancholy,* 2d ed. (London, 1715): *British Loyalty Displayed,* pp. 29–30; *Upon the Burning of Dr. Sacheverell's Sermons,* p. 68; *High Church Loyalty, A Song,* pp. 52–53; *An Excerpt from the Doctor Militant,* p. 17. For the Whig reaction to this position, see John Toland, *An Appeal to Honest People against Wicked Priests* (London, 1710?), pp. 1–2; Dennis[?], *The Danger of Priestcraft,* p. 21; Toland[?], *Jacobitism, Perjury, and Popery of High Church Priests* (London, 1710), pp. 3–4.

25. For his fears of clerical influence, see his letter to the earl of Sunderland (20 May 1710), *Letters,* p. 218; for his hostility to the Church of England party, see *F* 52. The image of the Anglican church is from a speech by Sacheverell, as cited by White Kennett, *A True Answer to Dr. Sacheverell's Sermon before the Lord Mayor* (London, 1709), p. 20.

26. For the reaction of Durham County, see HMC, *Portland,* 4:570. For the Tory attitude toward the Whig bishops, see the anonymous *Dialogue between Jack High and Will Low* (London, 1710), p. 9.

27. Addison's judgment of the rioters' personality and motivation is substantiated by historical fact. See the letter of Richard Ames (Bilston, 13 July 1715), in *House of Commons Journals* 18 (1714–18):227. So frequently did these riots occur that on 20 July 1715 the king—goaded by his Whig parliament—signed into law an act "for preventing tumults, and riotous assemblies; and for the more speedy and effectual punishing the rioters" (*HCJ* 18:232). See also *F* 14.

28. Oldmixon, *Maynwaring,* p. 289.

29. Cf. *S* 399.

30. Cf. *F* 7, *F* 32. Addison made fleeting satirical reference to the slogan (4 Sept. 1710, *T* 220) and implied that it was a political device useful in party polemics. (According to Percy, he alluded to it again in *S* 243 [8 Dec. 1711] although not visibly to the modern reader.) Despite Addison's reserve in 1710, the particular slogan called forth a vengeful rebuttal from other Whigs. Especially active that year was Hoadly; see, for example, his pamphlets: *The Election Dialogue, Serious Advice to the Good People of England,* and *True, Genuine Tory-Address,* in *A Collection of Several Papers,* pp. 123–24, pp. 27–33 et passim, and p. 2; *The Fears and Sentiments of All True Britains* (London, 1710), p. 10. See also Arthur Maynwaring, *Four Letters to a Friend in North Britain* (London, 1710), pp. 3 ff.; Toland, *An Appeal,* passim. For an earlier Whig answer, in 1707, to the Tory charge, see Francis Higgins, *The Church of England Not in Danger: . . . in a Sermon Preached at White-Hall, February 26, 1706/7* (London, 1707).

31. Stephen Poyntz to Secretary Stanhope, 8/19 Sept. 1716, in William

Coxe, *The Memoirs of the Life and Administration of Sir Robert Walpole,* 3 vols. (London, 1798), 2:81. Poyntz's schismatic fears were characteristic of those bruited among Whigs all through 1716 and earlier.

32. Francis Atterbury, *A Sermon Preached before the Honourable House of Commons at St. Margaret's Westminster, May 29, 1701* (London, 1701), pp. 19–20.

9. The Nature of Belief

1. Henry More, *Enthusiasmus Triumphatus* [1656], (London, 1712), pp. 45, 54; for Sprat's distinction, see Johnson's *Dictionary of the English Language* (London, 1755), s.v. "zeal."

2. Joseph Spence, *Observations, Anecdotes, and Characters of Books and Men,* ed. James M. Osborn, 2 vols. (Oxford, 1966), 1:82; *Addisoniana,* 2 vols. (London, 1803), 1:7. For the contents of Addison's Saturday papers on religion in the *Spectator,* see Bond's Introduction, p. lxiv. For his consistent statements on the right of free inquiry, see, e.g., *S* 237.

3. Addison's moral idealism is part of a lengthy tradition. See, e.g., Plato *Meno* 86C; Aristotle *Nicomachean Ethics* (ed. Richard McKeon; New York, 1941), 1178b; Cicero *De officiis,* trans. Walter Miller (London and New York, 1913), p. 19; and *De finibus,* trans. H. Rackham (London and New York, 1914), p. 459; Isaac Barrow, *The Pleasantness of Religion,* in *Works,* 1:1; John Tillotson, *The Wisdom of Being Religious,* in *Works,* 1:1; Robert Boyle, *Of the High Veneration Man's Intellect Owes to God* (London, 1685), pp. 65–66, 86 ff.; and *Some Motives and Incentives to the Love of God* (London, 1659), pp. 56–57; William Bates, *The Harmony of the Divine Attributes,* in *Works,* p. 94; William Derham, *Physico-Theology* [1711–12], in Letsome and Nicholl, *Defence,* 2:722; Richard Bentley, *Confutation,* p. 23; John Scott, *The Christian Life* (London, 1681), p. 110.

4. Joseph Glanvill, *Agreement of Reason and Religion,* in *Essays on Several Important Subjects in Philosophy and Religion* (London, 1676), p. 21; and *Logoy Threskeia* (London, 1670), p. 24; cf. Barrow, *Of the Virtue and Reasonableness of Faith,* in *Works,* 2:22; Edward Stillingfleet, *A Rational Account of the Grounds of the Protestant Religion* [1665], 2 vols. (Oxford, 1844), 1:323. The usual Anglican tradition is synthesized by Richard Hooker, *Polity,* 1. 14. 5.

5. John Locke, *Mr. Locke's Reply to the Right Reverend the Lord Bishop of Worcester's Answer to his Letter, concerning Some Passages relating to Mr. Locke's Essay of Human Understanding* (London, 1697), pp. 82, 96; *S* 465.

6. Bates, *Harmony,* in *Works,* p. 138. In making this statement, Bates has reworked a passage from the Royal Society, Boyle Papers, 1, fol. 86.

(Boyle's statement is cited by Richard S. Westfall, *Science and Religion in Seventeenth-Century England,* p. 174.) See also Robert South, *Christianity Mysterious, and the Wisdom of God in Making It So . . . ,* in *Sermons,* 1:416.

7. Tillotson, *Of the Trial of the Spirit,* in *Works,* 1:185. Cf. John Wilkins, *A Discourse concerning a New Planet* [1640], in *Mathematical and Philosophical Works* (London, 1708), p. 145. See also *S* 465.

8. Isaac Newton, *Mathematical Principles of Natural Philosophy* [1729], trans. Andrew Motte (Berkeley, Calif., 1934), bk. 3; *S* 237. For Addison's statement of indebtedness to the new science, see particularly *S* 420. For statements on its religious significance, see the following: Thomas Sprat, *The History of the Royal Society of London, for the Improving of Natural Knowledge* (London, 1667), pp. 15–19; Glanvill, *Modern Improvements of Useful Knowledge,* in *Essays,* pp. 1–2, 10; and *Usefulness of Real Philosophy to Religion,* in *Essays,* p. 11; William Fleetwood, *A Sermon Preached before the Gentlemen Educated at Eton College* (London, 1701), pp. 6–7; Bates, *Harmony,* in *Works,* p. 137; Boyle, *The Christian Virtuoso* [1690], in *Works,* 6 vols. (London, 1772), 5:513–14.

9. *An Oration in Defence of the New Philosophy* [1693], trans. Richard Rawlinson, in Addison, *Works,* 6:607–12.

10. Boyle, *Christian Virtuoso,* in *Works,* 5:515; and *Some Motives,* pp. 56–57; Addison, *An Oration.* Cf. Sprat, *History,* pp. 348–49; Glanvill, *Usefulness of Philosophy,* in *Essays,* p. 2 et passim; Newton, *Optics* [1704], 4th ed. corrected (London, 1730), pp. 344–45.

11. For Newton's statement, see *Optics,* pp. 344–45. Cf. Glanvill, *Usefulness of Philosophy,* in *Essays,* p. 10; Barrow, *The Being of God,* in *Works,* 2:80–81. See also *T* 119, *T* 221, *T* 236, *S* 10.

12. Boyle, *The Excellency of Theology, Compared with Natural Philosophy* (London, 1674), p. 6; cf. *S* 459.

13. Stillingfleet, *Origines Sacrae* [1662], 5th ed. (London, 1680), p. 338; see also John Williams, *The Possibility, Expediency, and Necessity of Divine Revelation* [1694–95], in Letsome and Nicholl, *Defence,* 1:155–56; Samuel Clarke, *A Demonstration of the Being and Attributes of God* [1704], in Letsome and Nicholl, *Defence,* 2:55. Throughout his sermons Tillotson maintained that the foundations of religious belief are "the belief of a God, and another life." Other orthodox Anglicans reduced natural Christianity to a single premise, namely, that God exists in all his attributes. See John Locke, *The Reasonableness of Christianity* (London, 1695), passim; Bentley, *Confutation,* p. 23; Wilkins, *Of the Principles and Duties of Natural Religion* [1675], 7th ed. (London, 1715), pp. 34–35.

14. Tillotson, *Of the Necessity of Good Works,* in *Works,* 3:338.

15. For Locke's statement of belief, see *Reasonableness of Christianity,*

pp. 26–27 et passim; for Locke and Addison on faith's assurance, see *An Essay concerning Human Understanding* (London, 1690), bk. 4, chap. 16, sec. 14; *S* 459. Cf. South, *Christianity Mysterious,* in *Sermons,* 1:411 ff.; Wilkins, *Principles,* pp. 342–43; Bates, *Harmony,* in *Works,* p. 137.

16. Cf. Tillotson, *Wisdom of Being Religious,* in *Works,* 1:12.

17. Benjamin Whichcote, *Moral and Religious Aphorisms* [1703], (London, 1930), no. 1121. For contemporary support of Addison's position, see the following: Locke, *Reasonableness of Christianity,* pp. 21, 283; Tillotson, *The Example of Jesus in Doing Good,* in *Works,* 1:154–55; and *Instituted Religion Not Intended to Undermine Nature,* in *Works,* 2:305, 307, 310–11; Gilbert Burnet, *Of the Propagation of the Gospel in Foreign Parts* [1704], in *An Account of the Society for Propagating the Gospel in Foreign Parts* (London, 1704), p. 18.

18. Cf. *S* 186, *S* 459. Addison's view of the relationship between faith and morality is essentially Latitudinarian. See Tillotson, *Concerning Our Imitation of the Divine Perfections,* in *Works,* 2:512; and *Instituted Religion Not Intended to Undermine Nature,* in *Works,* 2:310–11; South, *So God Created Man in His Own Image, in the Image of God Created He Him,* in *Sermons,* 1:25; Benjamin Hoadly, *Two Sermons upon St. Matthew 10:34* [1703], in *Several Tracts Formerly Published* (London, 1715), p. 89; and, in Letsome and Nicholl, *Defence,* the following: George Stanhope, *No Practical Precepts of the Christian Religion Unreasonable* [1702], 1:799–811; and *The Wisdom of the Christian Religion* [1702], 1:820; Samuel Bradford, *The Excellency of the Christian Revelation, As It Removes the Guilty Fears of Sinners, and Their Ignorance of God* [1699], 1:460–69; Clarke, *A Discourse concerning the Unchangeable Obligations of Natural Religion, and the Truth and Certainty of the Christian Revelation* [1705], 2:68–69, 70–71, 158.

19. Addison, *Of the Christian Religion* [1721], *MW,* 2:443.

10. The Proof for Divinity

1. John Dryden, Preface to *Religio Laici, or A Layman's Faith* [1682], in Dryden, *Poems,* vol. 1. The Latitudinarian voice is John Tillotson's, *Of the Trial of the Spirit,* in *Works,* 1:185.

2. Robert South, *Ecclesiastical Policy the Best Policy, or, Religion the Best Reason of State,* in *Sermons,* 1:56.

3. Tillotson, *The Wisdom of Being Religious,* in *Works,* 1:6. Cf. John Edwards, *A Demonstration of the Existence and Providence of God* (London, 1696), p. 3; *S* 565.

4. Cf. Thomas Burnet, *The Sacred Theory of the Earth* [Eng. trans.,

1684–90], 5th ed., 2 vols. (London, 1722), 1:188. For Addison's veneration of Burnet as the author of a new Holy Writ, see his poem *Ad Burnettum* [1698–99], *MW*, 1:284–89.

5. Nicolas Malebranche, *Christian Conferences* (London, 1695), p. 57. Cf. Augustine *De ordine* (trans. Robert P. Russell; New York, 1948), 2. 15. 42. For a comprehensive statement on the concept of order from the English Renaissance through the eighteenth century, see Maynard Mack, Introduction to Pope's *Essay on Man*, in *Poems of Alexander Pope* (London and New Haven, 1950, 1951), vol. 3.i.

6. *S* 543. Cf. Robert Hooke, *A Discourse of Earthquakes*, in *Posthumous Works*, ed. Richard Waller (London, 1705), p. 423; Tillotson, *The Wisdom of God in the Creation of the World*, in *Works*, 2:551; Robert Boyle, *A Disquisition about the Final Causes of Natural Things* (London, 1688), p. 40; William Bates, *Of the Existence of God*, in *Works*, p. 6; William Derham, *Physico-Theology* [1711–12], in Letsome and Nicholl, *Defence*, 2:575; Edwards, *Demonstration*, pp. 3–4; Burnet, *Sacred Theory*, 1:409–10; François de Salignac de La Mothe Fénelon, *A Demonstration of the Existence of God* (London, 1713), pp. 177–78.

7. Cf. Boyle, *Of the High Veneration Man's Intellect Owes to God* (London, 1685), p. 61.

8. Boyle, *Disquisition*, pp. 43–44. Addison's use of "the several glories of the heaven and earth" to prove God's existence has parallels in the following: Cicero *De natura deorum*, tr. H. Rackham (London and New York, 1933), pp. 137–39; Seneca *Of Benefits*, in *Works*, trans. Thomas Lodge (London, 1620), p. 80 (also his Epistle 90, pp. 378–79, and *Natural Questions*, p. 819). Cf. the Boyle lecturers in Letsome and Nicholl, *Defence:* Richard Bentley, *Confutation*, pp. 52–53; John Hancock, *Arguments to Prove the Being of God* [1706], 2:210; Josiah Woodward, *The Certainty of God's Being, and of His Universal Government* [1710], 2:498. See also Edwards, *Demonstration*, pp. 19–74; Edward Stillingfleet, *Origines Sacrae* [1662], 5th ed. (London, 1680), pp. 376–78.

9. Cf. John Locke, *An Essay concerning Human Understanding* (London, 1690), bk. 3, chap. 6, sec. 12; Boyle, *High Veneration*, pp. 25, 75–76; Derham, *Physico-Theology*, in Letsome and Nicholl, *Defence*, 2:581; William King, *De Origine Mali* (Dublin, 1702), p. 45; Tillotson, *Concerning the Advantages of an Early Piety*, in *Works*, 1:516; Benjamin Whichcote, *Moral and Religious Aphorisms* [1703], (London, 1930), no. 155.

10. John Ray, *The Wisdom of God Manifested in the Works of the Creation* [1691], 8th ed. (London, 1722), pp. 121–22; Derham, *Physico-Theology*, in Letsome and Nicholl, *Defence*, 2:625, 626–27.

11. Samuel Johnson, *The Lives of the English Poets* [1779–81], ed. George Birkbeck Hill, 3 vols. (Oxford, 1905), 3:245.

12. Boyle, *The Christian Virtuoso* [1690], in *Works,* 6 vols. (London, 1772), 5:515.

13. Boyle, *High Veneration,* p. 25. Cf. King, *De Origine Mali,* p. 45; Derham, *Physico-Theology,* in Letsome and Nicholl, *Defence,* 2:581; Tillotson, *Early Piety,* in *Works,* 1:516; Whichcote, *Aphorisms,* no. 155. Addison constantly softened the proof of natural philosophers for divine existence by recalling attributes of mercy and benevolence. From Isaac Newton, e.g., he borrowed the notion that the duplication of intricate organs in a living body was proof of divine existence; see *Optics* [1704], 4th ed. corrected (London, 1730), p. 378, and *S* 543. But unlike the scientist he also used the argument to emphasize divine generosity, for one eye or ear or leg or hand or claw would have been "sufficient for the subsistence and preservation of an animal." (This statement by Addison is a paraphrase of Stillingfleet, *Origines Sacrae,* p. 376.)

14. *S* 519; Locke, *Essay,* bk. 3, chap. 6, sec. 12; cf. Boyle, *High Veneration,* pp. 75–76. For the classic attack on the physico-theological argument, see Immanuel Kant, "Of the Impossibility of the Physico-theological Proof," in *The Critique of Pure Reason* [1781; 1787], trans. F. Max Müller (London, 1881).

15. For this portrait of man, see also *G* 117, *T* 156, *S* 111, *S* 219, *S* 237, *S* 349, *S* 387.

16. Bates, *The Immortality of the Soul,* in *Works,* pp. 39–43; Samuel Clarke, *A Demonstration of the Being and Attributes of God* [1704] and *A Discourse concerning the Unchangeable Obligations of Natural Religion, and the Truth and Certainty of the Christian Revelation* [1705], in Letsome and Nicholl, *Defence,* 2:4–5, 112–14; see also Tillotson, *Success Not Always Answerable to the Probability of Second Causes,* in *Works,* 1:337. The idea was also enunciated by the physico-theologians; see, e.g., Bentley, *Confutation,* pp. 4, 5, 6–8. Cf. John Wilkins, *Of the Principles and Duties of Natural Religion* [1675], 7th ed. (London, 1715), pp. 81, 167–70.

17. Francis Gastrell, *The Certainty and Necessity of Religion in General* [1697], in Letsome and Nicholl, *Defence,* 1:296; Locke, *Essay,* bk. 4, chap. 10, sec. 3. Cf. Ralph Cudworth, *The True Intellectual System of the Universe* [1678], 3 vols. (London, 1845), 3:54–55; Tillotson, *The Eternity of God,* in *Works,* 2:681–85; Burnet, *Sacred Theory,* 1:428–29; Bentley, *Confutation,* pp. 57–62; Boyle, *High Veneration,* p. 64; Isaac Barrow, *The Being of God proved from Universal Consent,* in *Works,* 2:115. Clarke used the idea repeatedly in his Boyle lectures, *Demonstration* and *Discourse,* in Letsome and Nicholl, *Defence,* 2:6–19, 67–68. For the classic attack on the argument from eternity, particularly as phrased by Locke, see David Hume, *A Treatise of Human Nature* (London, 1739), bk. 1, pt. 3, sec. 2.

18. Boyle, *High Veneration,* pp. 64–68; Tillotson, *Eternity of God,* in *Works,* 2:681–85. For scriptural authority, see Heb. 13:8; Rev. 1:8; 2 Pet. 3:8.

19. Tillotson, *Of the Immortality of the Soul,* in *Works,* 3:110; cf. Boyle, *The Excellency of Theology, Compared with Natural Philosophy* (London, 1674), p. 55; Bentley, *Confutation,* p. 15. See *S* 111 (cf. *S* 487); *Cato,* act 5, sc. 1; *S* 600.

20. Tillotson, *Of the Immortality of the Soul,* in *Works,* 3:31–34, 37–38, 39–43; Bates, *Immortality of the Soul,* in *Works,* pp. 31–53. The following sources supported one or more of Addison's three points: Benjamin Hampton, *The Existence of the Human Soul after Death* (London, 1711), pp. 31–32; Stillingfleet, *Origines Sacrae,* p. 386; and *A Letter to a Deist* (London, 1677), p. 6; South, *Who Knowing the Judgment of God . . . Have Pleasure in Them That Do Them,* in *Sermons,* 1:226–27; George Stanhope, *Death Abolished, and Life and Immortality Brought to Light by Jesus Christ* [1701], in Letsome and Nicholl, *Defence,* 1:698–99; Woodward, *The Reasonableness of the Christian Hope,* in Letsome and Nicholl, *Defence,* 2:554; Bentley, *Confutation,* p. 8. For Addison on the Platonic doctrine of immortality, see *Cato,* act 5, sc. 1; *T* 154.

21. 2 Cor. 3:18; Henry More, *The Immortality of the Soul* (London, 1659), bk. 3, chap. 1, axiom 29. Cf. Arthur O. Lovejoy, *The Great Chain of Being,* chap. 9.

22. Bentley, *Confutation,* p. 15. That all human faculties—including the intellective—would be enlarged in the "future, blessed state" was a current idea. See Tillotson's sermon "On the Happiness of a Heavenly Conversation" (as cited in *S,* vol. 5, p. 50 n.); and *The Present and Future Advantage of an Holy and Virtuous Life,* in *Works,* 3:58; Boyle, *Christian Virtuoso,* in *Works,* 6:789; South, *Christianity Mysterious, and the Wisdom of God in Making It So . . . ,* in *Sermons,* 1:416; Bates, *Of Death,* in *The Four Last Things* (London, 1691), p. 48.

23. Barrow, *The Maker of Heaven and Earth,* in *Works,* 2:154. Addison's concept of infinity as a clue to the divine attributes was borrowed from Locke, *Essay,* bk. 2, chap. 23, sec. 33.

24. His secular sources were Blaise Pascal, *Pensées,* sec. 2: "The Misery of Man without God" (72), and Newton, *Optics,* p. 345. He expresses his regard for Fontenelle and the theory of peopled planets in *S* 519.

25. Locke, *Essay,* bk. 4, chap. 12, sec. 11.

Afterword. Armored Genius

1. Joseph Spence, *Observations, Anecdotes, and Characters of Books and Men,* ed. James M. Osborn, 2 vols. (Oxford, 1966), 1:304, 62; cf. p. 333.

2. For Addison's relations with "superiors," see Spence, *Observations,* 1:333.

3. For the imputation of homosexuality, see Spence, *Observations,* 1:80, and Richard Steele, *Plebeian* 2 [1719], in *Tracts.* For want of evidence, the charge remains conjectural.

4. Spence, *Observations,* 1:62; Samuel Johnson, *The Lives of the English Poets* [1779–81], ed. George Birkbeck Hill, 3 vols. (Oxford, 1905), 2:147, 126.

5. To Alexander Pope, 29 Sept. 1725, Jonathan Swift, *Correspondence,* 3:103.

6. Johnson, *Lives,* 2:149.

APPENDIX. THE 1714 EDITION OF *The Trial of Count Tariff*

1. Appearing in London either at the very end of July or the beginning of August, *The Late Tryal and Conviction of Count Tariff* was "Printed for *A. Baldwin,* near the *Oxford-Arms* in *Warwick-Lane,* MDCCXIV. Price Three-pence." Because of the rarity of this piece and its bibliographical problems, we have preserved the original spelling, punctuation, and italics.

2. See Steele's *S* 555 for mention of the periodical's friends as recently as December 1712.

3. Abel Boyer, *History,* pp. 712–14; also see p. 680. By March 1714 St. John began to despair the queen's "outliving the next summer."

4. Boyer, *State,* 8:6 ff., 11–12, 14–17, 65–67.

BIBLIOGRAPHY

COLLATERAL PRIMARY SOURCES

Aikin, Lucy. *The Life of Joseph Addison*. London, 1843.

Anon. *An Answer to the Examiner's Cavils against the Barrier Treaty of 1709*. London, 1713.

———. *The Assiento Contract Considered*. London, 1714.

———. *A Collection of Petitions Presented to the Honourable House of Commons against the Trade with France*. London, 1713.

———. *The Consequences of a Law for Reducing the Duties upon French Wines, Brandy, Silks, and Linen, to Those of Other Nations. With Remarks on the Mercator*. London, 1713.

———. *The Criterion, or Touchstone, by Which to Judge of the Principles of High and Low Church*. London, 1710.

———. *A Dialogue betwixt Whig and Tory*. London, 1693.

———. *The Doctor Militant; or, Church Triumphant*. In *A Collection of Poems, for and against Dr. Sacheverell*. London, 1710.

———. *The Happiness of the Hanover Succession, Illustrated from the Conduct of the Late Administrators, Wherein Their Designs Are Farther Exposed, and Public Justice Demanded upon the Betrayers of Our Constitution*. London, 1715.

——— [Probably by Francis Hare]. *The Management of the War. In a Letter to a Tory Member*. London, 1711.

———. *Mr. Addison Turned Tory: or, The Scene Inverted: Wherein It Is Made to Appear That the Whigs Have Misunderstood That Celebrated Author in His Applauded Tragedy, Called "Cato," and That the Duke of M——'s Character, in Endeavouring to Be a General for Life, Bears a Much Greater Resemblance to That of Caesar and Syphax, Than the Hero of His Play. To Which Are Added, Some Cursory Remarks upon the Play Itself*. London, 1713.

———. *A Modest Enquiry into the Danger of the Church*. London, 1716.

———. *A New Catechism, with Dr. Hickes's Thirty-Nine Articles*. London, 1710.

———. *The Old and New Ministry Compared*. London, 1711.

———. *Remarks on the Barrier Treaty Vindicated. In a Letter to the Author*. London, 1713.

———. *Remarks on a False, Scandalous, and Seditious Libel, Intitled, The Conduct of the Allies, and of the Late Ministry, etc*. London, 1711.

——— [Attributed to Arthur Maynwaring by John Oldmixon in *The Life*

and Posthumous Works of Arthur Maynwaring (London, 1715), p. 248].
Remarks upon the Present Negotiations of Peace Begun between Britain and France. London, 1711.
———. *Revolution and Anti-Revolution Principles Stated and Compared, the Constitution Explained and Vindicated, and the Justice and Necessity of Excluding the Pretender, Maintained against the Book Entitled, Hereditary Right of the Crown of England Asserted*. London, 1714.
———. *St. Paul the Tentmaker. A Discourse Showing How Religion Has in All Ages Been Promoted by the Industrious Mechanic*. In *A Collection of State Tracts*, 3 vols. (London, 1705–7), vol. 2 (1705).
———. *A Satire on the Earl of Oxford, Lord Bolingbr——k, Mr. Moor, and Mr. Prior*. In *The Harleian Miscellany*, 12 vols. (London, 1808–11), vol. 11.
———. *The Sentiments of Our Forefathers Relating to the Succession of the Crown, Hereditary Right, and Nonresistance, Dedicated to All Those That Prefer Hereditary Right to a Parliamentary One, Notwithstanding the Latter Is Likely to Take Place*. London, 1714.
———. *Treason Unmasked; or, The Queen's Title, the Revolution, and the Hanover Succession Vindicated*. London, 1713.
——— [Probably by Philip Hunton]. *A Treatise of Monarchy, Containing Two Parts. . . . Done by an Earnest Desirer of His Country's Peace* [1643, 1689]. In *Harleian Miscellany*, vol. 6.
———. *Two Letters concerning the Author of the Examiner*. London, 1713.
Asgill, John. *Succession of the House of Hanover Vindicated, against the Pretender's Second Declaration in Folio, Intitled, The Hereditary Right of the Crown of England Asserted, etc.* London, 1714.
Barrow, Isaac. *The Reward of Honouring God*. In *Works*, vol. 1.
Bennett, Thomas. *Charity-Schools Recommended, in a Sermon Preached at St. James's Church in Colchester, on Sunday, March 26, 1710*. London, 1710.
Bentley, Richard. *A Sermon upon Popery*. London, 1715.
Berkeley, George. *Passive Obedience; or, The Christian Doctrine of Not Resisting the Supreme Power* [1712]. In *Works*, vol. 6.
Bradford, Samuel. *The Credibility of the Christian Revelation, from Its Intrinsic Evidence* [1699], in Letsome and Nicholl, *Defence*, vol. 1.
Bramston, William. *The Great Sin of Lukewarmness in Religion*. London, 1713.
Browne, Simon. *Joy and Trembling. A Sermon Preached in the Old Jewry, June 7, 1716*. London, 1716.
Burnet, Gilbert. *The Bishop of Salisbury's Speech in the House of Lords,*

on the First Article of the Impeachment of Dr. Henry Sacheverell. London, 1710.

———. *A Sermon Preached at the Funeral of the Honourable Robert Boyle; at St. Martin's in the Fields, January 7, 1691/2.* London, 1692.

Collier, Jeremy, trans. *Emperor Marcus Antoninus, His Conversation with Himself.* London, 1701.

Defoe, Daniel[?]. *An Essay on the History of Parties and Persecution in Britain.* London, 1711.

———. *An Essay upon Public Credit.* London, 1710.

——— [?]. *A Letter from a Member of the House of Commons to His Friend in the Country Relating to the Bill of Commerce.* London, 1713.

———. *The Letters of Daniel Defoe,* ed. George Harris Healey. Oxford, 1955.

Fleetwood, William. *A Sermon of the Education of Children, Preached before the Right Honourable the Lord Mayor, and Court of Aldermen, at Guild-Hall Chapel, on Sunday, November 1, 1696.* London, 1696.

Fontenelle, Bernard Le Bovier de. *A Conversation on the Plurality of Worlds* [Eng. trans., 1695]. London, 1769.

Hoadly, Benjamin. *The Measures of Submission to the Civil Magistrates Considered* [1705]. 5th ed. London, 1718.

[Jacob, Giles]. *Memoirs of the Life and Writings of the Right Honourable Joseph Addison, Esq.; with His Character by Sir Richard Steele.* 2d ed. London, 1724.

Lambe, Charles. *The Pretences for the Present Rebellion, Considered. In a Sermon Preached at St. Katherine Cree-Church and All-Hallows Barkin, on October 16, 1715.* London, 1715.

More, Henry. *An Antidote against Atheism* [1653]. London, 1712.

———. *Enchiridion Ethicum, the English Translation of 1690.* New York, 1930.

Ridpath, George. *Parliamentary Right Maintained; or, The Hanoverian Succession Justified.* London, 1714.

———. *The Peril of Being Zealously Affected but Not Well; or, Reflections on Dr. Sacheverel's Sermon, Preached before the Right Honourable the Lord Mayor, Aldermen, and Citizens of London, at the Cathedral Church of St. Paul, on the Fifth of November, 1709.* London, 1709.

Savile, George. *Cautions to Those Who Are to Choose Members to Serve in Parliament. To Which Is Added a List of Those That Voted for and against the Bill of Commerce.* London, 1713.

Senault, J. F. *The Use of Passions.* Translated by Henry, earl of Monmouth. London, 1671.

South, Robert. *False Foundations Removed, and True Ones Laid for Such*

Wise Builders as Design to Build for Eternity. In a Sermon Preached at St. Mary's, Oxon., before the University, December 10, 1661. In *Sermons,* vol. 1.
———. *Natural Religion, without Revelation, Shown Only Sufficient to Render a Sinner Inexcusable. In a Sermon Preached before the University at Christ-Church, Oxon., on November 2, 1690.* In *Sermons,* vol. 1.
Stanhope, George. *Those Christian Doctrines Not Incredible, Which Are (to Us) Incomprehensible* [1702]. In Letsome and Nicholl, *Defence,* vol. 1.
Tickell, Thomas. Preface to *The Works of the Late Right Honourable Joseph Addison, Esq.* [1721]. Birmingham, 1761.
Tillotson, John. *The Best Men Liable to the Worst Treatment, from Mistaken Zealots.* In *Works,* vol. 2.
———. *The Danger of Zeal, without Knowledge.* In *Works,* vol. 2.
———. *The Folly of Scoffing at Religion.* In *Works,* vol. 1.
———. *Religion, Our First and Great Concernment.* In *Works,* vol. 2.
Williams, John. *A Sermon Preached before the Society for the Propagation of the Gospel in Foreign Parts. At the Parish Church of St. Lawrence Jewry, February 15, 1705/6.* London, 1706.
Woodward, Josiah. *The Divine Light, Succour, and Comfort of the Christian Religion* [1710]. In Letsome and Nicholl, *Defence,* vol. 2.

SECONDARY SOURCES

Part I. In the Market Place

Ashton, T. S. *An Economic History of England: The Eighteenth Century.* London, 1955.
Beer, Max. *Early British Economics from the Thirteenth to the Eighteenth Century.* London, 1938.
Buck, Philip. *The Politics of Mercantilism.* New York, 1942.
Clapham, John. *The Bank of England.* Cambridge, 1945.
Clark, G. N. *The Later Stuarts.* Oxford, 1934.
———. "War Trade and Trade War, 1701–1713." *Economic History Review* 1 (1928):262–80.
Cragg, G. R. *From Puritanism to the Age of Reason.* Cambridge, 1950.
Cunningham, W. *The Growth of English Industry and Commerce in Modern Times.* Cambridge, 1892.
Dobrée, Bonamy. "The First Victorian," *Essays in Biography.* Oxford, 1925. Pp. 201–345.
———. "Addison," *English Literature of the Eighteenth Century, 1700–1740.* Oxford, 1959. Pp. 102–20.

Ehrenpreis, Irvin. *Swift, the Man, His Works, and the Age,* vol. 2, *Dr. Swift.* Cambridge, Mass., 1967.
Fussell, Paul. *The Rhetorical World of Augustan Humanism.* Oxford, 1965.
Gay, Peter. "The Spectator as Actor." *Encounter,* December 1967. Pp. 27–32.
Harkness, D. A. E. "The Opposition to the Eighth and Ninth Articles of the Commercial Treaty of Utrecht." *Scottish Historical Review* 21 (1924) :219–26.
Heckscher, Eli F. *Mercantilism.* Translated by Mendel Shapiro. London, 1935.
Hewins, W. A. S. *English Trade and Finance Chiefly in the Seventeenth Century.* London, 1892.
Jones, M. G. *The Charity School Movement.* Cambridge, 1938.
Lewis, C. S. "Addison." In *Essays on the Eighteenth Century Presented to David Nichol Smith in Honour of His Seventieth Birthday.* Oxford, 1945. Pp. 1–14.
Lipson, Ephraim. *The Economic History of England.* London, 1947.
Macaulay, Thomas Babington. "The Life and Writings of Addison" [1843], *Critical and Historical Essays.* London, 1907.
Novak, Maximillian E. *Economics and the Fiction of Daniel Defoe.* Berkeley and Los Angeles, 1962.
Paulson, Ronald. *The Fictions of Satire.* Baltimore, 1967. Pp. 120–28, 210–22.
Schollenberger, Johann. *Geschichte der schweizerischen Politik.* Vol. 1. Frauenfeld, 1906–8.
Seeley, John R. *The Expansion of England.* London, 1888.
Sombart, Werner. *The Quintessence of Capitalism.* Translated by M. Epstein. London, 1915.
Stephen, Leslie. *English Literature and Society in the Eighteenth Century.* New York and London, 1904.
Sutherland, James. *Defoe* [1937]. 2d ed. London, 1950.
Tawney, R. H. *Religion and the Rise of Capitalism* [1926]. New York, 1952.
Trevelyan, George Macaulay. *England under Queen Anne.* 3 vols. London, 1930–34.
———. *England under the Stuarts.* New York and London, 1933.
Troeltsch, Ernst. *The Social Teaching of the Christian Churches.* Translated by Olive Wyon. London, 1949.
Watt, Ian. *The Rise of the Novel.* London, 1957.
Weber, Max. *The Protestant Ethic and the Spirit of Capitalism.* Translated by Talcott Parson. New York and London, 1930.

Wilson, Charles H. *Anglo-Dutch Commerce and Finance in the Eighteenth Century.* Cambridge, 1941.

———. *Mercantilism.* London, 1958.

Wolf, John B. *The Emergence of the Great Powers, 1685–1715.* London, 1951.

Wright, Louis B. *Middle-Class Culture in Elizabethan England.* Chapel Hill, 1935.

Part II. On the Hustings

Cox, Richard H. *Locke on War and Peace.* Oxford, 1960.

Feiling, Keith. *A History of the Tory Party, 1640–1714.* Oxford, 1924.

Fink, Zera. *The Classical Republicans.* Evanston, Ill., 1945.

Gierke, Otto. *Natural Law and the Theory of Society.* Cambridge, 1934.

Holmes, Geoffrey. *British Politics in the Age of Anne.* London and New York, 1967.

Kemp, Betty. *King and Commons, 1660–1832.* London and New York, 1957.

Lamprecht, Sterling P. *The Moral and Political Philosophy of John Locke.* New York, 1918.

Laski, Harold J. *The Rise of Liberalism.* New York and London, 1936.

Laslett, Peter. Introduction to *Two Treatises of Government* [by John Locke]. Cambridge, 1960.

Loftis, John. *The Politics of Drama in Augustan England.* Oxford, 1963.

Plumb, J. H. *The Origins of Political Stability: England, 1675–1725.* Boston, 1967.

Ritchie, David. *Natural Rights: A Criticism of Some Political and Ethical Conceptions* [1895]. 3d ed. London, 1916.

Sabine, George H. *A History of Political Thought.* New York, 1937.

Stephen, Leslie. *A History of English Thought in the Eighteenth Century* [1876–80]. New York, 1927.

Sutherland, James. "The Last Years of Joseph Addison," *Background for Queen Anne.* London, 1939. Pp. 127–44.

Trevelyan, George Macaulay. *England under Queen Anne.* 3 vols. London, 1930–34.

Walcott, Robert. *English Politics in the Early Eighteenth Century.* Oxford, 1956.

Weston, Corinne Comstock. *English Constitutional Theory and the House of Lords.* London, 1965.

Williams, Basil. *The Whig Supremacy: 1714–60.* Oxford, 1942.

Williams, E. Neville. *The Eighteenth-Century Constitution.* Cambridge, 1960.

Winton, Calhoun. *Captain Steele*. Baltimore, 1964.
———. *Sir Richard Steele, M.P.* Baltimore, 1970.

PART III. IN THE PULPIT

Abbey, Charles J., and Overton, John H. *The English Church in the Eighteenth Century*. London, 1887.
Bennett, G. V. *White Kennett, 1660–1728*. London, 1957.
Bush, May Delaney. "Rational Proof of a Deity from the Order of Nature." *ELH* 9 (1942) :288–319.
Cragg, G. R. *From Puritanism to the Age of Reason*. Cambridge, 1950.
Davies, Horton. *Worship and Theology in England: From Watts and Wesley to Maurice, 1690–1850*. Princeton, 1961.
Harth, Phillip. *Swift and Anglican Rationalism*. Chicago, 1961.
Landa, Louis. "Jonathan Swift: 'Not the Gravest of Divines.' " In *Jonathan Swift, 1667–1967: A Dublin Tercentenary Tribute*. Edited by R. McHugh and P. Edwards. Dublin, 1967. Pp. 38–60.
———. *Swift and the Church of Ireland*. Oxford, 1954.
Lovejoy, Arthur O. *The Great Chain of Being*. Cambridge, Mass., 1936.
McKillop, Alan D. *The Background of Thomson's Seasons*. Minneapolis, 1942.
MacLean, Kenneth. *John Locke and English Literature of the Eighteenth Century*. New Haven, 1936.
Nicolson, Marjorie H. *The Breaking of the Circle: Studies in the Effect of the "New Science" upon Seventeenth-Century Poetry*. Evanston, Ill., 1950.
———. "The Early Stage of Cartesianism in England." *Studies in Philology* 26 (1929) :356–74.
———. *The Microscope and English Imagination*. Smith College Studies in Modern Languages, vol. 16, no. 4. Northampton, Mass., 1935.
———. *Mountain Gloom and Mountain Glory*. Ithaca, N.Y., 1959.
———. *Newton Demands the Muse: Newton's "Opticks" and the Eighteenth-Century Poets*. Princeton, 1946.
Raven, Charles E. *Natural Religion and Christian Theology*. Cambridge, 1953.
Sarton, George. *A Guide to the History of Science*. New York, 1952.
Stromberg, Roland. *Religious Liberalism in Eighteenth-Century England*. London, 1954.
Sykes, Norman. *Church and State in England in the Eighteenth Century* [1934]. Hamden, Conn., 1962.
———. *The Church of England and Non-Episcopal Churches in the Sixteenth and Seventeenth Centuries*. London, 1949.

———. *From Sheldon to Secker*. Cambridge, 1959.
Tulloch, John. *Rational Theology and Christian Philosophy in the Seventeenth Century*. London, 1874.
Westfall, Richard S. *Science and Religion in Seventeenth-Century England*. New Haven, 1958.
Willey, Basil. *The Seventeenth-Century Background* [1934]. London, 1949.

INDEX